PROFITING WITH FOREX

PROFITING WITH FOREX

The Most Effective Tools and Techniques for Trading Currencies

JOHN JAGERSON, CTA
S. WADE HANSEN, CTA

McGraw-Hill

New York   Chicago   San Francisco   Lisbon   London   Madrid
Mexico City   Milan   New Delhi   San Juan   Seoul
Singapore   Sydney   Toronto

2 3 4 5 6 7 8 9 0 DOC/DOC 0 9 8 7 6

ISBN 0-07-146465-4

This publication is designed to provide accurate and authoritative information in regard to the subject matter covered. It is sold with the understanding that neither the author nor the publisher is engaged in rendering legal, accounting, futures/securities trading, or other professional service. If legal advice or other expert assistance is required, the services of a competent professional person should be sought.
                    —*From a Declaration of Principles jointly adopted by a Committee*
                    of the American Bar Association and a Committee of Publishers

McGraw-Hill books are available at special quantity discounts to use as premiums and sales promotions, or for use in corporate training programs. For more information, please write to the Director of Special Sales, Professional Publishing, McGraw-Hill, Two Penn Plaza, New York, NY 10121-2298. Or contact your local bookstore.

Library of Congress Cataloging-in-Publication Data

Jagerson, John.
    Profiting with Forex : the most effective tools and techniques for trading
    currencies / by John Jagerson and S. Wade Hansen.
       p. cm.
    ISBN 0-07-146465-4 (hardcover : alk. paper)
    1. Foreign exchange futures. 2. Foreign exchange market.
    3. Currency convertibility. I. Hansen, S. Wade. II. Title.
    HG3853.J34 2006
    332.4'5—dc22
                                                           2005036706

CONTENTS

CHAPTER 16

Money Management   239

CHAPTER 17

Getting Started   249

Conclusion   253

APPENDIX

Fat Tails   255

ACKNOWLEDGMENTS

Putting this book together was a fun and demanding project, and we couldn't have done it without the following people:

Anne L. Hansen
Wendi Jagerson

Graham Anderson
Joseph Cervantes
Russ Francis
Stephen Isaacs
Jane Palmieri
John D. Wonnacott
R. Blake Young

Thanks for helping us put our dreams on the shelf.

John Jagerson
S. Wade Hansen

Life always has a fat tail.

—*Eugene Fama*
Professor of Finance
University of Chicago

Life always has a fat tail" is a statistician's way of saying, "You never know what life is going to throw at you so you had better be prepared for anything."[1] Nowhere is this statement truer than when you're looking at your financial future. Let us explain.

We are going to be surprised by both positive and negative events in our financial lives. The stock market is going to go up, and the stock market is going to go down. Inflation is going to rise and fall. Low interest rates are going to give us great deals on our home mortgages, and high interest rates are going to give us great returns on our CDs, savings accounts, and money market accounts. Knowing that all these things are going to happen is the easy part. It becomes increasingly difficult, however, when you are trying to determine when each of these things is going to happen. Wouldn't it be nice to protect the money you have and the profits you make no matter what happens? Well, you can in the Forex market. The Forex market enables you to make money no matter what is happening in the world around you. We are preparing for the unexpected by tapping into the profit-generating potential of the Forex market, and we believe you should too.

We first got involved in the Forex market after the dot-com bubble burst in the stock market. We wanted to find a way to diversify our portfolios so that we could take advantage of whatever market conditions presented themselves in the future. Now, we would love to say that we were instant successes and that we turned $1,000 into a cool $1 million overnight, but that would be ridiculous. We're not superheroes, and that's not how things happen in the real world. We had to learn some hard lessons and lose a lot of money as we progressed, but we did it, and you can too. From the time we got involved in the world's greatest financial market, we've taught thousands of people how to be successful in the financial markets

---

1 If you want to know what fat tails are, check out the appendix.

and developed investment education courses for the largest investment education company in the United States; we are now managing money in the Forex market for our investors. We've learned a thing or two along our journey, and we want to pass that along to you. Sure, you could set out on your own and try to learn all these lessons on your own, but why would you? We've got all the information right here to get you started and keep you making profits for years to come.

In this book, we use basic economic principles, technical analysis concepts, and a lot of common sense to explain what the Forex market is and why it does what it does. We approach the Forex market from a very practical standpoint. Instead of dwelling on the sophisticated economic principles that make the world go 'round, we choose to focus on the basics that easily translate into realistic and sensible investing decisions. We will look at the Forex market from a practical point of view—not a theoretical one. Theories are a great place to start because they point you in the right direction, but they don't tell you what to do in the market right now. You need a set of practical tools to make snap decisions in the Forex market. This book provides those tools.

Like every other financial market, the Forex market is constantly changing and evolving. If you change with it, you will be successful. If you stubbornly hold onto your preconceived theories, you won't be successful. If you just remember that the market is always right, you will do well.

We tell you some stories, teach you a few history lessons, and take a look into the future because once you see what forces shaped this financial world we live in and what forces are going to continue to shape it, you can be successful in it. We would also like to continue the discussion past this book. Once you've read the book, or as you are going through it, ask us your questions. Let us know what you think. Just drop us a line to say, "Hello." Our e-mail address is johnandwade@profitingwithforex.com. Or visit our Web site at www.profitingwithforex.com. Come be a part of the successful community of Forex investors.

PROFITING WITH FOREX

CHAPTER 1

Profiting with Forex

There is a Forex solution to every question you've ever asked about your financial future. We talk with people every day who want to know how they can take advantage of both the good times and the bad times in the economy. They want to know how to profit from the stock market when it is going up and how they can protect themselves when it is going down. They want to know how they can take advantage of the unprecedented economic growth in China, India, and other emerging markets. They want to know how to combat inflation to ensure that their retirement nest egg will continue to provide an enjoyable lifestyle. They want to know if there is anything they can do to offset rising oil prices. They want to know how to improve their budget when commodity prices—from the price of the orange juice they buy at the store to the price of the lumber for their new home—start to rise. Mostly, they want to make profits. And every time they ask us, we respond with one word: Forex.

Certainly, you could devote your life to learning to understand stocks, mutual funds, and options to take advantage of the ups and downs of the stock market. And you could learn about foreign bonds and exchange-traded funds to take advantage of the growth of the emerging markets around the world. Plus, you could master interest rate futures and government bonds to combat inflation. And to top it all off, you could dive into the commodities market to speculate on the wild swings in the price of crude oil and offset some risk in pork belly and soybean futures. But, really, who has time for all that?

If you're like most of us, you've got a 401(k), an IRA, or another type of retirement vehicle into which you are putting the majority of your savings. And that's a good thing. The stock market has done extremely well over the long term and deserves a place in your overall portfolio. But wouldn't it be nice if there were a way you could address all the other issues just mentioned without having to become a financial genius? Well, there is.

The Forex market enables you to have the best of both worlds. When stock prices go up, you can profit with the Forex market. When stock prices go down, you can profit with the Forex market. When emerging markets gain strength and begin to grow at exponential rates, you can profit with the Forex market. It doesn't matter if inflation levels are going up or if inflation levels are going down; you can profit with the Forex market. And as oil and other commodity prices fluctuate up and down and up and down, you can profit with the Forex market. You will be amazed at how easy it is to get involved and make money in this incredible market.

Finally, there is a way for all investors—no matter how big or small—to harness the world around them and secure their financial future. The Forex market is available to everyone, yet so few people know about this universal tool. As you read this book and learn more and more about the Forex market, we guarantee that you will ask yourself the same question over and over again, "Why in the world have I not been taking advantage of the Forex market until now?" Maybe you've never heard of the Forex market. Maybe you've heard of it but never really knew anything about it. Whatever the reason, today is your day to get started. Once you do, you'll never look back.

This book will introduce you to all the advantages of the Forex market and show you how to profit from it. It addresses the questions you have concerning your financial future. And, most importantly, it will show you how you can implement the things you learn in your own investing. The Forex market has changed our lives. It has changed the way we view the financial marketplace. We used to see obstacles and limitations. Now all we see are opportunities and freedom. The Forex market is the perfect supplement to our stock and bond investing. It enables us to profit from whatever is happening in the world around us. The Forex market is the solution.

WHAT IS THE FOREX MARKET?

The Forex market is the largest financial market in the world. Nearly $2 trillion worth of foreign currencies trade back and forth across the Forex market every day. Forex stands for the *for*eign *ex*change—the financial exchange on which governments, banks, international corporations, hedge funds, and individual investors exchange foreign currencies.

For instance, when you fly to another country, one of the first things you do when you get off the plane is look for a currency exchange counter where you can exchange your U.S. dollars for whatever currency is used in the country you are visiting—such as British pounds, Japanese yen, or euros. Why do you do this? Because you know that the cab driver, the hotel clerk, and the souvenir salesperson are all going to want you to pay them in their national currency, not U.S. dollars.

When you slide your U.S. dollars over to the teller and he or she slides back a stack of multicolored bills—let's face it, foreign money is a lot more colorful than the greenback—you have just participated in the Forex market. You exchanged one currency for another. Now, if you stop and think about all the people who travel, all the businesses that operate in multiple countries, and all the governments that are exchanging money, you can start to get an idea of how big the Forex market really is.

Those of you who travel abroad frequently have probably also noticed that the exchange rates at the currency counter at the airport never seem to be the same. They are constantly changing. Sometimes you get a lot more bang for your buck when you exchange your money, and sometimes you have to exchange a few more U.S. dollars just to get by. That is because exchange rates are constantly changing, and it is these changes in exchange rates that enable you to make a lot of money in the Forex market.

THE ADVANTAGES OF THE FOREX MARKET

The Forex market enjoys unparalleled advantages. You will find that some markets share similar advantages, but no one market on earth comes close to rivaling the protection, profit potential, and ease of use available in the Forex market. Take a look at the advantages you can find within the Forex market.

Market Size

The Forex market is the largest financial market in the world. (See Figure 1.1.) Nearly $2 trillion change hands every day. To give you an idea of what an awesome number that is, the New York Stock Exchange experienced record volume during the third quarter of 1998 and cleared only $1.9 trillion in volume—60 times less than the Forex market clears in a quarter. Being the largest financial market in the world is advantageous; it makes buying and selling currencies extremely easy because there are so many buyers and sellers out there. Imagine that you are trying to sell your home, and you had thousands of people standing at your front door—cash in hand— ready to buy the house. It wouldn't be too tough to sell the house.

The second advantage of the size of the Forex market is that investors are unable to manipulate it. Since potential manipulation is virtually nonexistent, you can be confident that the prices you are getting in the Forex market are fair prices.

FIGURE 1.1

Market size comparison (in millions of US$)

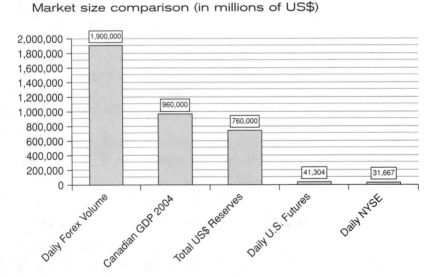

Source: Ouroboros Capital Management, LLC

Ease of Entry

You do not have to be rich to trade in the Forex market. Everybody deserves to be able to protect his or her financial future, and the Forex market makes this possible by offering an extremely low barrier to entry. In fact, you can open a Forex account with as little as $300.

Profit Potential

It doesn't matter if the value of the U.S. dollar is going up or down. You can make money in the Forex market. If you think its value is going up, you simply buy the U.S. dollar and make money all the way up. If you think its value is going down, you simply sell the U.S. dollar and make money all the way down.

Tax Advantages

When you invest in most financial markets, you must pay short-term capital gains tax if you take your profits within one year of purchasing a security. If you hold the security for more than one year before taking your profits, you must pay long-term capital gains tax. Currently, short-term capital gains are taxed at your current tax rate, and long-term capital gains are taxed at only 15 percent. Obviously, it is much better to pay less in taxes. In the Forex market—much to investors' delight—it doesn't matter if you take your profits one minute after you enter a trade or one month after you enter a trade. Sixty percent of your profits are taxed at long-term capital gains rates, while only 40 percent of your profits are taxed at short-term capital gains rates. That means you keep more of your profits in your pockets.

For example, imagine you made $10,000 on a six-month trade in the stock market and that you also made $10,000 on a six-month trade in the Forex market. Both trades occurred in taxable accounts, so you owe taxes on both. Assume you are in the 33 percent tax bracket.

Tax Treatment of the Stock Market Since you entered and exited your trade in the stock market within six months, you will have to pay short-term capital gains tax. If you are in the 33 percent tax bracket, you will have to pay 33 percent tax on of the profits. So for a profit of $10,000, you will end up paying $3,300 in taxes.

$$\$10,000 \times 33\% = \$3,300$$

While you did get to keep $6,700 of the original $10,000 profit, it is never fun to pay taxes.

Tax Advantages of the Forex Market   We all want to keep as much of our profit as we possibly can, and the Forex market allows us to do that. Even though you entered and exited your trade in the Forex market within six months—just as you did for your stock trade—only a portion (40 percent) of your profits is taxed as short-term capital gains. The remaining 60 percent of your profits get the benefit of being taxed as long-term capital gains. This means that you will have to pay 33 percent on only $4,000 and—according to current long-term capital gains rates—15 percent on $6,000.

Portion Taxed as Short-Term Capital Gains

$$\$10,000 \times 40\% = \$4,000$$
$$\$4,000 \times 33\% = \$1,320$$

Portion Taxed as Long-Term Capital Gains

$$\$10,000 \times 60\% = \$6,000$$
$$\$6,000 \times 15\% = \$900$$

Total Taxes Paid

$$\$1,320 + \$900 = \$2,220$$

You would have to pay only $2,220 with your Forex trade compared to the $3,300 you would have to pay with your stock trade. That is a savings of slightly more than 35 percent. Tax savings like that can add up quickly.

You can also accumulate profits quickly by investing in the Forex market within your IRA or other tax-deferred retirement account. Many investors are unaware they can trade anything but stocks and mutual funds within their retirement accounts because their brokers have conditioned them to focus only on these asset categories. Some brokers don't want to deal with the extra work that would come from allowing you to invest more freely. It isn't advantageous for them. On the other hand, other brokers believe that you should be able to choose where you put your money. Check with your brokerage firm and see if it offers self-directed options in its retirement accounts.

Trading Hours

The Forex market is open 24 hours a day nearly 5½ days a week. It doesn't matter if you're working or retired, a homemaker or a student, you can find a time that works for you to get involved in the Forex market. In fact, the Forex market is usually most active early in the morning and late and night. There are many part-time traders who are able to use these varied hours of market activity to their advantage by trading when they are not at work. The varied trading hours of the Forex market also benefit long-term investors because these investors are able to enter and exit their positions whenever the market dictates.

No Commissions

Every time you buy a stock, a bond, a mutual fund, or a home, you are paying someone somewhere a commission. In the Forex market, however, you never have to pay a commission. The price you see is the price you get. You don't have to factor in a little extra for the broker. You simply pay the listed price. No more, no less.

Increased Leverage

The Forex market allows you to control $100,000 with as little as $1,000. This means that you can make your money work harder for you in the Forex market than it can anywhere else. Imagine. You can keep all the profits from a $100,000 trade, and all you have to do is provide 1 percent of the money.

To put this in perspective, imagine that you are a real estate investor, and you see a $300,000 home that you believe is going to increase in value. If you could use the same amount of leverage in the real estate market as you can in the Forex market, you could buy that house with only $3,000 down and a potentially interest-free loan. That would be incredible. Any real estate investor in the country would do anything to get that kind of a deal, and that is exactly the opportunity you have in the Forex market.

Increased leverage is also the point that well-intentioned, but misinformed people point to when they say that investing in the Forex market is risky. Granted, this amount of leverage may seem aggressive, but the Forex market gives you the perfect antidote for the risks associated with increased leverage: guaranteed stops.

Guaranteed Stops

You have the ability in the Forex market to determine at exactly which price you would like to enter a trade and at exactly which price you would like to exit a trade—and these prices are guaranteed. A *stop*, or stop-loss order, is an order you place that instructs your broker to exit your trade if the price ever drops to a certain level. Think of a stop-loss order as a stop sign for your trade. If your trade ever reaches the stop sign—the price at which you would like to exit your trade—it immediately stops and exits so you can protect your money.

Guaranteed stops allow you to specify exactly how much you are willing to risk. Even though you are using great leverage, you still have the power to get out of a trade at any price you wish. You can't say that about the stock market. Sure, you can enter a stop order to take you out of a trade if the stock starts to move down, but you have no guarantee that you will get out at a certain price. It is really the luck of the draw for stocks. Not so in the Forex market. You have guaranteed stops under normal market conditions. There are some extreme events—like the outbreak of a war or extremely unexpected economic announcements—that may cause some slippage, but we have never personally experienced this.

MIND THE GAPS

If you've ever been to London and ridden the London underground, you are familiar with the charming reminder to "mind the gap." Every time the doors of the trains open, a soothing voice comes over the loud speaker and tells you to "mind the gap." This statement reminds you to watch your step as you step into and out of the trains because there is a gap between the train and the platform. Of course, this is just common sense. Nobody wants to plunge a leg down a ravine between a concrete platform and a steel train. Unfortunately, the ravines that exist in the investment landscape are not as apparent and aren't usually accompanied by courteous warnings of potential danger.

The key to developing and maintaining a well-balanced portfolio is learning how to mind and fill the gaps that are inherent in any market. Every market has gaps—the Forex included. But let's say you're investing in mutual funds in the stock market; you've made some great profits, but you'd like to fill some of the gaps. You will have to look outside the stock market to find the solution.

One gap that exists with mutual funds is that you can't buy or sell them until the market closes for the day. This can pose a problem on days when the market is rising quickly because you end up missing out on all of the positive movement. If you are investing in the Forex market, however, you can fill that gap because you can profit from your Forex trades while you are waiting to get into your mutual fund trades. You can fill the same gap when the stock market drops quickly. You can make money in your Forex trades to offset the losses you would incur in your mutual fund trades.

The Forex market offers unparalleled advantages. Many other financial markets offer some of the same advantages, but the Forex market offers them all. The Forex is the solution for the gaps in three widely used financial markets: the stock market, the bond market, and the futures market. Each of these markets offers the potential for making money, but once you see how they stack up against the Forex market, you'll be wondering why you haven't added the Forex market to your investing arsenal already.

The gaps you will see in all three markets are:

Commissions
Market hours
Liquidity
Taxes
Bear (downtrending) markets
Analysis overload

Forex Market versus Stock Market

Since most of you are familiar with the stock market, this is a good place to start. The stock market has been the traditional investment of choice for most retirement accounts. The accessibility of the stock market and the fact that the United States has the best stock market in the world make it a logical place for serious investors. Along with outstanding benefits, the stock market also has a few inherent gaps that the Forex market can fill. Some of these gaps are particularly relevant to the active investor who trades frequently. Others are important to every stock market investor.

Gap 1: Commissions   Each time you trade one of your stocks (or mutual funds), either by entering or exiting a position, you incur a commission charge. In most cases, the charge is much greater if you actually need to speak with a broker to execute your trade. Imagine that you own several shares of Google's (GOOG) stock, and you are concerned with the effects an upcoming earnings announcement might have on the value of your stock. You decide to call your broker to make a trade and ask for some advice. It's going to cost you.

We took an informal poll of the largest online stockbrokers and found an average charge of $50 per trade in this situation. Those kinds of fees can add up. Plus, that fee was only for the sell order. Had you wanted to purchase the stock, you would have had to pay twice that amount, or $100. Now imagine how much it would cost if you wanted your broker to help you execute several orders on multiple stocks. You get the idea.

By contrast, almost every dealer in the retail Forex market offers commission-free service. Plus, you can talk to most Forex dealers in person as many times as you need to for free. Most Forex commodity trading advisors also operate on a commission-free basis. You should certainly do your homework to make sure that you are dealing with a dealer who is giving you the best treatment, but most offer comparable arrangements.

Gap 2: Market Hours   The U.S. stock markets are open from 9:30 a.m. to 4 p.m. Eastern time Monday through Friday. This is right in the middle of business hours. Because most retail stock market investors are at work during these hours, many cannot enter stock trades during the day when the stock market is open. Instead, they have to "roll the dice" by placing orders when the stock market is closed and hope they will get into or out of their trades at a favorable price when the market opens the next day. If the stock opens at around the same price it closed at the previous day, you get a good price on your trade. If the stock opens at a much higher price than it closed at the previous day, you can get a very unfavorable price.

The Forex market is open 24 hours per day, from Sunday afternoon through the following Friday evening. Because the market is almost always open, you can enter your trades whenever you have time. And your orders will be filled within fractions of a second thanks to the multitrillion dollar volume the Forex market enjoys—even in the middle of the night. The exceptionally high volume that occurs on the Forex market also helps fill the next gap in the stock market.

Gap 3: Liquidity   Liquidity can be an issue when you are trading smaller stocks. *Liquidity* refers to your ability to sell, or liquidate, an investment you may be holding. If you can sell it quickly, the investment is a liquid investment. If you can't sell it quickly, the investment is an illiquid investment. Imagine that you own a small-cap or micro-cap stock, and you need to exit your position quickly. Chances are you will receive a much lower price for your stock than you were anticipating. This is especially the case if the stock is experiencing bad news.

Mutual funds, as we mentioned earlier, are not liquid during market hours because you can buy or sell them only once the market has closed. Some mutual funds even have restrictions on when you are eligible to sell them without incurring penalties. The lack of liquidity found in mutual fund investing can keep you out of trades that are making money or keep you in trades that are losing money.

The Forex market has more liquidity (buyers and sellers) than any other financial market. This means that if you want to get into a trade, there will always be somebody there to sell it to you. And when you want to get out of a trade, there will always be somebody there to buy it from you. And you can do all this at a reasonable price.

Gap 4: Taxes   Taxes are one of the biggest concerns any stock investor must address. Making profits every month in your investing is wonderful. But if you do not have your investments sheltered in an IRA or other protected account, you will be charged a short-term capital gains tax on all your profitable trades that lasted less than one year. In some cases, this can mean a tax hit of more than 30 percent. Most of you probably have the majority of your investments in tax-sheltered accounts. However, even tax-sheltered accounts have a gap. The drawback to these accounts, of course, is that you don't really have access to that money—without penalties—until you are 59½ years old. That's right. If you take your money out of a tax-sheltered account before you are 59½, you will have to pay an additional penalty—which currently stands at 10 percent. That can make a huge difference in your account balance.

By contrast, short-term Forex profits are taxed at a much lower rate. Each time you make a gain in the Forex market, as we outlined previously, 60 percent of your profits automatically qualify as long-term capital gains, while only 40 percent of your profits are considered short-term gains. And for those of you who are wondering, you can invest in the Forex market through a retirement account, like an IRA, as well. So, you can enjoy the best of both worlds.

Gap 5: Bear (Downtrending) Markets   Bearish stock market conditions are usually something that stock and mutual fund investors patiently endure. Some more advanced, and usually more wealthy, stock investors, however, are able to try to take advantage of bearish market conditions by shorting stocks. *Shorting a stock* means that you: first, borrow a stock from your broker; second, sell that stock on the open market at whatever the going rate is; third, wait and hope the stock drops in value; fourth, buy the stock back (hopefully at a lower price); and fifth, return the stock plus interest to your broker. If the stock declines in value while you are shorting it, you make money. If the stock increases in value while you are shorting it, you lose money. Shorting a stock is risky and expensive. Plus, not everyone qualifies to short stock. You have to have enough experience and enough money before your broker will even allow you to try to short stocks. Additionally, when you do short a stock you have borrowed from your broker, your broker charges you interest.

Perhaps the biggest drawback of shorting stocks is the "uptick" rule. If you see and want to take advantage of a stock that is dropping, you can't just jump in and immediately start shorting the stock. You have to wait until the stock creates an uptick. An *uptick* occurs when the stock trades at a price higher than it was previously. So if a stock drops from $50 to $49 to $48 to $47, it has not experienced an uptick, and you cannot short it. If, however, the stock rises back up to $48 after it has dropped to $47, it has experienced an uptick, and you can now short it. As you can imagine, most stocks that are falling tend to fall rapidly, and it is very difficult to find upticks. This can keep you out of a lot of trades even though you know the stock is going down.

Taking advantage of a downtrend in the Forex market is much easier than shorting a stock if you want to take advantage of a bearish market. It is as simple as this. If you think something in the Forex market is going up, you click on the "buy" button. If you think something in the Forex market is going down, you click on the "sell" button. How easy is that? You don't have to qualify for any additional trading permission. You don't have to ask your broker if you can borrow anything. And, most importantly, you don't have to wait for any nebulous upticks. If you see something headed down to the floor, you can jump in and take advantage of it any time you please. Imagine being able to take advantage of both uptrends and downtrends with just the click of a button.

Gap 6: Analysis Overload   The stock market offers an incredible selection of investments. There are literally tens of thousands of stocks and mutual funds to choose from. How in the world are you supposed to make an informed decision about which ones are the best to buy and which ones are the best to sell? Even your broker isn't able to stay on top of every stock and every mutual fund. To combat this problem, most of us have diversified our stock and mutual fund portfolios to cover a broad range in the market. This works pretty well because it lets you take advantage of movements in various segments of the market. It does, however, make it difficult to keep track of and load up on the stocks and mutual funds that are going to do well and dump the stocks and mutual funds that are not going to do as well.

The Forex market is much simpler to monitor. You really need to keep track of only eight different currencies. That's right: eight. Even if you don't have a lot of free time, you can keep track of something for which you need only two hands to count. (We talk more about the eight currencies you'll need to keep an eye on later in the book.)

Forex Gap   To ensure we are giving you a balanced view, and to emphasize that we are not issuing any type of Chicken-Little warning to pull out of the stock market, we want to highlight a gap in the Forex market that the stock market fills.

The overall Forex market is a trend-neutral market. This means that it moves up and down. But once you net out the ups and the downs, it is basically a flat market. The stock market, on the other hand is a predominantly uptrending market. This means that although the stock market fluctuates up and down, it has moved up over the long haul, as you can see in Figure 1.2. When a market is predominantly uptrending, it is generally easier to invest in for the long term without having to do a lot of thinking. You can just put your money in and trust that the market will go up.

However, this steady uptrend can also be counterproductive because it lulls investors into a false sense of security. If you believe the stock market is always going up, you probably are not going to pay as much attention to the market as you should. You don't have to look back any farther than the dot-com crash that started in 2000 to see this illustrated. Although the market has bounced back a bit since

FIGURE 1.2

Stock market trends: S&P 500 from 1959 through 2005, quarterly intervals

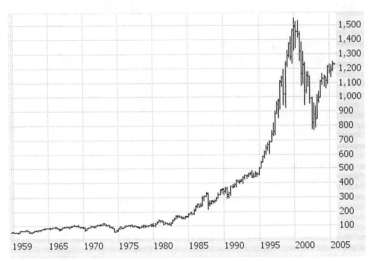

Source: Prophet.net

FIGURE 1.3

S&P five-year chart, monthly intervals

Source: Prophet.net

its low in 2002, it has still not recovered all its losses. (See Figure 1.3.) We are confident that the market will recover all its losses in the long term, but you could have saved yourself a lot of heartache if you had known about the Forex solution.

Keep investing in the stock market. Apply all the sensible rules and practices you have been taught. Then go one step further and really put the odds in your favor by minding the gaps with the Forex market.

Forex Market versus Bond Market

Almost everyone who has had an investment account has invested in the bond market. We feel confident saying this because, although most people don't know it, money market funds are part of the bond market. If you have ever had cash in an investment account that was not being used to buy stocks, mutual funds, and the like, your broker probably put your money in the money market.

The bond market—money market funds, municipal securities, Treasury securities, federal agency securities, corporate bonds, mortgage securities, and asset-backed securities—is generally considered to be a safe place to invest your money. Many even believe that you are guaranteed not to lose any of your principal in the bond market. While the bond market is certainly a conservative market and a great place to put your money, it is not a guaranteed market. While the likelihood is outrageously small, you could even lose some, or all, of your principal by investing in Treasury securities or the money market. And in any market in which there are no guarantees, there are bound to be gaps.

Gap 1: Commissions   Investors trade bonds through two markets: the over-the-counter (OTC) market and the secondary market. Bonds trade on the OTC market when they are first being issued. This means that if you buy a bond on the OTC market, you are buying the bond from the entity that will be paying you on the bond. Bonds trade on the secondary market once they have already been purchased and the person or entity that purchased the bonds wants to sell them to someone else.

The bond market, with the exception of U.S. Treasury bonds and notes—which trade on the Chicago Board of Trade (CBOT)—does not have a central exchange. Instead, bond dealers and brokers coordinate the sale and purchase of bonds through other bond dealers and brokers. To pay dealers and brokers for their services, bonds usually trade at a marked-up price. This means that you're going to pay a little extra to purchase the bond you want. On top of that, dealers and brokers may also charge an extra commission for unusual orders just to make it worth their while.

You already understand the benefits of operating in the commission-free environment of the Forex market, so we don't elaborate on that here. The same applies to all the gaps we discuss throughout the remainder of this section. Unless we have something more to add about an advantage of the Forex market regarding a particular gap, we won't repeat ourselves.

Gap 2: Market Hours   The CBOT trades U.S. Treasury bonds and notes on the trading floor each weekday from 7:20 a.m. until 2 p.m. CST and electronically each weekday from 6 p.m. to 4 p.m. CST the following day. Keep in mind that while it is nice to have access to the electronic market, most of the trading is done on the CBOT trading floor during business hours.

The rest of the bond market, which does not operate on a central exchange, can potentially operate on a 24-hour basis, but it usually doesn't. Most trading occurs during business hours because bond dealers and brokers need to be in their offices in order to transact trades.

Gap 3: Liquidity   Bonds are usually quite liquid during business hours. However, after business hours, liquidity can dry up quickly. This can be problematic if something happens later in the evening or during the night to affect the bond market. Prices will most likely have changed significantly before the beginning of the next business day, and you may be stuck with losses.

Gap 4: Taxes   While the Forex market stacks up well against some bonds with respect to tax issues, many bonds are far superior to the Forex market when you are analyzing tax consequences. Many bonds are issued as tax-free bonds, which means that you do not have to pay taxes on any of your profits. The profits from U.S. savings bonds can also be tax free if you use them for education.

Gap 5: Bear (Downtrending) Markets   Defining a bear market in the bond market is a subjective process. If you own bonds, bear markets occur when bond yields go up. If you don't own bonds, bear markets occur when bond yields go down. A bond yield is the total return you are going to get on your investment during the life of the bond. As the prices of bonds change, the bond yields also change. The more expensive a bond is, the lower the bond yield will be because you have to pay more for the same benefits. The less expensive a bond is, the higher the bond yield will be because you have to pay less for the same benefits.

When a bond's yield is rising, it means that the price of the bond is dropping. If you own the bond, this is bad news for you because, if you had to sell your bond right now, you would get less money than you originally paid for the bond and could end up losing money on the transaction. However, if you were simultaneously investing in the Forex market, you would be able to offset your losses in the bond market with your gains in the Forex market.

Similarly, when the bond yield is dropping, it means the price of the bond is rising. If you want to purchase the bond, this is bad news for you because you will have to pay more for the bond than you would have if you had purchased it yesterday. Again, simultaneously investing in the Forex market can help you offset some of the extra costs of buying a more expensive bond.

Gap 6: Analysis Overload   The bond market offers many varieties—money market funds, municipal securities, Treasury securities, federal agency securities, corporate bonds, mortgage securities, and asset-backed securities—of bonds to choose from. You can also choose from myriad bond funds offered by virtually every mutual fund family and investment bank. To make your decisions, you need to know which ones offer tax advantages, which ones are no-coupon bonds, when they expire, how frequently interest payments are disbursed, what the yield to maturity is, and so on. On top of that, you have to figure out the ratings scales for multiple-rating agencies. Learning whether an "A" rating is better than an "Aa2" rating will take some time and effort.

Forex Gap   Bonds make it very easy to determine exactly how much money you will make in the market during a given year. If a $1,000 bond has an annual coupon (interest) rate of 6 percent, you know you will receive $60 each and every year until the bond expires. This is quite an attractive feature to people on fixed incomes and those who know they have specific financial obligations they have to meet.

The Forex market is not as predictable. Because you have to monitor the market and make individual decisions about your investments, your returns are going to fluctuate. You certainly have the ability to make a lot more money in the Forex market, but your returns will certainly not be as predictable.

Most financial planners would suggest that you keep part of your money in the bond market. This is good advice. You will have to choose how you want to take advantage of the bond market—be it through individual bonds or bond funds—but you should definitely consider putting money in bonds. Of course, you shouldn't invest in any market without identifying how you are going to mind the gaps in that market. Once again, the Forex is the solution.

Forex Market versus Futures Market

It may seem strange to compare the Forex market to the futures market because Forex contracts are actually short-term futures contracts. But even though both markets have many of the same features, the retail Forex market has a few key added benefits you won't want to be without.

The futures market is also often called the *commodities* market because commodity futures make up a large portion of the market. In fact, the futures market was originally created to trade commodities. Nowadays, however, the futures market branches out much farther than commodities—corn, soybeans, orange juice, pork bellies (bacon), and so forth. You can now trade futures contracts on everything from the S&P 500 to the weather. That's right; you can trade weather contracts on the futures market.

A futures contract is a promise to deliver something—be it 100,000 barrels of oil or $100,000 cash—at a certain price on a certain date in the future in exchange for some sort of consideration. For example, if you owned a stack of gold bricks and you thought gold was going to be worth less one year from now than it is today, you might sell a futures contract on gold that states that the buyer of the futures contract has to buy your gold in one year at the same price it is selling at today. That way, if the price of gold does indeed go down, the buyer of the futures contract will still pay you the higher price in exchange for your gold.

You can also take advantage of the futures market when prices are going up. Suppose you knew that you had to buy a pile of gold bricks in one year, and you thought gold prices were going to go up. In this case, you could buy a futures contract from somebody who agrees to sell you their gold in one year at the same price at which it is trading today. That way, if the price of gold does indeed go up, you will be able to buy your pile of gold bricks at a discount because you would be buying it at the same price at which it was trading the previous year.

You can see that many of the benefits that are available to you in the Forex market are also available in the rest of the futures market. As good as the rest of the futures market is, however, there are still a few gaps the Forex market can fill.

Gap 1: Commissions

Most futures brokers charge a commission for each transaction to cover their costs and increase the bottom line. You will need to pay this commission when you enter a trade and when you exit a trade.

Gap 2: Market Hours

Most futures contracts trade in much the same way as the U.S. Treasury bonds and notes trade on the CBOT; they trade on exchanges that have both electronic trading platforms and physical trading floors. The trading floors, or pits, are open only during certain business hours. So if your broker transacts business only on the trading floor, you will have to meet the demands of its schedule. The futures market is available for after-hours trading on electronic markets, such as the GLOBEX, but you often have to pay extra fees to access these trading platforms.

Many different futures exchanges service the futures market, with each one specializing in different futures contracts. And each exchange has its own set of trading rules and schedules. You may have heard of a few of them. The Chicago Mercantile Exchange (CME) specializes in trading commodities futures, currency futures, and stock index futures. The New York Mercantile Exchange (NYMEX) is most well known for trading oil futures. And the New York Board of Trade (NYBOT) specializes in trading sugar, coffee, and U.S. dollar futures. While this is far from a comprehensive list, these are three of the major players.

Gap 3: Liquidity

Because most of the trading in the futures markets occurs in the trading pits, the liquidity of the futures market dries up somewhat during nonbusiness hours. Even though the market is available for trading during the night via the GLOBEX and other electronic exchanges, if no one is awake to be on the other side of your trade, it is going to be very difficult to buy or sell anything at a decent price. The Forex market, in contrast, provides dealers who are willing to guarantee they can fill your orders at a favorable price even in the off-peak hours when the market isn't seeing a lot of activity.

Gap 4: Taxes   This gap does not exist in the futures market because every futures contract receives the same tax treatment the futures contracts in the Forex market enjoy.

Gap 5: Bear (Downtrending) Markets   This gap does exist in the futures market, but it exists in a form that is slightly different from that in the stock or bond markets. While you can buy futures contracts when you think they are going up and sell them when you think they are going down, you do not have any guarantees on your exit prices. Imagine you had sold a futures contract on coffee because you believed that the price of coffee was going to decline during the next few years. Then, out of the blue, a little franchise called Starbucks exploded across the nation, and the demand for coffee soared. This increased demand pushed the value of your futures contract higher, and you were suddenly losing money. The futures market does not have guaranteed stops. You can set stop-loss orders, but the prices you establish in your stop-loss orders are not guaranteed to be met. If the price of coffee rises too fast, you may end up losing more money than you bargained for.

Gap 6: Analysis Overload   While there are certainly not as many investment choices in the futures market as there are in the stock market, you will still have to sift through a lot of possible contracts and news events to adequately track the futures market. Following is an example of some of the commodity futures con-tracts available through the futures market:

Grain and Oilseed Futures
- Corn
- Oats
- Soybeans
- Soybean meal
- Soybean oil
- Rough rice
- Wheat

- Barley
- Canola

Livestock Futures
- Cattle—live
- Lean hogs

Food and Fiber Futures
- Lumber
- Cocoa
- Coffee
- Sugar
- Cotton
- Orange juice
- Azuki beans
- Wool
- Silk
- Rubber
- Copper—high grade
- Gold
- Platinum
- Silver
- Lead
- Aluminum
- Nickel
- Palladium
- Tin
- Zinc

Petroleum Futures
- Crude oil—light sweet
- Heating oil No. 2
- Gasoline
- Natural gas

You get the idea. We haven't gotten into the financial futures contracts—like stock-index futures, single-stock futures, interest-rate futures, and so on.

Forex Gap   Because Forex contracts are futures contracts, there isn't really a Forex gap that the rest of the futures market can fill. You can get involved in the Forex market with less money than you need in the futures market, you can trade with high liquidity 24 hours per day, and you have guaranteed stops. It doesn't get much better than that.

In discussing both the stock and the bond market, we talked about how the Forex market is a nice complement to the investing you are already doing and that you should continue to invest in both the stock and bond markets. The futures market is really another story. You can easily replace all the investing you are doing in the futures market by investing in the Forex market. For example, if you believe commodity prices are going to be going up, instead of taking positions in multiple commodity futures contracts, you could place one simple trade to buy the Canadian dollar. Canada exports more commodities to the United States than any other country. In fact, Canada is the United States' largest trading partner. (We discuss this in more detail later in the book.) As commodity prices rise, the value of the Canadian dollar rises as well. So if you had a choice between putting a lot of money into various futures contracts that do not have guaranteed stops and putting a little bit of money into one Forex contract that has a guaranteed stop and great leverage, which would you choose?

The Forex market is an incredible profit-generating machine on its own, and it is especially effective at filling the inherent gaps in other financial markets. So if you're investing in the stock or bond market, ask yourself why you shouldn't also be investing in the Forex market. There's no good reason. Investing in either of these two markets without investing in the Forex market is like buying homeowner's insurance without buying an umbrella liability policy. Sure, most of the things that happen to your home will be covered by the homeowner's policy, but there are other major claims that won't be. Do your portfolio a favor, and give yourself all the opportunities available to protect what you have while making your money work even harder for you.

LIFE IS GOING TO HAPPEN

One thing we can guarantee is that the Forex market is going to continue to move because life is going to keep happening. Economies are going to cycle back and forth between years of growth and years of decline. Oil prices are going to keep going up and down and up and down. The stock market is going to go through bullish runs and bearish declines. We're going to be surprised by some of the things that happen, and others are going to seem like no big deal. But as long as the world keeps changing, you can make money in the Forex market.

To give you an idea of just how many announcement-based changes are scheduled to take place during the year, look at Table 1.1.

You don't have to know exactly how each one of these announcements affects the Forex market right now. But they do, and you can take advantage of them.

Actually, it is change that makes the Forex market function. Imagine if nothing ever changed—economies never heated up or cooled down, consumers never changed their tastes and preferences, terrorists never struck, and natural disasters never occurred. The values of currencies around the globe would never change. The global community could institute a set exchange rate for every currency, and you would never have to calculate an exchange rate again. As

TABLE 1.1

Annual Economic Announcement-Based Changes

Economic Announcement	Frequency of Announcement
Unemployment rate	Monthly
FOMC interest rate	Eight times per year
Gross domestic product (GDP)	Quarterly
Consumer confidence	Monthly
Consumer price index (CPI)	Monthly
Balance of trade	Quarterly
Current account	Quarterly
Index of leading indicators (LEI)	Monthly
Balance of payments	Quarterly
Durable goods orders	Monthly
Housing starts/building permits	Monthly
New home sales	Monthly
Factory orders	Monthly
Business inventories and sales	Monthly
Institute of Supply Management (ISM)	Monthly
Purchasing manager's index (PMI)	Monthly
Retail sales	Monthly

a matter of fact, this is exactly what the global community tried to do after World War II.

Following the war, most of the major global economies—with the exception of the United States—were in shambles. To address the issues at hand, 730 delegates from 44 different countries converged on the Mount Washington Hotel in Bretton Woods, New Hampshire, in July 1944 to discuss their options. In an effort to stabilize the global economy and help major European and Asian economies rebuild, these delegates agreed to peg their countries' currencies to the U.S. dollar, which in turn would be pegged to the price of gold at $35 per ounce.

Having pegged exchange rates allowed the signing countries of the Bretton Woods Agreement to develop international trade agreements and conduits without having to worry about floating exchange rates. It became much easier to exchange goods and services, and this relative ease of exchange led to a rapid reconstruction and expansion of formerly decimated economies.

While pegging currencies to the U.S. dollar worked for a few decades, the practice was ultimately discarded by larger economies because the world changed. European and Asian economies began to boom, the United States was involved in the Vietnam War, and the pegged currency system ceased to meet the needs of the member countries. It soon became apparent that currencies had to be allowed to float freely to accommodate the various changes each economy was experiencing.

Just as these global economies experienced mammoth changes during the decades following World War II, our financial situations endure changes all the time. To meet the demands of these changes in our lives, we want to have options so that we can choose whatever is going to fit our situation at the time and make alterations when necessary. The Forex market offers you this ability in your investing.

A few years ago my yoga instructor talked about the importance of being flexible. To illustrate what he was saying, he compared a healthy, live tree branch with a brittle, nearly dead tree branch—a concept he attributed to an ancient proverb from India. The healthy, live branch is flexible and can move back and forth, depending on the direction the prevailing forces in nature are pushing it. The brittle, nearly dead branch is not flexible, and if the prevailing forces of nature push it too far in any direction, it will break. In other words, if you want to be successful in life, you need to emulate the healthy, live branch and be flexible.

Rigidity in life can be unpleasant. Rigidity in the markets can be disastrous. Be flexible. Invest your money in more than one place. Put some in the stock market. Put some in the bond market. Put some in the Forex market. You will find it is easier to be flexible and react to changes in the global economy when your money is diversified.

DIVERSIFICATION

Broadway musicals run six days a week year in and year out. It doesn't matter if the lead actor or actress gets sick or if a chorus dancer sprains an ankle; the show must go on. And the show can go on because each cast has understudies who can step in and take the place of anyone who cannot perform. For instance, if the performer who plays the role of Simba in Disney's *The Lion King* gets sick and can't perform, there is another performer in the cast who has also learned the role of Simba and can step in at a moment's notice until the regular performer recovers. Most musicals also have a "swing." The swing is the most versatile performer in the cast and can play almost any role in the show. Often, the swing is called on to step into a role only moments before the curtain rises or after the show has already begun because someone has been hurt or becomes sick. Swings and understudies are essential to a Broadway musical's success because without them, the show can't always go on.

Just as the show must always go on when you're on Broadway, your portfolio and your purchasing power must always go on growing. Any setback in your investment portfolio or in your purchasing power can disrupt your plans for the future. So what do you do if one of your investments gets "sick" and can't perform as well as you had expected? Hopefully, you've diversified your portfolio, so one of your other investments can step in and pick up the slack in growth that your underperforming investment has created.

Most often, investors will diversify among a few mutual funds, some bonds, and cash. They do so because most financial planners you talk to will recommend a mix of these three vehicles. They recommend this mix because as mutual funds are losing value, bonds are usually gaining—or at least holding—their value, and cash is holding its value—unless, of course, inflation is rising. On the other side of the equation, as bonds are losing value, mutual funds will usually be able to pick up the slack. So in essence, bonds are the understudies for mutual funds, and mutual funds are the understudies for bonds. This is a great strategy within your bond and equity portfolio. Diversification decreases risk. Unfortunately, far too few investors are taking advantage of the "swing" of investment vehicles: Forex.

PROTECT AND MULTIPLY

Diversification into the Forex market provides a twofold financial benefit—it enables you to protect and multiply your money at the same time. Let's first talk about how the Forex market can protect your money. When financial professionals and institutions talk about protecting their money and assets, they often talk about hedging their risks.

Hedging (Protecting)

A hedge is a series of bushes or small trees that have been planted in a row to distinguish one plot of land from another. Medieval English landowners and privacy-starved celebrities are famous for their hedges. Medieval English landowners planted hedges because they wanted to define boundaries and create limits to protect their land. Celebrities plant hedges to provide a barrier between themselves and the paparazzi. But these two groups of people aren't the only ones who create hedges. In fact, everybody does it. Hedging— or protecting—your property or privacy is a natural instinct. We deposit our money in a bank to keep it safe. We keep our valuables in a safe or a safety deposit box to ensure that nothing bad happens to them. We lock our doors and install security systems to protect us from anything that may be dangerous. We put up fences around our yards. We put passwords on our computers. Basically, we protect everything we own.

Everything, that is, except the value of our money. We protect the money itself by placing it in banks, safety deposit boxes, and the like, but we rarely protect its value. The value of our money is exposed to at least one of two financial risks: market risk and inflation risk.

Market risk is the risk you accept when you put your money in the market—be it stocks or bonds. If the market crashes, the value of your investments will also crash. True, the broker handling your investments may be a strong company with impeccable standards, but the fiscal and ethical prowess of your broker has very little to do with the safety of your investments. Regardless of the strength of the firm you invest through, you are still exposed to market risk.

The Forex is the solution to market risk because you can offset your losses in the stock or bond market with your gains in the Forex market. You can place trades in the Forex market that will profit from the decline in the stock or bond market. By doing this, as your balance in your stock or bond account declines, the balance in your Forex account is increasing. When you look at your overall portfolio using this strategy, you will notice you have not lost any money. You hedged against the losses resulting from market risk by investing in a different market, the Forex.

"I've taken care of market risk," you may say. "I've put my money in CDs, money market accounts, and bonds. No matter what happens, I will never lose my principal." While this may be true, you have still accounted for only one of the two financial risks. You may never lose your principal, but conservative investments do not protect you from inflation.

Inflation risk is a risk you have to accept. You cannot escape it. Inflation decreases the purchasing power of money. This means that as inflation continues, you will be able to buy less and less for $1, and your savings and investments will lose their value. The price of U.S. postage stamps provides a great illustration of the effects of inflation. In 1960, the price of a stamp was less than 5 cents. Today, the price of a stamp is 39 cents. That is an increase of nearly 700 percent. Obviously, $1 bought a lot more in 1960 than $1 buys today, and that trend is only going to continue. If inflation rises at a higher percentage than the percentage of return you are receiving from your conservative investments, you are actually losing purchasing power even though you are making money.

The Forex is the solution to inflation risk because you can off-set your loss of spending power with your gains in the Forex market. Inflation affects the Forex market in a fairly predictable manner. Knowing this, you can make your Forex trades accordingly and profit from rising inflation. You can then take these profits, combine them with the profits from your other conservative investments, and nullify the effects of inflation.

Multiplying

While the Forex market is the perfect solution for hedging your other investments, it is also the perfect solution for multiplying your investment returns. You've seen how gains in the Forex market can offset the losses in other financial markets, but the real excitement begins when you are doing well in those other financial markets.

The stock market, for instance, is bound to go up some of the time, and, when it does, you can take advantage of that movement with your stock and mutual fund holdings. But it doesn't stop there. You can multiply your returns in the stock market by coupling them with your returns in the Forex market during the same period. Remember, you can make money in the Forex market when stocks and mutual funds are going up or down. It doesn't matter which direction the stock market is moving; the versatility of the Forex market allows you to be profitable regardless.

Too many people equate the Forex market with the stock market the same way they equate the bond market with the stock market. Generally, when the bond market is going up, the stock market is going down. And when the bond market is going down, the stock market is generally going up. This is why financial planners suggest that you hold both stocks and bonds in your portfolio. They tend to offset each other nicely. The Forex market doesn't work like that. It does not automatically move in the opposite direction from the stock market. It moves independently. This is what allows you to make money in the Forex market in both good and bad times in the stock market.

Take advantage of the Forex market to *multiply* your returns. Increase your earnings by utilizing the fabulous leverage available in the Forex market, and increase the percentage of your earnings that you will be able to keep in your own pocket that result from the tremendous tax advantages available in the Forex market.

THE FOREX CAN BE FICKLE

Although life may unfold in a fairly predictable manner, it is bound to throw you a curveball every now and then. Think about going to the produce section of your grocery store. When certain fruits and vegetables are in season, they cost much less than they do at other times of the year because there is such an abundant supply of them. On the other hand, those same fruits and vegetables, when they are out of season, can cost a lot more because there is a smaller supply of them, and they probably had to be imported from somewhere far. There are also times when the fruits and vegetables are in season but there aren't very many of them because it was a poor growing year that year, or a random disease attacked the crop. In cases like this, even though the fruits and vegetables are in season, they are still expensive.

The Forex market operates in much the same way. There will always be typical, expected movements in the market based on economic shifts. However, there will also always be unexpected hiccups in the market, which you aren't expecting, that can adversely affect your investments. These market surprises are nothing you should be afraid of. They happen to everyone. Luckily, the Forex market offers you tremendous advantages in protecting your assets and investments. You will have to be disciplined and prepared, but you can handle anything in this market.

It is also possible for you to take advantage of the unexpected changes in the Forex market. All too often we categorize surprises and changes in the investment world as negative experiences. Certainly, most people were surprised and lost a lot of money when the dot-com bubble burst in 2000, but there were also a lot of people— who understood what they were watching for—who made a lot of money during the incredible rise in the stock market during the 1990s and held onto it. The same holds true in the Forex market. People may be surprised if the value of the U.S. dollar suddenly plummets, but those who understand and know what to watch for can capitalize on that movement and walk away with tremendous profits.

THE SKEPTIC'S FAQ

A healthy dose of skepticism is a good—and sometimes essential— trait in today's world. We work in an environment in which most of the people around us are ardent stock and stock option investors. Almost every one of them with whom we have discussed the Forex market has asked us why they should get involved with it when they are already involved in the stock and stock options markets. They want to know if it is really as exciting as they have heard. As we explain our reasons and rationale, we are usually able to convince them to at least take a look at Forex. We don't win everybody over, and that's okay. The most exciting thing for us is that they are asking good questions. These are intelligent people who sincerely want answers so that they can make informed decisions. And we assume, since you are reading this book, that you are too.

To try to help answer some of the questions you probably have, we have compiled a list of the questions we hear most frequently and our responses to them. If you still have questions after you're through reading this list, send us an e-mail at faq@profitingwithforex.com, and we'll respond to your questions personally.

Why haven't I heard of the Forex market before?

The Forex market has been readily available to retail investors for only the past few years. While banks and other large institutions have been taking advantage of the Forex market for many years, retail investors have had access to the market only since the late 1990s—and that access was extremely limited for the first few years. Not until recently has it become quite simple to enter and enjoy the benefits of the Forex market. Plus, a lot has changed in the past few years. Accordingly, many of the Forex books that were written a few years ago are now out of date.

Unfortunately for most retail investors, they were too preoccupied to notice that a tremendous new market had been made available to them. They were too worried about their stock accounts declining after the dot-com disaster to be looking at other investment opportunities. Plus, financial planners and stockbrokers didn't do much to promote the Forex market. Why would they? Most of them don't understand how the Forex market works, and it doesn't benefit them to tell you about it. Financial planners and stockbrokers don't make any money when you invest in the Forex market, but they do make a lot of money when you invest in the stock market; they make commissions.

If you're looking for big-name credibility in the Forex market, look no further than the most famous stock market investor who ever lived: Warren Buffett. In Berkshire Hathaway's 2003 annual report to shareholders, Buffett explained, "During 2002 we entered the foreign currency market for the first time in my life, and in 2003 we enlarged our position, as I became increasingly bearish on the dollar." This turned out to be an incredibly profitable move for the company. In 2003, while Berkshire Hathaway made a pretax gain of only $448 million in common stocks, it made a pretax gain of $825 million in foreign exchange contracts. Not too bad for its second year of investing.

Isn't the leverage in the Forex market too dangerous?

Leverage can be extremely dangerous if you use it incorrectly. Anybody who tells you something different is trying to sell you something or doesn't truly understand what leverage is. With that said, you can eliminate excess danger by understanding and using leverage wisely. You do not need to use all of the leverage available to you to be profitable in the Forex market.

The same concept applies to many things in our lives. Take electricity for example. By itself, electricity is extremely dangerous—to the point that it can kill you if you are not careful. But because we have learned how to harness its incredible power, electricity has revolutionized the way we live. We all know that there is a potential danger inherent in using electricity, but we use it anyway because we are confident that we have set up the appropriate safeguards to prevent us from being injured. The same holds true for the available leverage in the Forex market.

Earlier in the book, as we were discussing the advantages of the Forex market, we mentioned the concept of guaranteed stops. Stop orders allow you to specify the exact price at which you would like to exit a trade. It doesn't matter if you are using a lot of leverage or just a little bit of leverage; you can specify exactly where you want to get out with your stop order. And it doesn't matter if you want to risk a few hundred dollars in your trade or a few thousand dollars; you can set your stop order to take you out exactly where you want to exit the trade. You are in complete control.

Leverage is a great tool for accumulating wealth. And just like any other tool, you need to know how to properly use it to be effective. Don't be afraid of it. Learn about it. Figure out what it is and how it works. Then see how you can apply it in your investing to take full advantage of it.

Don't you need to be an economist to make money in the Forex market?

You do not need to be an economist to profit in the Forex market. This is a common misconception. All you need is a basic understanding of a few simple concepts and a lot of common sense. In fact, it's much easier to follow the news that is affecting the Forex market than it is to follow the news that affects the stock market. To fully understand and analyze all that is happening in the stock market, you need to have a solid grasp of financial accounting, and you need to follow all the earnings and news releases posted by the companies that comprise the stock market, the analysts who dissect the stock market, and the government agencies that regulate the stock market. To fully understand and analyze the Forex market, all you need to do is read the newspaper and watch the evening news.

The same events that affect your daily life affect the Forex market. If you are paying attention to the world around you on a daily basis, you are tuned in to what is affecting the Forex market.

Certainly, you need to know what you are looking for to truly make money, and we are going to get you started in your Forex education. You don't have to be looking for a lot. You don't need to learn any new calculations. You just need to learn some basic cause-and-effect scenarios. Anyone can do this.

Don't you have to be rich to invest in the Forex market?

The Forex market is surprisingly inexpensive to get involved in. When you're investing in the stock market, most brokers require you have a minimum investment of $2,000. You have to have that much money invested with the firm to make it worth it for the broker to take on your account. It's different in the Forex market. Thanks to the wonderful leverage you enjoy in the Forex market, you can open an account with as little as $250.

Having more money to begin with is always a nice advantage because you can make more money if you have more money. But let's face it. We don't all have a lot of money. We would, however, like the money we do have to be working for us. Reasonable Forex investors are not going to turn their $250 into $25,000 overnight, but they can get started.

For those of you looking for a specific recommendation of how much to get started with, we believe that you should open your account with at least $2,500. Starting with less than $2,500 seems to make people a bit too cavalier in their investing because they figure they can afford to lose the small amount they put into their accounts. And we have seen too many traders blow up several $500 accounts when, if they would have just waited until they could start with a larger account, they would have taken their investing more seriously and been more conservative.

What if I don't have a lot of time?

Join the crowd. Nobody seems to have a lot of time these days. And what time we do have available seems to come at different times for different people. Some people are available during the day. Some are available at night. Whether you're a morning person or an evening person and whether you have only a couple of minutes per day or a couple of hours, you can make the Forex market work for you.

The Japanese yen, Australian dollar, and New Zealand dollar are all great currencies to trade during the evening hours in the United States because the sun is just rising on all the economies these currencies represent. Usually, the market is busiest for a particular currency when the economy represented by that currency is awake and running. Most of the news that will affect a currency will be released during the country's business hours.

For the morning people among us, the British pound, Swiss franc, and euro each provide excellent opportunities to make money. In the early hours of the U.S. business day, the economies and businesses in Europe are still up and running—which generates a lot of activity in the Forex market. This is especially true for the U.S. dollar versus the euro. The currency pair of the U.S. dollar and the euro is the most heavily traded currency pair in the world. So when both the European and U.S. markets are open, this pair is bound to be moving.

Once you have asked all your questions about the Forex market, it is time to get involved and learn more. Is the Forex market perfect? Of course not. Nor is any other financial market. But the Forex market comes closer than any other market out there. We want to prove it to you. We're serious about your asking us questions. We want to address any concern you may have that is holding you back from taking advantage of the world's greatest market. It is that important. See for yourself what a difference a little diversification makes.

TAKING ADVANTAGE OF THE FOREX MARKET

Everybody can take advantage of the Forex market. You've already seen how easy it is to get involved in this market and enjoy the tax advantages, improved leverage, and 24-hour access it provides. The next step is learning what makes the market tick. Once you understand why the Forex market does what it does, you can put yourself in a position to profit from it.

In the Forex market, professionals use two types of analysis to both evaluate what the markets are doing and determine where the markets will be going in the future: fundamental analysis and technical analysis. *Fundamental analysis* is the study of the factors that affect the economies represented by the various currencies. For example, inflation rates and oil prices affect the economy of the United States and therefore affect the value of the U.S. dollar. We discuss exactly how each of these fundamental factors affects the value of the U.S. dollar later in this book. The important thing to understand at this point is that the U.S. dollar generally has a fairly predictable reaction to changes in fundamental economic factors. And if you know what those reactions are going to be, you can profit from them.

Technical analysis is the study of a currency's price movements on a chart. Forex investors will use charts like the one shown in Figure 1.4 to forecast what they believe will happen next in the market.

Using charts is an effective way of distilling what has happened in the Forex market into an easy-to-use format. For example, if the price is moving higher on the chart, it will most likely continue to move higher unless something happens to change its direction. It's like Newton's first law of motion—an object in motion tends to stay in motion unless acted upon by some other force. Technical analysis helps you identify which direction the price is currently moving and when it might change direction.

Both fundamental analysis and technical analysis can help you be profitable in the Forex market. Unfortunately, most professionals who use fundamental analysis swear by it and scoff at technical analysis. And vice versa for most professionals who use technical analysis. However, we have a different point of view. We figure that if you have both types of analysis available to you, why not use both? Certainly you have a better chance of success if you use all the tools that are available to you. To illustrate, imagine you are back in your

FIGURE 1.4

Chart of the EUR/USD, daily intervals

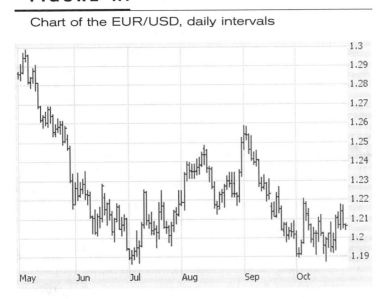

Source: Prophet.net

junior high shop class and you have the assignment of building a birdhouse. On the table in front of you is a stack of wood, a pile of nails, a hammer, and a saw. We are sure that if you really wanted to, you could build that birdhouse without using the saw. You could break the wood apart using the hammer and then nail the pieces together. You could also build that birdhouse without using the hammer. You could saw the wood into nice, clean pieces and then whack the nails as hard as you could with the side of the saw blade to put the pieces together. Of course, if you are a rational individual, neither one of these alternatives sounds appealing. You are going to use both the hammer and the saw to build a beautiful, high-quality birdhouse. The same concept holds true when you are investing in the Forex market. It would be silly not to use all the tools at your disposal.

In this book we introduce you to a wealth of tools you can use to make profits in the Forex market. We are confident in these tools because we use them on a daily basis as we manage money in the Forex market for our clients through our Commodity Trading Advisor (CTA)—Ouroboros Capital Management, LLC, and as we produce content and products for the largest investor-education company in the United States, INVESTools Inc.

Before we dive into the intricacies of the fundamental analysis and technical analysis tools you have at your disposal, however, you need to have an understanding of the basics of the Forex market. Once you understand Forex lingo, how the Forex market works, and the genesis of the Forex market, you will be able to apply the specific fundamental and technical tools and techniques we show you to enjoy the incredible profit potential this market offers.

CHAPTER 2

Basic Lingo Lesson

Before we delve any deeper into the exciting possibilities that exist in the Forex market, we need to get you up to speed on the language used in the Forex market. Most of us are quite comfortable with the lingo of the stock market because we've participated in it in one form or another through retirement and investment plans. While the lingo in the Forex market is similar in many respects—a profit is still a profit—there are some subtle differences. Don't worry. As far as vocabulary lessons go, this one is quite a lot of fun. Honestly. And there are only three terms you need to understand: pip, currency pair, and contract (or lot).

PIP

While some of you may recognize "Pip" as a character in Charles Dickens' *Great Expectations*, we hope you will become more intimately acquainted with the pips in the Forex market because you will be using them to determine your profits and losses. A *pip*, or point, is the smallest unit of measurement in the Forex market. For instance, when you are buying or selling something, you quote the price in dollars and cents, and the cents extend out to only two decimal places—e.g., $1.25. In the Forex market, however, most quotes are carried out to four decimal places—e.g., 1.2500. The last decimal place is called a pip. So if the exchange rate moved from 1.2500 to 1.2509, we would say that the price moved up 9 pips. You make money when the pips move your way in a trade.

As with most rules in life, there is an exception to the rule of exchange rates being carried out to four decimal points. Any exchange rate that contains the Japanese yen or the Thai baht as one of the currencies will only be carried out to two decimal places. If you want to know why, you will have to take it up with the International Organization for Standardization (ISO). Yes, there is such an organization. It is located in Geneva, Switzerland, and you would be amazed at the fields it affects—from health care and electrical engineering to ship building and metallurgy.

CURRENCY PAIR

We wouldn't have a Forex market if we weren't able to compare the value of one currency with the value of another currency. It is this comparison that drives prices. Forex contracts are always quoted in pairs. The euro versus the U.S. dollar (EUR/USD) is the most heavily traded currency pair. The U.S. dollar versus the Japanese yen (USD/JPY) is another popular pair. Table 2.1 contains the most common currency pairs, their trading symbols, and their nicknames.

One distinction you do need to make when looking at a currency pair is which currency is the base currency and which currency is the quote currency. The *base currency* is the first currency listed in the pairing. For example, the base currency in the EUR/USD pair is the euro, which is listed first. The base currency represents the strength or weakness of a currency as shown in Figure 2.1. As the lines on the chart of the EUR/USD move higher, it means the value of the euro in relation to the U.S. dollar is getting stronger.

TABLE 2.1

Currency Pairs, Their Trading Symbols, and Their Nicknames

Currency Pair	Trading Symbol	Nickname
Euro vs. U.S. dollar	EUR/USD	Euro
Great Britain pound vs. U.S. dollar	GBP/USD	Pound, sterling, or cable
U.S. dollar vs. Swiss franc	USD/CHF	Swissie
U.S. dollar vs. Japanese yen	USD/JPY	Yen
U.S. dollar vs. Canadian dollar	USD/CAD	Loonie
Australian dollar vs. U.S. dollar	AUD/USD	Aussie
New Zealand dollar vs. U.S. dollar	NZD/USD	Kiwi

FIGURE 2.1

Uptrending EUR/USD, hourly intervals

Source: Prophet.net

When the lines on the chart of the EUR/USD move lower (see Figure 2.2), it means that the value of the euro in relation to the U.S. dollar is getting weaker.

The same principle applies to the USD/JPY pair (see Figure 2.3) or any other currency pair. The U.S. dollar is the base currency in the USD/JPY pair. So as the lines chart of the USD/JPY move higher, it means that the value of the U.S. dollar in relation to the Japanese yen is getting stronger. And if the lines in the chart of the USD/JPY were to move lower, that would mean that the value of the U.S. dollar in relation to the Japanese yen was getting weaker.

The *quote currency* is the second currency listed in the pairing. For example, the quote currency in the GBP/USD pair is the U.S. dollar, which is listed second. The quote currency is important because it is the currency in which the exchange rate is quoted. To illustrate, when you say the exchange rate between the British pound and the U.S. dollar is 1.7533, you are saying that it costs $1.7533 to purchase £1. The same principle applies to the USD/CHF pair or any other currency pair. The Swiss franc is the quote currency in the USD/CHF pair. So when you say that the exchange rate between the U.S. dollar and the Swiss franc is 1.2468, you are saying that it takes 1.2468 Swiss francs to purchase $1.

FIGURE 2.2

Downtrending EUR/USD, hourly intervals

Source: Prophet.net

FIGURE 2.3

Uptrending USD/JPY, hourly intervals

Source: Prophet.net

CONTRACT (OR LOT)

In the stock market, when you want to buy something, you buy a share of stock. In the Forex market, when you want to buy something, you buy a *contract*, or a *lot*. You use the term *contract* because the Forex market utilizes currency futures contracts. There is no way to buy a share of the U.S. dollar the way you would buy a share of Google in the stock market. When you trade in the Forex market, you are trading contracts to buy and sell various currencies.

Contracts are divided into two categories: mini contracts and full-size contracts. A mini contract controls 10,000 units of whatever the quote currency in the currency pair is. So, for instance, if you were to buy one mini contract on the EUR/USD, you would control $10,000 because the U.S. dollar is the quote currency in the pair. If you were to buy one mini contract on the USD/JPY, you would control ¥10,000 because the Japanese yen is the quote currency in the pair. A full-size contract controls 100,000 units of whatever the quote currency in the currency pair is. As you can see, a full-size contract is ten times larger than a mini contract. Being able to choose between either mini or full-size contracts allows you to tailor your investing to best meet your investment style and strategy.

Make sure you take the time to feel comfortable with the lingo of the Forex market. If you have a solid foundation of knowledge, you'll be much better off in your investing. So now that you've got the basics, let's take a look at what makes the Forex market tick, how it came to be, and how you can use it to protect and increase your money.

CHAPTER 3

How the Forex
Market Works

The Forex market, just like every other market in the world, is driven by supply and demand. In fact, understanding the concept of supply and demand is so important in the Forex market that we are going to take a step back into Economics 101 for a moment to make sure we're all on the same page. Having a good grasp of supply and demand will make all of the difference in your Forex investing career because it will give you the ability to sift through the mountain of news that is produced every day and find those messages that are most important. So how do supply and demand affect the Forex market?

Supply is the measure of how much of a particular commodity is available at any one time. The value of a commodity—a currency in this case—is directly linked to its supply. As the supply of a currency increases, the currency becomes less valuable. Conversely, as the supply of a currency decreases, the currency becomes more valuable. Think about rocks and diamonds. Rocks aren't very valuable because they are everywhere. You can take a walk down a country road and have your choice of hundreds or even thousands of different rocks. Diamonds, on the other hand, are expensive because there aren't that many of them in circulation. There is a small supply of diamonds in the world, and you have to pay a premium if you want one.

On the other side of the economic equation, we find demand. *Demand* is the measure of how much of a particular commodity people want at any one time. Demand for a currency has the opposite effect on the value of a currency than does supply. As the demand for a currency increases, the currency becomes more valuable. Conversely, as the demand for a currency decreases, the currency becomes less valuable. To get a good idea of the effects demand can have on something's value, you have to look no further than Tickle Me Elmo. When Tickle Me Elmo was first released, there was an insanely high demand for the toy. Mothers and fathers were trampling each other to grab and pay for Elmo before someone else could wrestle it from their arms so they could make sure they had everything on their kid's holiday list. For those who weren't fast or aggressive enough to get Tickle Me Elmo at the store, paying outrageously high prices on eBay was their last resort. Huge demand had made this red, giggling doll much more valuable than it would have been if nobody's child had wanted it.

To illustrate how supply and demand interact to determine an ideal exchange rate in the Forex market, we use a standard supply and demand graph (see Figure 3.1). Supply is represented by a solid diagonal line that is directed up from a low point at the left to a high point at the right. Demand is represented by a dotted diagonal line that is directed down from a high point at the left to a low point at the right. The y, or vertical, axis represents price. The x, or horizontal, axis represents the quantity of supply and demand. Finally, the ideal exchange rate is represented by the point at which the two diagonal

FIGURE 3.1

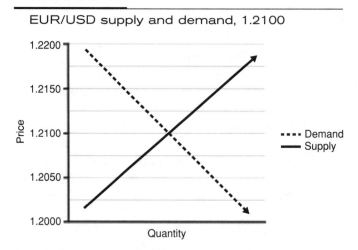

EUR/USD supply and demand, 1.2100

Source: Ouroboros Capital Management, LLC

lines intersect. In this case, the supply and demand graph indicates that the ideal exchange rate for the EUR/USD pair is $1.2100.

To illustrate an increase in either supply or demand, all you have to do is move the corresponding line to the right along the *x* axis. So if supply is increasing, you move the diagonal supply line farther to the right. If demand is increasing, you move the diagonal demand line farther to the right. To illustrate a decrease in either supply or demand, you simply do the opposite. All you have to do is move the corresponding line to the left along the *x* axis. If supply is decreasing, you move the diagonal supply line farther to the left. If demand is decreasing, you move the diagonal demand line farther to the left.

As we discussed, as supply increases, the ideal price decreases. You can see in Figure 3.2 that as the diagonal supply line moves farther and farther right—illustrating an increase in supply—the intersection of the two lines moves lower and lower on the *y* axis. This tells us that the ideal exchange rate is getting lower and lower.

Conversely, as shown in Figure 3.3, as the diagonal supply line moves farther and farther left—illustrating a decrease in supply—the intersection of the two lines moves higher and higher on the *y* axis. This tells us that the ideal exchange rate is getting higher and higher.

Moving the diagonal demand line left and right will have similar effects on the exchange rate. As demand increases, the ideal price increases. So when you move the diagonal demand line farther and

FIGURE 3.2

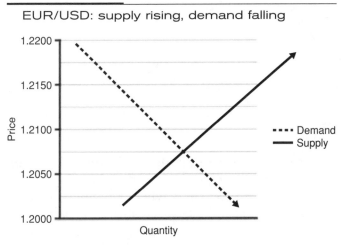

EUR/USD: supply rising, demand falling

Source: Ouroboros Capital Management, LLC

FIGURE 3.3

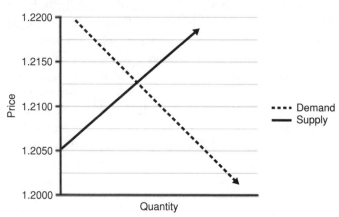

EUR/USD: supply falling, demand rising

Source: Ouroboros Capital Management, LLC

FIGURE 3.4

EUR/USD: demand rising, price rising

Source: Ouroboros Capital Management, LLC

farther right—illustrating an increase in demand—the intersection of the two diagonal lines moves higher and higher. (See Figure 3.4.)

You can also see (in Figure 3.5) how when you move the diagonal demand line farther and farther left—illustrating a decrease in demand—the intersection of the two diagonal lines moves lower and lower.

FIGURE 3.5

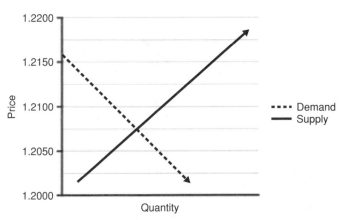

EUR/USD: demand falling, price falling

Source: Ouroboros Capital Management, LLC

FIGURE 3.6

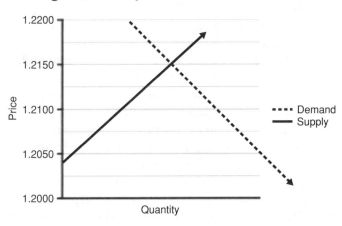

EUR/USD: demand rising, supply falling, price rising dramatically

Source: Ouroboros Capital Management, LLC

The instances in which you see a dramatic shift in the ideal price level come when both the supply and demand lines are moving. For instance, if demand for a currency suddenly increases while supply is decreasing, the ideal price level will climb very quickly. (See Figure 3.6.)

FIGURE 3.7

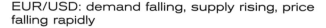

EUR/USD: demand falling, supply rising, price falling rapidly

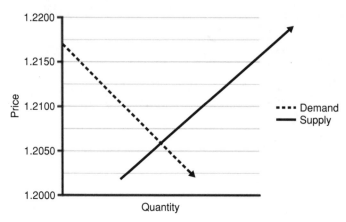

On the flip side, if demand for a currency suddenly falls off while supply is increasing, the ideal price level will fall just as quickly. (See Figure 3.7.) Supply and demand work efficiently in tandem.

Take a moment to make sure you feel comfortable with the concept of supply and demand and how these graphs represent the interaction between the two because we use these graphs to explain why the Forex market does what it does and how you can profit from it.

Understanding the movement of the Forex market is relatively simple because the same forces of supply and demand you experience in your life every day play a significant role in determining the exchange rates in the Forex market. Take oil prices, for example. When demand for oil goes up or the supply of oil drops off, oil prices go up. As oil prices go up, gasoline and natural gas prices go up. As gasoline and natural gas prices go up, you end up spending more to drive around town and to heat your home. And as you spend more and more on oil-based products, your budget gets leaner and leaner. The same factors that affect your budget affect the budgets of the world's largest corporations and governments.

One country that suffers from rising oil prices just the way you do is Japan. Japan imports nearly 100 percent of its oil. It's not known for its booming oil reserves, so it doesn't have much of a choice. Therefore, any oil Japan wants to use to produce electronics, cars, and other goods must be bought at whatever the going rate is. But that's just the beginning. Japan's economy relies on its ability to export the goods it creates to other countries, like the United States. As you've noticed driving around town, it costs a lot of money to transport your groceries, your kids, and yourself from one place to another. It costs even more when you have to ship your goods across the Pacific Ocean. Every car, DVD player, and computer Japan produces is becoming more and more expensive to ship to consumers. So when you look at it, Japan is getting hit on both sides. It has to import all its oil at inflated prices to create its goods, and then it has to pay inflated prices to ship all the goods it creates.

So what impact does all this have on Japanese goods? It makes them more expensive. If Japanese companies have to pay more to produce their products and then have to pay more to distribute their products, they are going to have to charge more for their products so that they can cover their expenses and make a profit. As products become more and more expensive, consumers are able to buy less and less. And as consumers buy less, companies make less money, which leads to all sorts of economically negative outcomes. Now, let's take a step back and look at what all this has to do with the exchange rate of the Japanese yen.

Looking through the lens of supply and demand, you can see how an increase in the price of oil would affect the value of the Japanese yen. Oil is priced and sold in U.S. dollars. As oil becomes more expensive, purchasers in Japan have to convert more and more of their Japanese yen into U.S. dollars so they can pay for their oil. This increases the supply of Japanese yen in the Forex market and subsequently lowers the value of the Japanese yen. To compound the problem, as Japanese goods become more expensive and fewer and fewer people can afford to buy them, the demand for Japanese yen falls. Since you must purchase Japanese products in Japanese yen, you have to sell whatever currency you have to buy Japanese yen. The fewer products you buy, the fewer Japanese yen you need. And when you don't need something, you stop demanding it. Rising supply plus falling demand equals a decrease in the value of the Japanese yen.

The price of oil and its effect on the Japanese yen is just one example of how supply and demand affects the Forex market. We look at many other fundamental factors that influence the Forex market in the coming chapters. The important thing now is that you feel comfortable with the concept of supply and demand. Once you are comfortable with this most basic and most important concept of economics, you will be unstoppable in the Forex market.

So, every time you analyze the Forex market, all you have to do is ask yourself how supply and demand are going to be affected by what is going on.

CHAPTER 4

Genesis and Growth of the Forex Market

The Forex market emerged from a changing global financial landscape, and it continues to change and adapt within that same volatile landscape. As it continues to develop, it is bound to demonstrate the same traits and reactions that have characterized it to this point. Knowing that the Forex can be predictably fickle, we have recognized the importance of learning about the genesis and growth of the Forex market so that we can better understand why it behaves the way it does today and how it is going to behave in the future. You have to understand the market before you can profit from it.

You must realize that we are not referring to a stale chronology of key events and dates that mark various changes in the Forex market when we talk about its genesis and growth. We couldn't care less about specific dates and locations. We don't want to know when things changed. We want to understand *why* they changed. The dates aren't going to move ahead in time and affect tomorrow's market, but the same forces that shaped the history of the Forex market are bound to shape its future.

Many of the economic forces that shaped the Forex market took time to develop, and they played themselves out slowly over a number of years. Only those who were not paying attention can claim that any of these forces snuck up on them unawares. Other economic forces play themselves out every day and shape the news we hear and the immediate profits and losses we stew over.

You only have to do one thing to be profitable in the Forex market. Well, maybe two things. First, you have to accept the fact that history repeats itself—often with a new twist, but it repeats itself nonetheless. Second, you have to act on your knowledge of the past. Don't worry. We're going to get to the specifics of implementation a little later in the book, but you've got to learn a few things first.

The Forex market is an impartial observer of political philosophies, social attitudes, and personal prejudices. Because the Forex is borderless and impartial, only two primary drivers motivate major market participants: risk reduction and profits. In other words, the Forex gives you the tremendous ability to sift through all the noise and misinformation in the global community and find the basic economic factors that are driving the market. We must warn you, however, that as these concepts become clearer, you will find times when you seem to be the only person thinking rationally. Irrational exuberance, to use a phrase coined by Alan Greenspan, former chairman of the Federal Reserve, is a very real part of the national and global marketplace. But if you've learned your lessons from history, you will recognize that all this has happened before, and you will be able to profit from your knowledge in the Forex.

THE MODERN GOLD STANDARD

The U.S. dollar used to be on a gold standard. The idea behind a gold standard is to attach the value of a currency to a fixed amount of gold that is then held in trust by the government. When you think about it, the little pieces of paper you carry around in your wallet really aren't worth a whole lot. Certainly, it costs some money to print and distribute paper money, but why is a piece of paper with "$20" printed on it worth twenty times more than a piece of paper that is the same size, shape, and color with "$1" printed on it? It used to be worth more because the piece of paper with $20 printed on it was a promissory note from the U.S. Treasury for $20 worth of gold. You could literally exchange the paper money in your pocket for gold if you wanted to. This is obviously no longer the case, but this is where paper money in the United States got its start.

The U.S. dollar is not the only currency to have been fixed or pegged to a certain amount or weight of a precious metal. The British pound was once worth one troy pound (12 troy ounces) of sterling silver. This is why a pound is called a pound and where it originally got the nickname "sterling."

The dollar was pegged at one time to both silver and gold, but a glut of silver—thanks to the mining boom—flooded the market, drove its value down, and eventually broke the government's peg to silver. This break didn't happen immediately, though. The powerful silver producers' lobby successfully forced the U.S. government to temporarily maintain the value of silver by purchasing huge amounts of it from producers for several years. Finally, after the pressure from outside the silver producers' lobby eclipsed the pressure from within, the administration changed its policies regarding the relationship between the U.S. dollar and silver and dumped the peg. Although we still see powerful lobbies exerting pressure on the U.S. government to affect the value of the U.S. dollar, the sheer size of the Forex market usually precludes this from happening. It takes an astronomical amount of pressure to move the Forex market, and individual governments and institutions are often incapable of mustering enough force on their own. This evens out the playing field for everyone involved in the market.

From 1900 to 1934, the U.S. dollar was fixed to a gold standard of $20.67 per ounce of gold. In 1934, President Franklin D. Roosevelt artificially reduced the value of a dollar by changing the exchange rate from $20.67 per ounce of gold to $35 per ounce. This was a 69 percent drop in the value of the U.S. dollar. Instead of being able to buy an ounce of gold for $20.67, you now had to come up with an extra $14.33 to buy the same ounce of gold. But, in reality, even if you could afford the price increase, you still wouldn't be able to buy any gold. To maintain control of the artificial devaluation he had imposed on the U.S. dollar, Roosevelt also made it illegal for U.S. citizens to own gold—aside from incidental gold jewelry or gold used in industrial applications. This may sound extraordinary, but it is true. And, as a result of this decision, the U.S. Treasury ceased production of gold coins and destroyed a limited run on the famed 1933 illegal double eagle $20 gold coin. This prohibition lasted until the 1960s.

While a dramatic, artificial change in the value of the U.S. dollar may seem a bit extreme, Roosevelt had good reasons to make the change. Roosevelt devalued the dollar to promote domestic economic growth by making U.S. exports more attractive to foreign buyers. If you are a British consumer and your British pound is worth one U.S. dollar, you will be able to buy $1 worth of U.S. goods with your British pound. However, if your British pound is suddenly now worth two U.S. dollars, you will be able to buy $2 worth of U.S. goods with your one British pound. The more you can buy with your money, the more you are likely to buy.

This short explanation illustrates just one of the two primary problems symptomatic of a metallic-monetary standard: the standard is only as good as the government that sets it. Roosevelt could have arbitrarily set the new gold standard at almost any value he chose. However, a government decree cannot decide the true value of gold or any other precious metal. The gold market ultimately decides the value of gold. The second problem inherent in a metallic-monetary standard is the supply of the metal itself can fluctuate wildly. When gold is flooding the market, like it was during the gold strikes in California and Australia during the 1850s, the inherent value of the gold decreases. When the accepted value of gold is pegged to a certain dollar amount, however, the increase in the supply of gold can lead to inflation.

As unstable as the peg of $35 per ounce of gold was in the middle of the twentieth century, it turned out to be the pillar of stability the rest of the world reached out to at the end of World War II. The war had devastated the economies of Europe and Japan, and members of the global economy had to establish some common ground to facilitate rebuilding. They found this common ground in the value of the U.S. dollar that was pegged to gold. Leaders from around the world agreed—through the Bretton Woods Accord—to piggyback on the strength of the U.S. dollar by pegging the values of their currencies to the value of the U.S. dollar. This was a convenient way to maintain stability in the global market, but it turned out to be only a short-term solution. Pegging currencies to one another requires an extraordinary amount of financial prudence and stability from all parties involved, and it proved to be too much for the signing members of the Bretton Woods Accord. The global economy is a dynamic place. Believing the world will always be stable is shortsighted and naive.

At the time the Bretton Woods Accord was signed, most currencies were allowed to fluctuate only within a narrow band of 1 percent of the value of the U.S. dollar. This meant that when an economy developed an outstanding balance of payments with another economy—because it had imported more goods from that country than it had exported to it—the resulting debit could be offset by transferring gold to that country to bring the books back into balance. However, if a country does not have enough gold to reconcile its international accounts, it has two choices. It can increase the amount of goods and services it is exporting, or it can devalue its currency. Actually, thanks to the Bretton Woods Accord, a country had only one choice because it had to maintain its currency's peg to the U.S. dollar, which meant it couldn't devalue its currency. So if a country developed an account deficit and wasn't able to increase its exports by adjusting the value of its currency, it was stuck. The interesting thing is, as fate would have it, that the country that first ran into this quandary was the United States—the peg itself.

In the 1960s, the United States began printing money to finance both the war in Vietnam and President Lyndon B. Johnson's Great Society social welfare programs. Johnson referred to "guns and but-ter" as he told the American people that the government could easily finance the expenses of the war—the guns—while still providing for the needs of people back home—the butter. In essence, Johnson convinced the voting public that they could have their cake and eat it too. Unfortunately, as time went by, the government had to print more and more money just to stay afloat. And as more and more money began to enter the system, inflation began to creep higher and higher.

At this time, thanks to Roosevelt's mandatory devaluation of the U.S. dollar in the 1930s, Americans were still unable to privately own gold. Europeans and others, on the other hand, were able to own gold, and they put this to their full advantage. Remember, gold was pegged to the U.S. dollar at a rate of $35 per ounce of gold. The inter-esting thing is that this peg existed only within the United States. Outside of the United States, where individuals could actually own gold, there was a thriving gold market. And, as open markets do, this gold market allowed the value of gold to fluctuate to a much higher price than $35 per ounce thanks to inflation in the United States.

Inflation decreases the value of a currency. As a currency becomes less and less valuable, you are able to purchase less and less with it. So if the value of gold had been allowed to fluctuate in the United States, gold would have cost more and more as the U.S. dollar became worth less and less.

Suppose you are the French government, or any other govern-ment that owes money to the United States, and the French franc, or any other currency, is worth about $1 because it is pegged to the dollar. You also know that you can exchange $35 for one ounce of gold in the United States. So you go ahead and you exchange 35 French francs for 35 U.S. dollars and then trade in your U.S. dollars for one ounce of gold. Well, at this point, you can bring your gold back to France and exchange it on the thriving European gold market for 50 French francs per ounce. You now have a profit of 15 French francs. Let's see. You didn't have to risk anything, and you made 15 French francs? That's an appealing system, and that's exactly how it worked. There was no risk in the exchange rate between the French francs and the U.S. dollars because the currencies were pegged to each other. There was also no risk in the exchange rate between the U.S. dollars and the gold because the two values were pegged to each other. Then you could sell the gold for what it was really worth on the open market instead of the artificially low price of $35 per ounce. It was like printing free money. All you had to do as a foreign government was make a few exchanges, and you would have free money that you could use to pay down your debts. If you had a deal like that available to you, wouldn't you take it? Of course you would. And governments around the world began to make a rush on the United States' gold deposits.

President Richard M. Nixon, who had inherited Johnson's inflationary legacy, recognized that the country's gold reserves were getting dangerously low and decided to take action. On August 15, 1971, Nixon "temporarily" moved the U.S. dollar off the gold standard. This meant that foreign governments, international corporations, and the like could no longer exchange their U.S. dollars for gold. It also meant the little green pieces of paper people were carrying around in their wallets were no longer backed by gold, or any other precious metal for that matter. U.S. dollars were now backed only by the good faith of the U.S. government to make good on all its financial obligations.

While U.S. dollars backed only by good faith may seem commonplace today, it was an extremely frightening prospect for the governments of other countries at the time. Remember, the United States was printing money at an alarming rate to finance its debts, and inflation was rising. And if your country's currency was pegged to the value of the U.S. dollar, your country's currency was losing value just as quickly as the inflation-plagued U.S. dollar was losing value. These foreign governments knew their economies stood little chance of surviving an inflationary crisis, so they did the only thing they could—they attacked the peg.

> In recent weeks, speculators have been waging an all-out war on the American dollar. (Nixon, "The Challenge of Peace," address to the nation outlining a new economic policy, August 15, 1971)

A Congressional subcommittee said today that the United States dollar is "overvalued" in relation to other currencies and urged that, one way or another, it be devalued. (*New York Times*, August 7, 1971)

The United States dollar was under speculative attack in world money markets yesterday. In Frankfurt, Milan, London, Zurich, Amsterdam and Tokyo, among other major financial centers, the pressure was heavy as nervous traders sold dollars and sought local currencies. (*New York Times*, August 13, 1971)

The dollar is under severe pressure in major financial markets in Europe and Japan . . . In this atmosphere, impressive sums are moving speculatively, betting that the dollar will be devalued. Large companies are hedging in order not to lose money should this occur. . . . Respectable voices in the financial community and in academia are asserting with some vehemence that the dollar is overvalued and that this situation should be corrected. . . . Most observers expect us to do something (probably to devalue the dollar), and foreign governments and private traders are now behaving under the assumption that we will do something; this heightens the speculative fever. (Memorandum from the Acting Assistant Secretary of State for Economic Affairs Milton Katz to Secretary of State William Pierce Rogers, August 13, 1971)

It's not whether it would happen, but when. This was the way many European authorities were talking about devaluation of the dollar. (*New York Times*, August 1, 1971)

The only way these foreign governments could protect the value and integrity of their own currencies was to attack the value of the U.S. dollar and push for devaluation. These efforts would ultimately lead to the end of the pegged currency system in Europe and Japan. The European countries attempted to adjust the peg with the U.S. dollars and remain pegged to one another, but these attempts eventually failed, and the European currencies were forced to float freely.

A free-floating system allows currencies to rise or fall in value based on the economic forces of supply and demand. This movement allows countries to achieve an appropriate balance between the value of their currencies, and it provides opportunities to profit with the Forex market. Since the early days of semifloating and free-floating currencies in the 1970s, the Forex market has passed through what we believe was its adolescence and has now entered its adulthood. Although it is clear that the Forex market is still moody, erratic, and sometimes patently insane, these same traits are what make the Forex market an ideal forum for generating profits.

IT HAS ALL HAPPENED BEFORE

Many of the same forces and anomalies that have affected the Forex market in the past are bound to continue affecting the Forex market in the future. If you can learn from the events of the past, you can take advantage of the events in the future. To understand the full range of influences that can affect the Forex market, we examine three Forex case studies. In these case studies you will see how pressure from without, pressure from within, and pressure from a few can have a tremendous impact on the value of a currency.

Pressure from Within—President Reagan's 1982 Push for a Strong Dollar

The most significant pressures exerted on a currency often come from within a country's own economy and political system. The U.S. dollar experienced these pressures when Ronald Reagan won the presidency in the early 1980s. One of the issues he had campaigned on in 1980 was inflation. The Carter administration had been plagued by double-digit inflation rates, and Americans were fed up with losing value in their savings and investment accounts. To combat inflation, Reagan pledged that he would fight for a stronger U.S. dollar, and fight he did. In January 1981, it took $1.3271 to buy one German deutsche mark. The deutsche mark was the forerunner to the euro and provides one of the best historical comparisons for the value of the U.S. dollar. By February 1985, the U.S. dollar had soared in value to the point where it cost only $0.6423 to buy one German deutsche mark. That is an increase in the value of the U.S. dollar compared to the German deutsche mark of more than 100 percent. For those of you who are interested, that is a difference of 6,848 pips. Using $2,000 in margin to buy one contract in today's Forex market, you could have made $68,480, or a 3,424 percent return, on your investment. Not too shabby. You probably wouldn't have been able to catch all that movement, but you have to remember that it took place during the space of three years. Certainly you would have been able to recognize the dominant strong U.S. dollar

FIGURE 4.1

DEM/USD, early 1980s decline

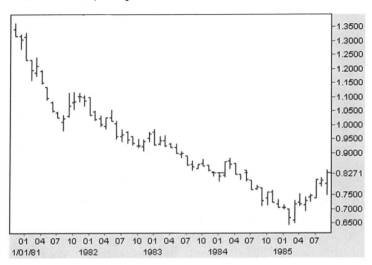

Source: Prophet.net

trend at some point during those three years and cashed in on the movement. (See Figure 4.1.)

As the value of the U.S. dollar skyrocketed, imports surged. A stronger U.S. dollar makes it much easier for Americans to buy goods from other countries because those goods are relatively inexpensive compared to the U.S. dollar. This new buying power led to a surge of spending within the United States, and other economies were more than happy to meet consumer demand by shipping cars, paper, raw materials, electronics, and so on to the United States. These were the halcyon days of the Sony Walkman, Toyota Corolla, and Honda motorcycles. While this surge of inexpensive foreign goods was thrilling for consumers, U.S. producers began to feel the pinch of aggressive price cutting from competitors who had a distinct advantage through the strengthening value of the U.S. dollar. American producers were simply unable to compete.

Faced with falling profits, American producers petitioned the federal government to take action to bring the U.S. dollar back into a more favorable balance with the world's currencies. Washington heard the pleas of its citizens and by January 1988, the Federal Reserve, or the Fed, managed to return the U.S. dollar to an exchange rate of

$1.3035 versus the German deutsche mark. This in turn made U.S. exports more affordable to foreign buyers. Unfortunately for U.S. producers, the import-export business landscape had been changed forever as efficient distribution channels had been created into and out of developing manufacturing economies. And ever since, Americans have had access to a never-ending stream of inexpensive products from foreign producers.

Two Forex market characteristics played themselves out beautifully during the strong-dollar years of the Reagan administration. The first is the Forex market's tendency to overreact and swing the pendulum from one extreme to another. When Reagan first took office and began to take steps to strengthen the U.S. dollar, most people hoped the dollar would increase in value but that it would find a balance with other world currencies. Instead, the U.S. dollar became too strong, and the administration had to take corrective measures to avoid an economic catastrophe at home. The second characteristic illustrated in this example is the Forex market's affinity for long-term trends. None of the remarkable movements of the U.S. dollar occurred overnight. Each move took years to fully mature. You can see in Figure 4.2, which shows the EUR/USD (remember, the German deutsche mark was the forerunner of the euro) from 1980 through

FIGURE 4.2

DEM/USD, 1980s recovery

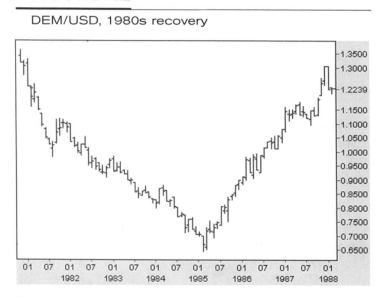

Source: Prophet.net

1988, how smoothly the chart went down as the U.S. dollar was becoming stronger and how smoothly it went back up as the U.S. dollar lost some of its strength.

Pressure from Without—the 1992 Failure of the British Pound

Maintaining a currency's pegged, or predetermined, value is incredibly difficult because there are so many different pressures acting on the world's economies. As the world becomes smaller and more interconnected, governments have to focus more and more on what is occurring in the countries around them. Issues, such as the price of labor in China, that used to have no impact whatsoever on global economies are suddenly of utmost importance. And, eventually, governments are forced to recognize that they are no longer the sole masters of their fate. One country that believed it could withstand the onslaught of the forces of globalization and absorb its effects was Great Britain. In 1992, Great Britain was part of the exchange rate mechanism (ERM), which fixed the trading ranges of participating European currencies into a trading band that was allowed to fluctuate by 15 percent. If a currency began to deviate outside of the band, the central bank responsible for the economy represented by that currency was obligated to begin buying or selling the currency to make it conform.

This is a great example of a fundamental flaw of government and academic economic philosophy. There are many reasons why a currency will lose a significant amount of value. Trying to identify which reason is currently affecting the value of the currency is usually an exercise in futility. If governments could effectively manipulate the Forex market on a consistent basis, there would be no need for a Forex market. Managing an out-of-control currency's decline and bringing it back to a predetermined value through a campaign of either purchasing or selling it, over the long term, is extremely difficult. Usually, the currency is out of control because something in the global economy is out of balance and needs to be rectified, and in the case of Great Britain in the early 1990s, it was the British economy.

Around this time, speculators—with hedge fund magnate George Soros in the lead—began to recognize the inherent weakness in the British economy and attack the British pound. Soros and the other traders knew that the Bank of England could not prop up a falling currency for long. The forces working against the British

pound were just too great. To attack the British pound, these speculators began selling it at an astonishing rate. They did this because
they knew that the Bank of England was buying British pounds in
an attempt to support the value of the currency. They also knew that
the bank could only buy so many British pounds before it became so
saturated that it would no longer be able to prop up the currency.
And this is exactly what happened. Finally in September 1992, the
Bank of England reached its capacity to prop up the value of the
British pound by purchasing it and abandoned the 15 percent restric-
tion imposed by the ERM. (See Figure 4.3.)

From September 1992 though January 1993, the British pound
fell from a high of approximately $2.0100 per British pound to $1.4063.
That is an astonishing 6,037 pips in just five months. Imagine if you
had sold the GBP/USD in mid-1992. You would have walked away
having made approximately $60,370 on a measly $2,000 margin—
that's 3,018 percent. Although it is highly improbably that you could
have entered your trade at the extreme high and exited your trade
at the extreme low, it is easy to believe that you could have caught at
least part of that movement and doubled your money because many
did just that.

F I G U R E   4.3

GBP/USD, monthly intervals

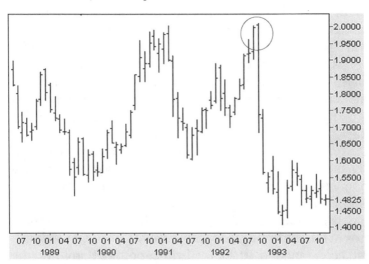

Source: Prophet.net

Once again, the economic factors that led up to the collapse of the British pound were not unveiled to the rest of the world overnight. News agencies had been reporting on them for months. Rarely does the Forex market sneak up on you when it comes to macroeconomic news and events. Knowing this should allow you to protect yourself and profit from any coming catastrophes because you will have ample warning of what is coming. George Soros saw the writing on the wall, so to speak, and traded against the British pound. Anybody who was paying attention could have done the same thing. You certainly couldn't have made as large and aggressive a trade as Soros did, but you could have significantly improved the balance in your own portfolio. Would you like to know how Soros made out on his bearish bet? It turns out that it paid off to the tune of approximately $1 billion in profits. Not bad for a day's work.

Pressure from a Few—NAFTA's "Guaranteed Bonds" and the Mexican Peso (1994)

In 1994, the Mexican economy was enjoying unprecedented success. In the late 1980s, the Mexican government had been pushing to increase the total amount of foreign capital that was being invested in the country, and it was working. Previously, almost all foreign investment in Mexico had been directed toward the country's small oil industry. But through 1994, foreign investment had been increasing. The idea behind this campaign was that close ties to first world economies—especially that of the United States—would have a lifting effect on the Mexican economy that would help create wealth and prosperity for the Mexican people.

While the basic aims of the Mexican government were noble, the returns to foreign investors were less appealing. Investors want profits, and when their investments begin to lose value, they tend to move their money to greener pastures. In the case of these foreign investors who had pumped so much money into the Mexican economy, they were, for the most part, pleased with the performance of the investments themselves. Where they became dissatisfied was in trying to convert the profits from these investments from Mexican pesos to whatever currency they held their primary accounts in. Every time they tried to convert their Mexican pesos into another currency, they lost money because the value of the Mexican peso was steadily declining.

Faced with a declining peso and unhappy foreign investors, the Mexican government made the fateful decision to step into the Forex market and attempt to artificially support the value of the Mexican peso by offering short-term bonds called "tesebonos." Issuing bonds in and of itself was not a strange or radical idea. The United States issues billions of dollars worth of bonds every year. The interesting—and ultimately disastrous—thing about these bonds was that instead of being based on the Mexican peso, these bonds were based on the U.S. dollar. That's right. If you had purchased one of these tesebonos, you would not have received your regular interest payments in Mexican pesos. Rather, you would have received them in U.S. dollars.

Initially, these short-term bonds were attractive to foreign investors, and the sale of them succeeded in temporarily boosting the value of the peso as demand picked up and the current account deficit was satisfied. However, tying the bonds to the U.S. dollar exposed the Mexican government to an even greater amount of exchange-rate risk.

In the Mexican presidential election of 1994, Ernesto Zedillo defeated the incumbent Carlos Salinas to take control of the country. One area in which Zedillo's views differed from those of the out-going president's was currency control. Salinas—as illustrated by his issuance of tesebonos bonds—believed in tight currency control. Zedillo, believing the country's newfound economic prosperity would continue, thought that the Mexican peso should be free-floating. His decision to allow the Mexican peso to float freely in December 1994 came to be known as "the December mistake." Most experts agree that the Mexican peso, which was overvalued, could have been carefully brought down to a more reasonable level through the use of proper monetary controls, but the currency was simply unable to weather the instant vacuum created by the lack of government support and control. Subsequently, the Mexican peso lost two-thirds of its value within a week.

As you can imagine, this spooked the market. Investors began to pull their money out and flee the Mexican market in a national fire sale. Billions of pesos flooded the market as even the investors in the "guaranteed" tesebonos bonds began to sell fearing that the Mexican government would not be able to live up to its obligations. Fortunately for them, President Bill Clinton decided to bail out the Mexican economy by granting the Mexican government a $50 billion loan that would enable the government to meet its obligations.

The Mexican peso has still not fully recovered from "the December mistake." Before the end of 1994, every U.S. dollar was worth approximately 3 Mexican pesos. After the end of 1994 and still today, every U.S. dollar is worth approximately 10 Mexican pesos.

PROFITING FROM HISTORY

Every economy on earth, especially that of the United States, is susceptible to each of the pressures we discussed in this chapter. Whether the pressures come from within or without, they are going to affect the values of the currencies in the Forex market. The benefit you have is that you know these things are going to affect the market, and you can take advantage of them. And as you have seen in the previous examples, you do not need to be camped out in front of your computer to make profits and be successful. Most major moves in the Forex market occur over an extended period of time.

Once you know what you are looking for, you can easily identify and enter profit-generating trades. You would be surprised at how often market-altering events, like the ones we just discussed, occur in the Forex market. Remember, life happens, and the Forex market is always going to be moving. In the following chapters, we show you the major fundamental factors that are driving the Forex market today, give you the background you will need to fully understand how and why these factors are affecting the market, and teach you how you can take advantage of them to protect your assets and generate tremendous profits.

CHAPTER 5

Fundamental Analysis Tools

Fundamentals move the Forex market. Fundamentals affect the supply of a currency. Fundamentals affect the demand for a currency. Fundamentals are where it all begins. If you can get a handle on fundamental analysis, you are well on your way to making profits in the Forex market.

When you start to think of everything that occurs around the world every day—from the performance of the Japanese stock exchange to the number of barrels of oil Saudi Arabia produces—you start to realize that there are literally thousands of fundamental factors that could have an impact on the Forex market at any given time. That is quite an overwhelming thought. Nobody could possibly keep track of every little thing that happens. And believe us, they don't. Some Forex investors may be focusing on commodities prices, while others are focusing on the stock market in London. What is important to one investor may not be important to another, and that is okay. To be successful in the Forex market, you do not have to monitor everything that happens everywhere around the world all the time. You only need to stay on top of the big stuff.

In this section, we outline a few fundamental factors we believe belong in the category of "the big stuff." Many different fundamental factors have affected the Forex market in the past. And while some of those same fundamental factors will most likely play a role in shaping the future of the Forex market, many won't. We focus on six fundamental factors that will play a significant role in driving the Forex market in the future. We want to point out up front, however, that these six factors do not comprise a comprehensive list of everything that will affect the Forex market in the future. We couldn't possibly provide such a list. What we have done is create a solid foundation on which you can build. Can you make profits utilizing only the fundamental tools we illustrate in the coming pages? Yes. However, what is likely to happen is you will begin your investing by utilizing a few of these fundamental analysis tools, and you will naturally expand into more and more tools as you are exposed to the Forex market. It is a natural process. Never stop learning. And if you invest correctly, you never will. In fact, we would like to help you get started. Visit www.profitingwithforex.com for additional fundamental analysis reports and commentary.

You will remember that we believe it is in your best interest to begin your investing with fundamental analysis but that you need to follow that up with technical analysis to have a complete investment strategy. Keep that in mind as you learn about these fundamental analysis tools because we discuss technical analysis next.

Each fundamental analysis tool is based on an underlying fundamental factor (see Table 5.1) that can give you a glimpse into the future movements of the U.S. dollar. Tracking the changes in these fundamental tools will give you advance warning of reversals and continuations in the movement of the U.S. dollar.

This table contains the six fundamental factors and the eight fundamental tools. Anybody can watch eight fundamental tools, especially when five of the eight are updated only once a month or less. Plus, these are all things you are aware of anyway in your daily

TABLE 5.1

Fundamental Factors and Fundamental Tools

Fundamental Factor	Fundamental Tool
U.S. government	Interest rates
	Treasury international capital (TIC) data
Inflation	Consumer price index (CPI)
U.S. stock market	S&P 500
China and other emerging markets	U.S. dollar vs. Chinese yuan (USD/CNY)
	Balance of trade
Oil	Crude oil futures
Breaking news	News media

life. You know when oil and gas prices are going up. You know when commodity and grocery prices are going down. You're aware of these things because they affect your life. Well, now paying attention is going to pay off in two big ways. Paying attention when things are going well in the U.S. economy will help you make great profits in the Forex market. Paying attention when things aren't going so well in the U.S. economy will help you offset the hits your pocketbook may take with profits in the Forex market. Life is going to happen. Pay attention and take advantage of it, regardless of what happens.

The U.S. Government

The government of the United States has more impact on the value of the U.S. dollar than anything else. We know this is a fairly obvious statement, but you never want to discount the obvious in the Forex market. More often than not, if you simply focus on the obvious, you will be profitable.

The U.S. government, through its spending and policy decisions, has an overwhelming impact on the economy of the country. It doesn't matter if Congress is proposing adding benefits to a new social program or the Federal Reserve (the Fed) is looking to change its monetary policy; the economy is going to be affected. And when the U.S. economy is affected, the Forex market reacts. Don't feel that you have to be glued to C-SPAN 24 hours a day to be profitable. You don't. You should, however, pay close attention to two major fundamental factors controlled exclusively by the U.S. government: the national debt and federal interest rates.

THE FUNDAMENTAL FACTOR

The single largest investor in the U.S. economy is the U.S. government. It may seem a little unusual to refer to the U.S. government as an investor in its own economy, but it is because it has a stake in what happens in the economy. And as you might expect, the U.S. government is extremely interested in receiving as high a return on its investment as it possibly can. Politicians like their jobs, and they want to keep them. They keep their jobs by being reelected. They get reelected by keeping their constituents happy. They keep their constituents happy by providing them with a robust economy and the social programs they are calling for. To do all this, the government needs money, and the government receives money from only one source: taxes. Now while comprehensive social programs make constituents happy, high taxes don't. Therefore, politicians hope for and do everything they can to foster a robust economy because it accomplishes two things for them. It gives their constituents something to cheer about, and it provides more tax revenues without their having to increase the tax rates. Paying 25 percent in taxes when you are earning $100,000 is much better for the government than paying 25 percent in taxes when you are earning $75,000. To summarize, all this is really just a long way to say that it is in the best interest of the politicians who run the U.S. government to stimulate the economy, and you can count on them to try their hardest to do so.

The U.S. government manages its investment in the U.S. economy in several ways. However, the two most important with regard to the Forex, as we mentioned earlier, are the national debt and federal interest rates.

THE NATIONAL DEBT

The national debt is an interesting and often misunderstood component of the United States' economic picture. Debt has enabled the U.S. economy to grow and expand at a substantial rate, but it has also exposed the U.S. economy to additional risks. As of this writing, the U.S. national debt is $8,270,134,498,375.29.[1] That's a huge number. Any time a number has that many commas, you know you need to pay attention. Some people say you need to pay attention because a number that large is encouraging for the economy while others say you need to pay attention because a number that large is dangerous for the economy. Because there are so many diverging viewpoints, we think it will be helpful to look at the national debt from a few different perspectives.

The U.S. government is no stranger to national debt. The federal government first incurred a national debt after the Revolutionary War. Each of the 13 original states had managed to accumulate quite a bit of debt during the war as each one financed troops and supplies

---

1 As of March 15, 2006, Bureau of the Public Debt, United States Department of the Treasury, www.publicdebt.treas.gov/opd/opdpdodt.htm.

for the colonial army. After the war, the states began to groan under the weight of the debt. At the same time, the federal government was struggling to establish its legitimacy and power, and Alexander Hamilton saw the debt situation of each state as an opportunity to engender some unity among the states. He proposed that the federal government issue bonds to raise money so it could pay off and assume the debts of each state. A national debt would allow everybody who had fought together to become a nation to work together to pay down the debt. After quite a bit of convincing, Hamilton succeeded, and the national debt was born. And of course, it has been with us ever since.

The U.S. government almost succeeded in erasing the national debt in the early nineteenth century, but the Civil War pushed the debt level to new heights as it topped $3 billion. This was just the beginning of the uptrend. As the country weathered World War I, the Depression, and World War II, the national debt continued to climb. At the end of World War II, it had risen to above $250 billion. As the cold war escalated in the 1980s, the rate at which we added to the national debt also escalated. The country was actually adding $1 trillion to the national debt every four years. The stock market boom, the end of the cold war, and the strong economy of the 1990s finally did give the government a chance to catch up on some payments. And for the first time in nearly 30 years, we enjoyed a budget surplus. However, the terrorist attacks of September 11, 2001, and the subsequent wars in Afghanistan and Iraq changed all that, and the U.S. government has been posting record deficit numbers ever since. As you've noticed, the national debt tends to rise most rapidly during times of war. The United States' military is an incredibly expensive service to finance—especially when it is active.

Many alarmist groups with an agenda to advance would have you believe that any national debt whatsoever is evil and dangerous. While their message may be extreme, we do have to hand it to them for their creativity. If you've ever been near Times Square in New York City, you've seen this creativity firsthand. "The National Debt Clock" keeps track of the total national debt and "Your Family Share" of the national debt. While this clock is entertaining, it doesn't address the reasons for the government to incur debt or the real risks associated with that debt.

The national debt is not risky because it is large. When you look at it in perspective, you see that it is only 65 percent of the United States' annual gross domestic product (GDP). If you were to look at this percentage comparison in terms of your personal income and budget, it would be the equivalent of saying that what you owe on your mortgage is equal to 65 percent of what you are going to make this year. A national debt that is equal to 65 percent of GDP is not disproportionately larger than the national debt of other industrialized nations. So if the number $8,270,134,498,375.29 by itself isn't risky, what is?

The national debt is risky because we, as a nation, depend so heavily upon it. The American way of life seems to revolve around consumption and instant gratification. That is all fine and good when we're able to access the financing. The problems arise when the financing dries up.

The national debt is held by private individuals, institutions, and other governments. The percentage of our national debt that is held by other governments is significant. Of the $4.8 trillion that private investors hold, foreign governments hold more than $2.5 trillion. If these foreign governments ever became disenchanted with the United States and decided to divest themselves of their U.S. debt holdings, it would be catastrophic for the U.S. economy. Money flow would dry up, and the government would have to scramble to keep running. Foreign governments deciding to liquidate their U.S. debt would be like having your mortgage company call you up and tell you it is no longer willing to hold the mortgage on your house and that you need to find a way to pay it off right now. You can imagine the chaos that would ensue.

In the meantime, however, having foreign countries hold such a significant percentage of our national debt provides many advantages, the best of which is the interest it gives these foreign countries in the economy of the United States. Those countries who own U.S. debt have a vested interest in seeing the U.S. economy succeed so they can be paid on their debt holdings. This is why investing in U.S. bills, notes, and bonds is viewed as a virtually risk-free investment. Everybody has a stake in them, and nobody wants to lose any money.

Foreign Countries and U.S. Debt

So why do some foreign countries invest so heavily in U.S. debt? One reason is to enable the country—like China—that is holding the debt to deflate the value of its own currency relative to the U.S. dollar. This makes it easier for these economies to export goods and services to the United States. Let's look at how that works. It's like a two-for-one sale at the supermarket. There are probably many things at the market you don't buy on a regular basis because they are too expensive. However, when you see those items on a two-for-one sale, it is much easier to justify buying them because you figure you are paying only half as much as you normally would. The same concept holds true when you are looking to import goods or purchase locally produced goods. Most people in the United States like to buy products that are made in the USA whenever they can. But when products that are made in Asia and elsewhere are two, three, even four times cheaper to buy than the products that were made in the USA, our wallets, more often than not, make the ultimate purchasing decision.

One reason that these products from Asia are so inexpensive is the cheap labor that is available in many Asian countries. Another reason is that many Asian governments artificially suppress the value of their currencies to make it easier for other countries to buy Asian goods. If you can exchange 1 U.S. dollar for 20 Chinese yuan, you are going to buy a lot more Chinese goods than if you can exchange 1 U.S. dollar for only 10 Chinese yuan. One of the means by which these governments are able to suppress the value of their currencies is by buying U.S. debt. Once again, it is an exercise in supply and demand. When a foreign government buys U.S. debt, it has to first exchange its currency for U.S. dollars because you can buy U.S. debt only in U.S. dollars. This exchange increases the supply of the foreign currency at the same time as it increases demand for U.S. dollars. As the supply of the foreign currency increases, it becomes less valuable. And as the demand for the U.S. dollar increases, it becomes more valuable. As the values of each currency change—one moving higher and the other moving lower—these foreign governments are able to keep the values of their currencies low.

While many governments do, or have, engaged in this practice, it is difficult to maintain for a long period of time—especially when they are operating in a dynamic global marketplace like the Forex. We saw a great example of this concept in reverse earlier in this book as we saw how George Soros and other speculators pushed to devalue the British pound.

Foreign governments also hold significant U.S. dollar reserves because many of the world's commodities are priced only in U.S. dollars. The most important of these commodities is oil. The exchange rate for oil is quoted and sold solely in U.S. dollars. This means that every country that does not use the U.S. dollar as its national currency is obligated to convert its currency into U.S. dollars any time it wants to buy oil. When the value of the U.S. dollar is low, this exchange works to the benefit of the foreign countries. However, when the value of the U.S. dollar is high, foreign countries end up paying even more for their oil than they normally would. Imagine that one euro used to be worth $1.20 and that oil was selling for $60 per barrel. That means it would have cost €50 to buy one barrel of oil.

$$\$60 \text{ per barrel} \div \$1.20 \text{ per euro} = €50$$

Now imagine that the value of the U.S. dollar has increased to the point where one euro is only worth $1.00, but oil prices have remained constant at $60 per barrel. If you do the math, you will see that even though oil doesn't cost any more in U.S. dollars, it costs a lot more in euros. It would now cost €60 instead of €50 to buy one barrel of oil.

$$\$60 \text{ per barrel} \div \$1.00 \text{ per euro} = €60$$

So the price of oil didn't change, but any country that uses euros suddenly had to pay 20 percent more for its oil. That is a huge jump and one that could happen very easily. It doesn't take much to make big changes in the Forex market. So to protect themselves from this risk, foreign countries will maintain huge U.S. dollar–based reserves, a large portion of which is held in U.S. debt. No matter how high or low the value of the U.S. dollar rises or falls, the value of the U.S. dollar–based reserves held by foreign investors will remain equal to the value of the U.S. dollar.

The Risks of Foreign-Held U.S. Debt

Foreign countries hold U.S. debt for numerous reasons. And as long as those reasons remain valid in the future, these same foreign countries will continue to buy U.S. debt, and the United States will be able to continue its practice of debt financing. But if what exists now changes and foreign governments no longer need to hold such large reserves of U.S. dollar–based assets, the U.S. government could be in for a tight credit pinch.

Suppose those countries that are trying to deflate the value of their currencies decide one day to change their monetary policies and let their currencies float freely. While this would be better for U.S. producers, it would mean that the foreign countries would no longer need to buy as much U.S. debt. This would be a real blow to the U.S. government. If the government doesn't have anyone to sell

its debt to, it has no way of financing government programs—
unless it wants to raise taxes, which is never a very appealing solution. However, raising interest rates to allure more investors of U.S.
debt isn't very appealing either. We talk about how the U.S. government controls interest rates a bit later in the chapter, but first let us
explain why the U.S. government would have to raise interest rates.

All investors are looking for the maximum amount of profit
they can receive with the least amount of risk. Because of this, we
all look from investment to investment to see which one is going to
give us the best rate of return. And if U.S. debt doesn't appear to be
as good of an investment deal as something somebody else is offering, nobody is going to buy new U.S. debt. To combat this problem
and make U.S. debt more alluring to foreign governments and
other investors, the U.S. government raises the interest rates it will
pay on U.S. debt, thereby increasing profits for investors. While
this is an effective way to lure new investors, raising interest rates
also slows down the economy because it becomes much more
expensive to borrow money. We all love to earn interest, but we all
hate to pay it.

Another risk the U.S. government faces is a change in the pricing
standards of major commodities—like oil. If the Organization of
Petroleum Exporting Countries (OPEC) decided to price its barrels
of oil in euros, for instance, euro-based economies would no longer
have to hold such large reserves of U.S. dollar–based assets. They
wouldn't have to worry about currency fluctuations affecting the
price of their oil so they wouldn't have to hedge against that risk any-
more. This would dramatically reduce a large portion of the market
of buyers of U.S. debt.

Saddam Hussein, the former president of Iraq and former head of
its oil industry, tried this once in 1998. He declared that Iraqi oil prices
would be denominated in euros instead of U.S. dollars. Fortunately
for the United States, the practice did not spread beyond the borders
of Iraq. But just to make sure that the practice won't spread anytime
in the near future, the U.S. government—after taking control of Iraq
in 2003—changed the denomination of Iraqi oil back to U.S. dollars.
However, there is always the possibility that OPEC or some other
large producer of oil may make a change in the future. And if someone does make a change, you can be sure the markets will react.

To see how the Forex market may react to the threat of a decline
in the demand for U.S. debt, you need look no further than the reaction of the EUR/USD pair when the Central Bank of the Russian

FIGURE 6.1

EUR/USD reserve adjustment reaction, daily intervals

Source: Prophet.net

Federation announced on March 19, 2005, that it was readjusting its foreign reserve ratio from approximately 90 percent U.S. dollars and 10 percent euros to 80 percent U.S. dollars and 20 percent euros. The subsequent weeks saw the EUR/USD exchange rate slam on the brakes and flatten (see Figure 6.1) after previously being in a dramatic downtrend. The effect of the Russian announcement didn't last long, however, as investors realized that the news wasn't quite as big as it had initially seemed. However, this does illustrate how sensitive the Forex market is to this risk. Even though the market eventually sifted through the news and determined it wasn't that important, it made people stop and stand still until they could get their bearings.

While the announcement by the Central Bank of the Russian Federation turned out to have minimal effects, continuing announcements from other central banks will not. These announcements are bound to come as many central banks have already tested the waters with a few reports and statements. As globalization continues to draw the world into a closer and more tightly woven network, foreign central banks will have to diversify their holdings in order to reduce their dependency on the U.S. government and economy. When that happens, be ready to make some profits in the Forex market.

THE FUNDAMENTAL TOOL: TIC DATA

As you can imagine, the U.S. government is extremely interested in keeping track of who is buying U.S. debt and how much of it each buyer holds. To meet this objective, the U.S. Treasury has the assignment of tracking and cataloging this information. It does so through the Treasury international capital (TIC) system. TIC data tell us how much debt the U.S. government has sold, who has purchased it, and how much the purchasers hold in total.

By watching the trends in TIC data, you can anticipate how the U.S. dollar is going to react in the future. TIC data are usually released by the Department of the Treasury on the eleventh business day of the month at 9 a.m. Eastern time. Remember, you don't have to worry if foreign investment in U.S. debt is increasing or decreasing to make profits in the Forex market. You just want to see it move.

Here is how changes in the TIC data look on our supply and demand charts for the U.S. dollar. We'll begin with a basic supply and demand chart (see Figure 6.2).

When the TIC data show that foreign governments and others are increasing the amount of U.S. debt they are purchasing, you know that demand for the U.S. dollar is increasing because you have to buy U.S. debt in U.S. dollars. As demand for the U.S. dollar increases, the value of the U.S. dollar also increases. You can see how the price point for the U.S. dollar increased as we increased the demand for the U.S. dollar in Figure 6.3.

FIGURE 6.2

U.S. dollar—basic supply and demand chart

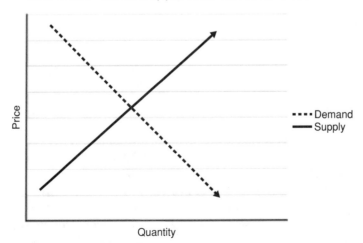

Source: Ouroboros Capital Management, LLC

FIGURE 6.3

U.S. dollar–demand rising

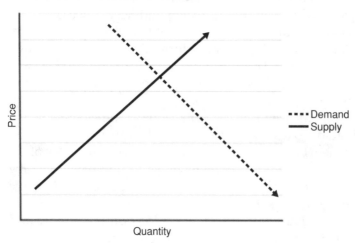

Source: Ouroboros Capital Management, LLC

FIGURE 6.4

U.S. dollar–demand falling

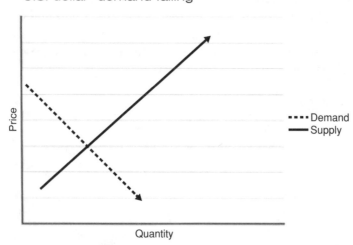

Source: Ouroboros Capital Management, LLC

When the TIC data show that foreign governments and others are decreasing the amount of U.S. debt they are purchasing, you know that demand for the U.S. dollar is decreasing. As demand for the U.S. dollar decreases, the value of the U.S. dollar also decreases. You can see how the price point for the U.S. dollar decreased as we decreased the demand for the U.S. dollar in Figure 6.4.

FIGURE 6.5

USD/JPY, weekly intervals

Source: Prophet.net

Let's take a look at the USD/JPY pair to see an actual example of how the Forex market reacts to TIC data (see Figure 6.5). During 2000 and 2001, the U.S. dollar was strengthening compared to the Japanese yen. This meant that the Japanese government—the largest foreign holder of U.S.-based assets—had less incentive to buy U.S. debt as the dollar was strengthening already, and the Japanese government didn't have to do anything else to try to suppress the value of its currency. You can see in the TIC data that Japanese buying of U.S. debt actually slowed and total holdings declined.

By contrast, during the U.S. economic slowdown after 2002, the U.S. dollar began losing value. This was not good news to exporting countries like Japan because the weaker the U.S. dollar is, the fewer foreign goods U.S. consumers can buy. So to ensure that the Japanese yen remained economically viable, the Japanese government began to increase its buying of U.S. debt. See Figure 6.6 for an example of how the Forex market reacted.

What we look for as currency traders is a confirmation from foreign countries of the current trend of the U.S. dollar. If the U.S. dollar is getting stronger and you see foreign governments, like Japan, reduce their rate of investing in U.S.-based assets, you know those governments are confident that the current bullish trend of the U.S. dollar will continue. The opposite scenario also applies. If

F I G U R E   6.6

USD/JPY, weekly intervals

Source: Prophet.net

the U.S. dollar is getting weaker and you see foreign governments increase their rate of investing in U.S.-based assets, you know those governments are confident that the current bearish trend of the U.S. dollar will continue.

Looking for confirmation of the trend of the U.S. dollar by observing foreign sentiment is important. If you do not see a confirmation of the current trend, there is a good chance the current trend of the U.S. dollar is not as strong as it looks and may turn around soon.

INTEREST RATES

As we've been talking about U.S. debt, we've been focusing mainly on the foreign countries who buy U.S. debt. That seems only natural. If the United States issues debt, then there must be somebody or some other country on the other end of the transaction that is buying the debt. Oddly enough, however, more often than not the party on the purchasing end of the transaction is the U.S. government—specifically, the Federal Reserve. It seems a little strange, but the largest holder of U.S. debt is the U.S. government. To put this into perspective, of the more than $8.2 trillion of U.S. debt outstanding, the U.S. Federal Reserve holds more than $3.4 trillion of it. That is almost half the total U.S. debt. This is a great example of why you can't just point to the total U.S. debt and say that number is too big and too risky. It's hard to believe that the government would ever default on itself as the largest holder of U.S. debt. Now, you're probably asking yourself why the Federal Reserve owns this much U.S. debt, and the answer is: interest rates.

The Federal Reserve (the Fed) utilizes the U.S. debt it holds to execute its monetary policy. The Federal Reserve is responsible for maintaining interest rates at the level determined by the Federal Open Market Committee (FOMC). To do this, the Fed uses its supply of more than $3.4 trillion to buy and sell billions of dollars worth of U.S. debt every day on the open markets. If the Fed wants to raise interest rates, it sells more U.S. debt than it buys. If the Fed wants to lower interest rates, it buys more U.S. debt than it sells.

Before central banking, the economy was subject to extreme booms and busts. Economic booms brought on rampant inflation and a subsequent economic bust. And as the Great Depression and subsequent recessions have proven, it is very difficult to pull the economy out of a downslide. Fortunately for us, we have a central bank that can step in and temper both the boom and bust cycles. While the system may not be perfect, it has provided an economic environment that is generally less risky—which provides the best possible environment for consistent prosperity.

Imagine that the Fed believes that the economy is growing too fast and could overheat. If it overheats, inflation could take off and the economy could stall and decline. To combat this scenario, the Fed will attempt to remove money from the economy. The less money there is floating around the economy, the less people can spend. And the less people can spend, the more slowly the economy begins to move. So to remove money from the economy, the Fed sells U.S. debt. As the Fed hands over the U.S. debt to purchasers, it takes their money and holds it in reserve outside of the flow of the general economy. All of this reduces the supply of money. And as the supply of money decreases and demand increases or remains the same, the value of money increases, and the Fed can charge a higher percentage of interest for it.

The same principles apply when the Fed believes that the economy is slowing down too much and could stall out. If it stalls out, a recession or depression could set in and hold down any potential recovery. To combat this scenario, the Fed will attempt to inject money into the economy. The more money there is floating around the economy, the more people can spend. And the more people can spend, the faster the economy begins to move. So to inject money into the economy, the Fed buys U.S. debt. As the Fed hands over cash to sellers in exchange for U.S. debt, it takes the debt and holds it in reserve outside of the flow of the general economy. All this, in turn, increases the supply of money. And as the supply of money increases and demand remains the same, the value of money decreases, and the Fed cannot charge as high an interest rate for it. While buying and selling U.S. debt is only one method the Fed can employ to control interest rates, it is an effective and widely used one.

THE FUNDAMENTAL TOOL: THE TARGET INTEREST RATE

U.S. interest rates have a more direct effect on the value of the U.S. dollar than any other fundamental factor. Raising the target interest rate will cause the U.S. dollar to become more valuable, and dropping the target interest rate will cause the U.S. dollar to become less valuable. Knowing this, you will want to pay close attention to the target interest rate.

Here is how changes in the target interest rate look on our supply and demand charts for the U.S. dollar. We'll begin with a basic supply and demand chart (Figure 6.7).

FIGURE 6.7

U.S. dollar—basic supply and demand chart

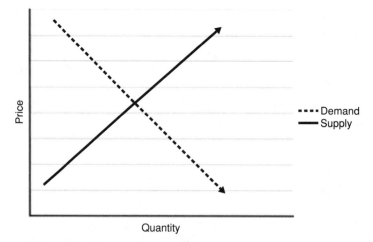

Source: Ouroboros Capital Management, LLC

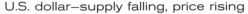

FIGURE 6.8

U.S. dollar—supply falling, price rising

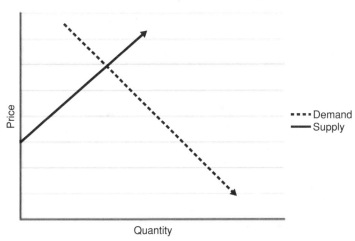

Source: Ouroboros Capital Management, LLC

When the Fed decides to increase the target interest rate, you know that the supply of U.S. dollars will be decreasing because the Fed sells U.S. debt and keeps U.S. dollars in reserve to raise interest rates. As the supply of U.S. dollars decreases, the value of the U.S. dollar increases. You can see how the price point for the U.S. dollar increased as we decreased the supply of U.S. dollars in Figure 6.8.

When the Fed decides to decrease the target interest rate, you know that the supply of U.S. dollars will be increasing because the Fed buys U.S. debt and injects money into the economy to lower interest rates. As the supply of U.S. dollars increases, the value of the U.S. dollar decreases. You can see how the price point for the U.S. dollar decreased as we increased the supply of U.S. dollars in Figure 6.9.

The chart in Figure 6.10 illustrates the effect of rising interest rates on the value of the U.S. dollar from December 2004 through November 2005—a period in which the Fed moved the target interest rate from 2.0 to 4.0 percent. It is important to note that the rising value of the U.S. dollar compared to the euro occurred despite a rising U.S. budget deficit and a skyrocketing trade deficit. But even with all the negative economic baggage, the U.S. dollar was still able to rise on the shoulders of the interest rate.

Before the Fed began to raise interest rates in 2004, it had been on a mission to lower interest rates and keep them low in an effort

FIGURE 6.9

U.S. dollar—supply rising, price falling

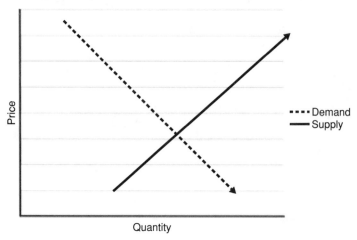

Source: Ouroboros Capital Management, LLC

FIGURE 6.10

EUR/USD, daily intervals

Source: Prophet.net

to stimulate the U.S. economy. The chart in Figure 6.11 illustrates the effects falling interest rates had on the value of the U.S. dollar compared to the Swiss franc. The Fed began lowering interest rates in early 2001. And by the time it was through in 2004, it had dropped interest rates from almost 6 percent all the way down to 1

FIGURE 6.11

USD/CHF, weekly intervals

Source: Prophet.net

percent. These persistent rate cuts bombarded the U.S. dollar, and it continued to lose value until the Fed reversed its stance and began to raise interest rates once again.

Interest rates in the United States are only half of the equation. To maximize your profits in the Forex market, you need to be aware of the interest rates that are affecting the currency on the other side of the currency pair. This means that if you are looking at the GBP/USD pair and the United States is beginning to lower its interest rates while Great Britain is maintaining or raising its interest rates, you should be placing trades that will capitalize on an increase in the value of the British pound. In the chart in Figure 6.12, you can see the effects of exactly this situation. While the United States was steadily lowering its interest rates to 1 percent from 2001 to 2004, Great Britain was maintaining its interest rates at well above 4 percent. This interest rate differential created an increase in demand for the higher-yielding British pound and an increase in supply of the lower-yielding U.S. dollar. When you put these two factors together, you can see that the resulting trend in favor of the British pound was significant.

The logic behind this extreme price movement of the GBP/USD is the same logic that affects your choice of banks when you are deciding where to put your savings. When you put your money into a savings account, you want to know what the interest rate will

FIGURE 6.12

GBP/USD, weekly intervals

Source: Prophet.net

FIGURE 6.13

AUD/JPY, weekly intervals

Source: Prophet.net

be for the money in your account. If one bank is offering to pay you 1 percent on your money while the other bank is offering to pay you 4 percent on your money, you are obviously going to choose the bank that is paying you a higher return. So it goes in the Forex market. If you can get a higher percentage return by buying British pounds and selling U.S. dollars than you can get by buying U.S. dollars and selling British pounds, you are going to buy the British pounds.

This same relationship is true of other currency pairs. For example, in Figure 6.13, you can see one of the highest-yielding currencies from 2001 to 2005—the Australian dollar—compared to the lowest-yielding currency—the Japanese yen. Because the Australian dollar offered an extremely high yield of more than 5 percent compared to the Japanese yen which offered a lower yield of nearly 0 percent, the trend favored the Australian dollar. These trends are relatively long lasting and are quite easy to identify.

USING THE TOOLS

TIC data and target interest rates enable you to decipher what is happening with the United States' national debt and what effect it will have on the U.S. dollar. Keeping track of these two tools is quite simple as TIC data are updated only once a month, and the FOMC holds only about eight meetings per year to determine interest rates. When new information from either of these two tools is available, read about it and ask yourself the question, "How does this information affect the supply of and demand for the U.S. dollar?" Once you answer that question, you can forecast where you think the currency pairs that are crossed with the U.S. dollar are going to move in the future. By monitoring these two tools, you can position yourself to make huge profits in the Forex market over the long term.

Remember that these fundamental tools are only the beginning of the tools you will be using in your Forex investing. We still have seven more fundamental tools to go—not to mention the technical analysis tools we discuss later on. You will need all these tools to implement a comprehensive trading strategy. At this point, you should have a good foundation laid, and we will continue to build on that foundation and bring everything together so you can go out tomorrow and take advantage of the world's greatest market.

CHAPTER 7

Inflation

In the absence of the gold standard, there is no way to protect savings from confiscation through inflation. There is no safe store of value.

—*Alan Greenspan*

We have all heard our grandparents and our parents tell us stories of how much cars, homes, and groceries used to cost "back in the day." Your grandparents can't believe how expensive everything has become, and you have a hard time believing your grandparents bought their first house for less money than you paid for your first car. But regardless of your generation, we have all come to accept the fact that prices are going to go up and that there is not much we can do about it. We have all accepted inflation.

THE FUNDAMENTAL FACTOR

Inflation is a general increase in price levels. Nowadays it seems like prices are always going up. Rising prices are normal. But why do they always go up? Inflation is a product of two things: the supply of money and the demand for things that exist within an economy. As the supply of money increases, there is more money floating around that people can use. And, invariably, when there is more money floating around, people are going to spend it. The problem is that there is only so much stuff we can buy. The global economy produces only a certain amount of goods and services. And when those goods and services are gone, they're gone. Knowing this, we all try to buy the goods and services before everyone else does, and we are willing to pay a higher price for them. And so the prices go up.

Some say that inflation is a natural part of the economic cycle and that it is actually good to see inflation because it is a sign that the economy is doing well and growing. Others say that any level of inflation is too much inflation. Prices should stay the same because any time prices move higher, your money is instantly worth less than it was before the prices went up. Both sides of the inflation argument have a point.

Inflation usually occurs during times of economic prosperity. The better the economy is doing, the better businesses and employees are doing. And the better businesses and employees are doing, the more money they have and the more money they spend. So when you look at it this way, inflation is a natural by-product of a strong, healthy economy and shouldn't be feared. Even so, how do you know when you've got too much of a "good" thing? Can you really have too much money floating around?

The French discovered the answers to these questions in the 1700s. John Law, a fugitive from Great Britain, made his way to the Continent and eventually gained the confidence of the French king. In their discussions about the economy of France, Law told the king that there was an easy way to bolster the economy: print more money. It seems to make sense. If you need to buy something, you need money. And if you need money, you should just print it. That way you get the goods and services you want, and those who provide the goods and services get the money they want. The king was so impressed with this idea that he decided to implement it, and the French began printing money.

To fully appreciate this, we need to take a step back and look at the evolution of money. We've all heard the stories of seashells and other precious objects being used as money. As societies advanced and progressed, however, they switched to a more standardized form of money: precious-metal coins. These coins were denominated by their actual weight and the value of the metal with which they were made. In other words, the coins in of themselves had some intrinsic value. The problem with precious-metal coins, however, is that there is only so much precious metal on the earth, and it is an arduous task to find, mine, and refine it. Paper money, on the other hand, is quite easy to print, and print, and print.

Paper money is also known as *fiat currency*. A *fiat* is an official decree or law. So fiat currency is so named because it requires an official decree or law to classify it as money. In a sense, it almost seems comical to take a piece of paper, write a few numbers on it, and say that it is worth hundreds of times more than an ordinary piece of paper that size is normally worth. But there was more to it than that. These pieces of paper money were actually promissory notes that were backed by gold and other precious metals that were kept in a vault somewhere. These paper notes were just easier to carry around. Imagine trying to carry your wages home if you were paid in gold bricks.

Unfortunately, most fiat currency doesn't stay tied to a pile of gold sitting in a vault somewhere because the stuff is just too easy to print. If you need more, you just have to run the presses for a minute or two, and, voilà, you have more money. This is exactly what happened to the French in the 1700s. Once they saw how easy it was to print money, they just kept printing more and more of it. But as more and more money entered the economy, prices kept getting higher and higher. Eventually some of the French people realized what was going on and began to hoard gold and silver coins. They would spend the paper money as soon as they could, but they wanted to hold onto something of value. Eventually the crazed French speculators and profiteers inflated the fiat bubble so massively that it burst. Prices came crashing down, and the French economy was left to lie in ruin. Inflation, which had been allowed to run unchecked, killed the economy.

If any of this sounds eerily familiar, you'll remember that the U.S. dollar used to be backed by gold when it was on the gold standard. However, President Nixon took the U.S. dollar off the gold standard in the early 1970s, and now the U.S. dollar is backed by the full faith and trust of the U.S. government. The presses at the U.S. mint continue to run, and we've seen our fair share of "irrational exuberance." We are not predicting a massive collapse of the U.S. economy here. We're just pointing out that rising inflation is a sign of a healthy economy, but it needs to be monitored very closely. And you'll notice that the Fed does monitor it—like a hawk, some would say.

The Fed monitors inflation because it understands that rising inflation can erode the value of the U.S. dollar. To get an idea of the eroding power of inflation, all you have to do is look at the cost of postage stamps in post–World War I Germany.

After World War I, the allies determined that the Germans owed those whom they had fought against reparations for the damage they had caused. The allies set this amount at 132,000,000,000 gold marks. Before the war, one gold mark had been worth just under $0.29, so the Germans owed the Allied Forces the equivalent of $31,428,571,428. Germany had no way of repaying this debt. And when it defaulted on its payments, France and Belgium moved in and occupied some of Germany's most economically fertile regions. This sent the economy into a tailspin, and the German mark eventually became worthless.

This cataclysmic decline is beautifully illustrated by the cost of postage stamps in Germany. In April 1921, it cost approximately 0.60 German marks to mail a letter from one city to another. By December 1923, it cost approximately 100,000,000,000 marks to mail a letter from one city to another. Can you imagine paying $100 billion to mail a letter? While this is an extreme example, it does make an important point. Inflation erodes the value of money.

COMBATING INFLATION

The Federal Reserve combats inflation with a variety of tools. One of these tools is the target interest rate. As the rate of inflation increases, the Fed will usually take action by raising interest rates. Again, one of the things the Fed does to raise interest rates is sell U.S. debt. As more and more people buy U.S. debt, more and more money is taken out of the economy, and the rate of inflation usually slows down. If people don't have the money to spend, prices will typically not continue to rise.

As we learned in the previous section, if the Fed wants to entice people to buy U.S. debt, it has to raise the interest rates it will pay on that debt. And when the Fed raises interest rates, the value of the U.S. dollar usually increases. In fact, this series of events usually plays out like clockwork, and you can take advantage of it in your Forex investing. When you see inflation rising (we'll show you how to track that in a moment), watch to see what the Fed does with interest rates. If it raises interest rates, you can put yourself in a position to take advantage of a strengthening U.S. dollar.

$$\text{Increasing inflation} \rightarrow \text{Higher interest rates} \rightarrow \text{Strengthening U.S. dollar}$$

If for some reason the Fed doesn't raise interest rates, you can put yourself in a position to take advantage of a declining U.S. dollar.

$$\text{Decreasing inflation} \rightarrow \text{Lower interest rates} \rightarrow \text{Weakening U.S. dollar}$$

The Fed will also take action if the rate of inflation decreases. To combat deflation, the Fed will often lower interest rates in order to inject money into the economy by encouraging borrowing. When you see this happening, you can put yourself in a position to take advantage of a declining U.S. dollar. Regardless of the trend of inflation, you can profit from it in the Forex market. During times of inflation, those profits can help offset the cost of rising prices in your day-to-day life. During times of deflation, you get to take advantage of not only lower prices and a U.S. dollar that stretches a lot farther but also the additional profits from your Forex trading.

Combating inflation by raising interest rates is not always easy to accomplish. Sometimes rising inflation is accompanied by a declining economy—rising unemployment or economic recession. This phenomenon is known as *stagflation*. Stagflation presents the Fed with myriad difficult decisions. It can raise interest rates to combat the inflation. But if it does, it will likely slow the economy down even more because it will be much more difficult to obtain new money to invest in expansion. If, on the other hand, the Fed chooses not to raise interest rates, inflation could continue to rise and erode the value of the U.S. dollar until the economy collapses under its own weight.

The United States faced this scenario in the 1970s as oil prices quadrupled at the same time as unemployment rates were rising and the economy was slowing down. Paul Volcker, who became chairman of the Fed in April 1979, decided to combat inflation at the potential cost of exacerbating unemployment rates. From the beginning of 1979 through the end of 1980, the Fed raised interest rates from 10¼ percent all the way up to 20 percent. This extraordinary jump in interest rates may look appealing if you are only getting 3 percent on your money in your money market account right now, but you have to remember that the high interest rates were accompanied by double-digit rates of inflation that were eroding the value of the profits you made on your interest payments as quickly as you received them. Fortunately for Volcker and the rest of the United States, the interest-rate hike coupled with other economic factors worked out, and the United States was able to shake off its inflationary chains for a little while.

Now that you've got a handle on what inflation is, how it comes about, and the affect it can have on the U.S. dollar, let's take a look at the simplest, most effective way you can monitor inflation in the United States.

THE FUNDAMENTAL TOOL: THE CONSUMER PRICE INDEX (CPI)

The consumer price index is the standard measure of inflation in the United States. The U.S. Bureau of Labor Statistics compiles the CPI, and it is composed of a basket of goods and services that are representative of those things a standard American household consumes on a regular basis. The CPI tracks the changes in the prices of each of the goods and services within the basket and reports the overall change in a single percentage. If the CPI is rising, you know prices for goods and services are rising—which means inflation is rising. If the CPI is falling, you know the prices for goods and services are falling—which means inflation is declining.

The CPI tracks the following major categories of goods and services:[1]

- *Food and beverages:* breakfast cereal, milk, coffee, chicken, wine, service meals, and snacks
- *Housing:* rent of primary residence, owner's equivalent rent, fuel oil, bedroom furniture
- *Apparel:* men's shirts and sweaters, women's dresses, jewelry
- *Transportation:* new vehicles, airline fares, gasoline, motor vehicle insurance
- *Medical care:* prescription drugs and medical supplies, physicians' services, eyeglasses and eye care, hospital services
- *Recreation:* televisions, pets and pet products, sports equipment, admissions
- *Education and communication:* college tuition, postage, telephone services, computer software and accessories
- *Other goods and services:* tobacco and smoking products, haircuts and other personal services, funeral expenses

As you can see, this is a fairly comprehensive list of the things we consume on a daily basis. Knowing this, you can be quite confident that the inflation information you receive from the CPI will be accurate.

To get an idea of why Americans are so accustomed to inflation, look at the trend shown on the chart in Figure 7.1; it represents the CPI since 1913. You will notice a few years during the Great Depression

---

1 Consumer Price Indexes, Frequently Asked Questions, U.S. Department of Labor, Bureau of Labor Statistics, www.bls.gov/cpi/cpifaq.htm, March 18, 2006.

FIGURE 7.1

U.S. CPI, 1913 to 2005

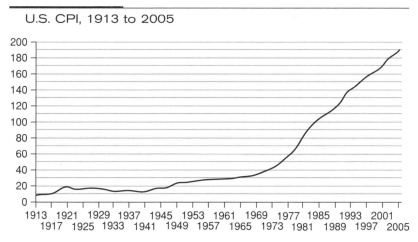

Source: U.S. Department of Labor

when the CPI actually declined, but once the country entered World War II, there was no looking back. In fact, the CPI has grown by an average of more than 3.4 percent during the past 90 plus years.

While the overall trend shows the CPI moving higher, some years do experience a larger percentage gain in prices than others. It is these abnormally large increases in the value of the CPI that you want to be watching for. As you monitor the vacillation of the CPI, you will be able to forecast what effects you believe these movements will have on the value of the U.S. dollar. Here is how changes in the CPI look on our supply and demand charts for the U.S. dollar. We'll begin with a basic supply and demand chart shown in Figure 7.2.

When the CPI is increasing in value, you know that inflation is rising and that the U.S. dollar is becoming worth less. You can see in Figure 7.3 how the price point for the U.S. dollar decreased as we increased the supply of U.S. dollars.

When this happens, the Fed is likely to jump in and raise interest rates to combat the inflation. You can see in Figure 7.4 how the price point for the U.S. dollar increased as we decreased the supply of U.S. dollars.

When the CPI is decreasing in value, you know that inflation is declining and that the U.S. dollar is becoming worth more and more. This increase in value is usually the result of a limited supply of U.S. dollars in the marketplace. See again Figure 7.4 for the effects.

FIGURE 7.2

U.S. dollar–basic supply and demand

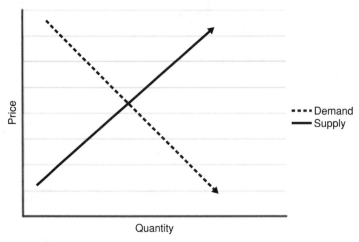

Source: Ouroboros Capital Management, LLC

FIGURE 7.3

U.S. dollar–supply rising, price falling

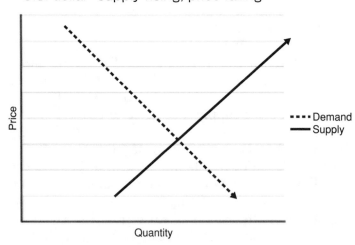

Source: Ouroboros Capital Management, LLC

When this happens, the Fed is likely to jump in and lower interest rates to inspire more borrowing and curb deflation. As the Fed lowers interest rates, the supply of money in the economy increases. See again Figure 7.3 for these effects.

FIGURE 7.4

U.S. dollar—supply falling, price rising

Source: Ouroboros Capital Management, LLC

Let's take a look at the EUR/USD pair to see an actual example of how the Forex market reacts to CPI data (see Figure 7.5). During the two years following the bursting of the dot-com bubble, inflation

FIGURE 7.5

EUR/USD, weekly intervals

Source: Prophet.net

rates slowed down, and the Fed began to drop interest rates in an attempt to spur the U.S. economy on to new growth. This decrease in inflation and subsequent drop in interest rates weakened the value of the U.S. dollar, and it began to decline in relationship to the euro.

Since the euro is listed first in this pair, the chart moved higher as the euro became stronger and the U.S. dollar became relatively weaker. As with most moves based on fundamental factors, this trend lasted for multiple years and moved hundreds of pips. Inflation rates do not change overnight. The U.S. economy is a lumbering giant, and it takes a lot of persuasion to get it to change directions.

USING THE TOOLS

One thing you have to remember about the relationship between the CPI and interest rates and the relationship between interest rates and the value of the U.S. dollar is that there is going to be some time lag between movements in the CPI and changes in the value of the U.S. dollar. Once the CPI numbers are released, the Fed has to wait until its next scheduled meeting to adjust interest rates. Only after the Fed adjusts interest rates can the Forex market price in the actual value of the rate adjustment.

We need to make one caveat here. Most of the time in the Forex market, investors will try to guess what is going to happen and adjust the values of each currency accordingly. For example, if investors believe that the Fed is going to raise interest rates in response to the CPI data that just came out, they will start moving the market before the Fed has a chance to react. Sometimes these investors guess right, and they make huge profits because they were ahead of the market. Sometimes these investors guess wrong, and they have to scramble to cut their losses. Don't feel like you need to be the first one to jump into a potential trend. There are still plenty of profits to be made by letting others take the big risks.

CHAPTER 8

The U.S. Stock Market

The U.S. stock market is the barometer of economic health in the United States. If the economy is doing well, the stock market is going to be doing well. And if the U.S. economy and stock market are doing well, the U.S. dollar is probably doing well. The world's financial markets are all related, and if you can learn how to take advantage of the benefits of one, you will be in a much better position to take advantage of the benefits of the others.

The real magic of the Forex market unfolds when you combine it with other profit-generating markets—like the U.S. stock market. The Forex market enables you to accelerate your stock market profits when the market is doing well, and it enables you to offset your losses when the stock market is performing poorly. Most of us invest in the stock market in one way or another. If you do nothing else with the Forex market, you should utilize it to complement your stock market investing and supercharge your return on investment.

THE FUNDAMENTAL FACTOR

The U.S. stock market is the largest and strongest stock market in the world. Because of this, the U.S. stock market attracts investors from around the globe. One requirement each one of these global investors must meet in order to invest in the U.S. stock market is to hold his or her account in U.S. dollars. You cannot buy stocks on the U.S. stock market with euros, Japanese yen, or British pounds. You must buy stocks with U.S. dollars. And for most foreign investors, this means they will have to exchange their native currencies for U.S. dollars.

When the stock market is doing well, more and more foreigners clamor to invest their money in the United States. This means that they will have to exchange their currencies for more and more U.S. dollars, which will boost the value of the U.S. dollar. Conversely, when the stock market isn't doing so well, more and more foreigners—and Americans alike—look for other investment opportunities. When this happens, the value of the U.S. dollar drops as investors increase the supply of U.S. dollars by selling them to buy other currencies.

Historically, the U.S. stock market has been seen as a relatively safe and productive place to put your money. The stock market enjoys the benefits of a phenomenon called *upward drift*. The productivity of companies combined with inflation and other factors cause stock values to rise over the long term. In fact, during the past 50 years, the stock market has returned an average gain of more than 12 percent per year. (See Figure 8.1.)

So the stock market always goes up, except when it doesn't. In other words, the stock market is cyclical. While the market has historically gone up most of the time, there are years—about 25 percent of the time—when it goes down. It ebbs and flows as market

FIGURE 8.1

Dow Jones Industrial Average, upward drift

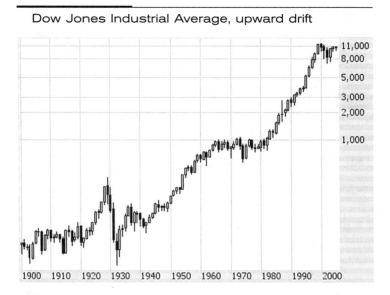

Source: Prophet.net

participants vacillate between levels of confidence and doubt, excitement and fear. Interestingly enough, stock market booms and busts are both fueled by the same emotional volatility. It just depends on which direction that volatility is focused. During stock market booms, investors' emotions run wild, and everybody gets overexcited to the point of investing in stocks that are selling at ridiculous prices. During stock market busts, investors' emotions also run wild, and everybody panics to the point of selling stocks that are trading at a great value. Sometimes there is not a lot of rhyme or reason to what happens in the stock market, but you can prepare yourself to take advantage of either situation.

During good times in the stock market, everybody who is picking stocks or funds looks like a genius. It is surprisingly easy to make money when the stock market is going up. You don't have to put a lot of thought into it. It just seems to happen naturally. Times like these in the stock market give you an excellent opportunity to enhance your returns in the Forex market. All investors live for the moments when they can make money in both their stock funds and the Forex market.

Exciting as this prospect may be, the Forex market becomes even more useful when the stock market is losing value. Virtually nowhere else does the Forex market serve as the perfect hedge for your investments than in the stock market. If you are a longer-term investor who enjoys the long-range returns of the stock market but who doesn't enjoy watching your account value drop whenever the stock market cycles through a downturn, you can offset your losses in the Forex market. If you have all your money invested in the stock market, you are completely at the mercy of the movements of the stock market. If you diversify your investments a little bit, however, and put the majority of your money in the stock market and a portion of it in the Forex market, you can retain more control of your financial future. Diversifying your money enables you to react to the movements of the market, regardless of its direction.

Most financial planners will talk about long-term growth in the market during the space of 20, 30, or 40 years. This is appropriate if you have that long to invest, but one thing many financial planners leave out of the discussion is what happens to your portfolio if you have been investing and getting steady returns for 29 years but in year 30 the market crashes. Imagine you were planning to retire at the end of 2002 and you had accumulated $1 million in your account by the beginning of 2000. But then the market suddenly took a turn for the worse. And as the next two to three years dragged on, you were forced to sit back and watch 40 percent of your $1 million portfolio vanish. Suddenly, your retirement looks a lot less certain. This is the type of market risk we are all exposed to in our stock investing. We're not trying to be doomsday advocates here, but we do believe it is important to monitor and manage your risks when you're trading.

Because the stock market does tend to drift steadily higher over the long term, we are not going to spend a lot of time talking about how to take advantage of the upward movements of the stock market. They seem to happen naturally. Instead we are going to focus on those economic forces that push the stock market down. Being able to recognize what moves the stock market down and how to counteract those movements in the Forex market will do two things for your portfolio: First, it will help you recognize the danger signs and prepare for the downturns. Second, by offsetting your stock market losses in the Forex market, you are able to hold onto some of your stock market positions so that when the market does turn around and start to head higher, you are already in.

It seems like the word of choice to describe busts in the stock market is *black*. There was Black Friday in 1869, Black Thursday in 1929, and Black Monday in 1987. When you top off those bleak, black days with an overinflated dot-com bubble, you've got a great overview of the darker moments of the stock market's history. And when you start to look at the majority of the negative movements in the stock market, you begin to notice a clear pattern emerging time and time again. The stock market tends to fall as it reaches new heights and virtually everyone in the market jumps on the bandwagon to take advantage of the profits.

Contrarian theory suggests that when an overwhelming majority of investors begins thinking alike, the majority is bound to be proven wrong in the not-too-distant future. And in most cases, contrarians are correct. It works like this. People who are participating in the stock market start seeing the stock market go up, and they get excited. Some jump in to take advantage of the early movements, but others stay on the sidelines so they can see if the market confirms that it is really moving higher. As the market begins to move higher and higher, more and more investors jump in because they now believe in the upward movement. Finally, near the top of the uptrend, the rest of the investors who have been sitting it out on the sidelines decide they can't afford to miss out on any more profit-making opportunities, and they jump into the game.

At about the same time that the last holdouts are jumping in, the investors who have been enjoying the bullish run throughout the entire uptrend decide it is now time to take their profits and run. As these investors start taking their profits, other investors look around and decide they should start taking their profits now too so they can avoid any potential downturns in the market. The selling generated by these groups of investors eventually begins to pull the market down, and people start to panic. Suddenly, there is a mass fire sale as investors try to unload their positions, and the market crashes.

This cycle of boom and bust happens over and over again in the stock market. And it follows the same patterns nearly every time. If you can learn to recognize these patterns, you can start taking advantage of them.

THE FUNDAMENTAL TOOL: THE S&P 500 VIA THE SPY

The S&P 500 is the most widely recognized U.S. market index in the world. It represents 500 of the largest companies that are traded on the U.S. stock markets. And the easiest way for retail investors like you to track the movements of the S&P 500 in your own trading is through the Standard & Poor's Depositary Receipts, or SPDRs (ticker symbol SPY)—an exchange-traded fund (ETF).

An ETF is a lot like a mutual fund in that the ETF is like a large container that holds numerous stocks within it. By holding so many different stocks within the fund, an ETF offers instant diversification in the stock market. ETFs also have numerous advantages over mutual funds. They usually have lower fees associated with them, you can trade them anytime during the market day instead of having to wait until the end of the market day, and you can protect them with stop loss orders—orders that tell your broker to automatically sell the ETF if the price drops to a certain level. To give you an idea of how low the fees actually are, you will have to pay only about 10 cents each year for every $100 you have invested.[1] That is one-tenth of one percent.

The SPY holds stock from each of the 500 large-cap stocks that make up the S&P 500. This is why it tracks the S&P 500 so well. It

---

1 State Street Global Advisors, About Spiders, American Stock Exchange, www.amex.com/spy/ aboutSPY.html, March 17, 2006.

is like a mini version of it. The SPY was first introduced to the market in 1993 and has gained in popularity ever since. It now trades an average of more than 80 million shares every day.

As we mentioned at the beginning of this chapter, the S&P 500 is the barometer for the U.S. economy. If good things are happening in the economy, the S&P 500 is going to react positively. If bad things are happening in the economy, the S&P 500 is going to react negatively. It is rather unfortunate in a way because we get hit doubly hard during poor economic periods. It is not only the economy that gets hit but also the stock market as well. However, it is this close correlation between the economy and the S&P 500 that makes the SPY such a great tool.

Think about it. Wall Street employs some of the brightest and most talented people in the country. And every day, these people run around and watch everything that is happening in the world around them and distill the information down into simple buy and sell decisions. It doesn't matter if it is a new bill being introduced on the floor of the Senate or AAA anticipating more motorists driving during the Memorial Day holiday, the investors on Wall Street are paying attention and telling us whether those things are good or bad for the economy. If the news is good for the economy, Wall Street will let us know by sending prices higher. If the news is bad for the economy, Wall Street will let us know in a hurry by sending prices screaming downward. In essence, watching the S&P 500 via the SPY is like employing a think tank with hundreds of thousands of analysts who are all telling you what is going on. That's a pretty good deal.

All that is left for you to do is watch to see if the market is going up or down. It's that easy. Once you've determined that, you can then determine how the U.S. dollar is likely to react to the situation. Let's take a look at our supply-and-demand graphs again to plot this out visually. We begin again with a basic supply and demand chart (see Figure 8.2).

When the S&P 500 is going up, you know that the economy is doing well and that the U.S. markets are becoming more attractive to foreign investors. To get involved in the U.S. markets, however, these foreign investors need to convert their native currencies into U.S. dollars. As they do so, they will be increasing the supply of their native currencies in the market while increasing the demand for U.S. dollars in the market. As demand for the U.S. dollar increases, the value of the U.S. dollar will also increase. You can see

FIGURE 8.2

U.S. dollar–basic supply and demand

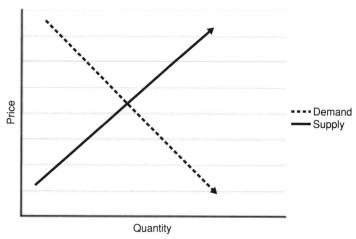

Source: Ouroboros Capital Management, LLC

FIGURE 8.3

U.S. dollar–demand rising, price rising

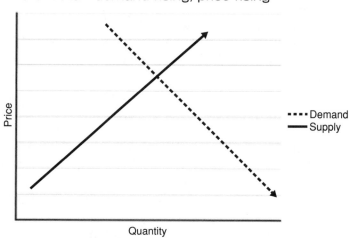

Source: Ouroboros Capital Management, LLC

in Figure 8.3 how the price point for the U.S. dollar increased as demand increased.

When the S&P 500 is going down, you know that the economy is doing poorly and that the U.S. markets are becoming less attractive to foreign investors. As the U.S. markets become less and less

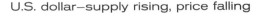

FIGURE 8.4

U.S. dollar—supply rising, price falling

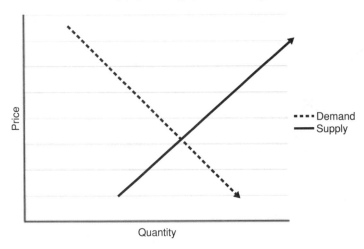

Source: Ouroboros Capital Management, LLC

attractive, foreign and domestic investors alike will begin looking for other places to invest their money. If those places happen to be outside the United States, these investors will need to convert their U.S. dollars into some other currency. As they convert their U.S. dollars, they increase the supply of U.S. dollars on the Forex market, and the value of the U.S. dollar decreases. You can see in Figure 8.4 how the price point for the U.S. dollar decreased as supply increased.

The meteoric rise in the S&P 500 during the inflating of the dot-com bubble in the late 1990s and its subsequent decline after the beginning of the new millennium is a perfect example of what you can be watching for to increase the profits in your portfolio. As you can see in Figure 8.5, the S&P 500 made gargantuan gains from 1995 through 2000.

During this same time period, the U.S. dollar was getting stronger and stronger every day, and this is just what you would expect. As more investors began flocking to the U.S. stock market, demand for U.S. dollars skyrocketed. You can pick just about any currency pair with the U.S. dollar in it and see how strong it was becoming. We've chosen the EUR/USD in Figure 8.6 to illustrate how quickly the U.S. dollar was gaining strength.

FIGURE 8.5

S&P 500, monthly intervals

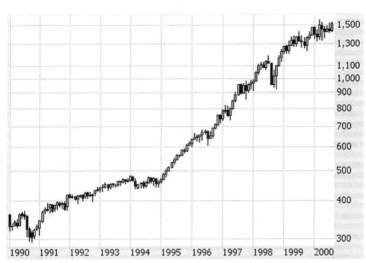

Source: Prophet.net

FIGURE 8.6

EUR/USD, monthly intervals

Source: Prophet.net

After the dot-com bubble burst in 2000, the stock market of the high-flying 1990s turned into a money pit. Dot-com company bankruptcies, corporate scandals, terror attacks on U.S. soil, and a host of other factors contributed to the downfall of the S&P 500—which endured a loss of more than 40 percent of its value. Panic is nothing new on Wall Street, and when it sets in, people take full advantage of it.

With the U.S. stock market falling apart, investors began looking for other places to put their money where they would feel more comfortable and confident that it would make a better return. As they began to leave the U.S. markets, they had to exchange their U.S. dollars for other currencies. This engorged the Forex market with a fresh supply of U.S. dollars, and the U.S. dollar began to lose value. Once again, you can look at just about any currency pair that includes the U.S. dollar and see the U.S. dollar losing strength. One thing you will also notice is that the turnaround from strong U.S. dollar to weak U.S. dollar didn't happen overnight. It took a while for investors to lose confidence in the S&P 500 and accept that it wasn't going to bounce back in the immediate future. Looking at the EUR/USD chart in Figure 8.7, you can see the slow turnaround in sentiment toward the U.S. dollar before the euro takes control and rises higher.

FIGURE 8.7

EUR/USD, monthly intervals

Source: Prophet.net

USING THE TOOLS

The easiest way to monitor the S&P 500 via the SPY is to invest in it. Now, you certainly don't have to do that, and nobody knows if that would be a great investment in the future, but we all tend to pay closer attention to those things in which we have a stake. Seeing how the stock market is affecting your own portfolio will give you a clear perspective on what is happening in the economy and market-place.

Whether you invest in the SPY or not, you do need to keep track of its movements. You don't have to watch its value tick up and down all day on your computer screen, but you do need to watch it. Start by watching it on a weekly basis. While the Forex market will immediately react to some short-term movements in the U.S. stock market, it is more susceptible to the longer-term influences of the stock market. The charts in this chapter reflect what happened during the space of a few years, so you shouldn't have any trouble catching the movements if you keep track of the S&P 500 each week.

CHAPTER 9

China

China has emerged as the next great world power. With a population of more than one billion, an eager and inexpensive workforce, and incredible natural and economic resources, China has quickly discovered the influence it exerts on its fellow global superpowers. A decade or two ago nobody would have imagined the anti-Western communist regime that sat at the head of the world's most populous nation would ever enact policy changes that would open the country's doors to the Western world, but it did. And the world has never and will never be the same. We are witnessing a once-powerful dragon experience a complete and consuming resurrection.

THE FUNDAMENTAL FACTOR

The landscape of the global economy changed forever when China opened its labor force and marketplace to the rest of the world. Every developed nation on earth benefits from the burgeoning labor force in China and the goods it produces. Many of the goods in your home and a majority of the goods you consume—especially if you shop at Wal-Mart—are produced in China. Even if you don't see a sticker on the bottom of something indicating it was made in China, chances are at least a portion of whatever you are holding had to be shipped across the Pacific Ocean. If you've ever visited the ports of Hong Kong, Shanghai, or Southern California, you can attest to the awesome number of containers that are moving back and forth from China to the United States. American consumers have an insatiable appetite for inexpensive goods, and Chinese companies and laborers are more than happy to provide those goods.

Chinese manufacturers have access to a growing workforce sprouting out of a population of more than one billion people. Most of these laborers are young, energetic men and women who are leaving their homes and families in China's rural regions in pursuit of money and a higher standard of living in the cities. Fortunately for manufacturers, the higher standard of living in the cities is still extremely inexpensive compared to what we are used to here in the United States. Because of this difference in the costs of maintaining an acceptable quality of life, Chinese manufacturers do not need to pay their laborers as much as U.S. manufacturers have to pay theirs. This gives Chinese manufacturers the ability to pass those savings along to their end customers through reduced prices on all their goods, and consumers around the world are always on the lookout for the next great deal. Think about your own shopping and purchasing habits. If you can buy a domestic product for $100 or buy virtually the same product offered by a Chinese producer for $50, you are most likely going to buy the $50 product. No matter how much we may say we like to buy locally produced goods, more often than not we are going to make our decision based on the impact it will have on our pocketbook, not on the impact it will have on a U.S. producer.

Developed countries around the world continue to send more and more money to China, and China continues to ship more and more goods to those developed countries. And as the money keeps rolling in, profits for Chinese firms are soaring, and the owners and employees of these companies are reaping the benefits. Increasing profits lead to further development and expansion, which lead to greater economies of scale in production, which lead to less expensive products, which lead to greater demand, which leads back to increasing profits. It is the upward profit spiral that keeps gaining strength as it cycles through and feeds off its own success. Western consumption is driving Eastern growth.

Consumption isn't a growing phenomenon confined only to the Western world, however. As Chinese companies continue to enjoy increasing profits that they then pass along to their new and established employees, consumption in China continues to rise. It is really a simple relationship between incomes and outflows. The more money the Chinese workforce earns the more money the Chinese workforce is likely to spend. So demand for consumer products is rising not only in the United States and other large countries but also in China.

All of this is incredibly profitable for the Chinese government, and it is in the best interest of the Chinese government to ensure that this type of growth continues. Experts are drawing comparisons between the current Chinese growth cycle and the hypergrowth of the Japanese economy between 1950 and 1990 but with one caveat—the Chinese are experiencing growth on a much larger and faster scale than the Japanese ever dreamed possible. The chart in Figure 9.1 illustrates the growth rate of the Chinese gross domestic product (GDP) during the past four years compared to the growth rate of the U.S. GDP. The Chinese GDP has grown at the unheard of rate of more than 9 percent each quarter, and has been one of the reasons that global growth has looked so great in the recent past.

The Chinese government has every incentive to ensure that this growth continues. It makes the Chinese government look good, it puts money in the government coffers, and it keeps the Chinese citizenry happy. Sustaining long-term growth at levels this high, however, is not a simple task. Frequently under circumstances like these, the economy will continue to grow, but its rate of growth will

FIGURE 9.1

Chinese GDP growth rate compared to the U.S. GDP growth rate, 2002–2005

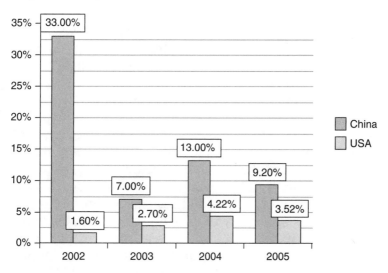

Source: Ouroboros Capital Management, LLC

slow down as time goes by because as demand for the goods and products of an economy go up, the demands for the currency that represents that economy also go up. As the demand for the currency goes up, the value of the currency usually goes up, which makes it more expensive to buy the goods and products of that economy. And as it becomes more expensive to buy those goods, demand has a tendency to decline, and the economy slows down. Naturally no government likes to see its economy slow down, and the Chinese government is no exception. It wants to maintain the country's export dominance, but the only way to do that is to manipulate the currency system—which is an expensive and complicated process. To maintain the degree of control the Chinese require, the government has to commit billions of dollars to peg its currency—the Chinese yuan—to the U.S. dollar.

Pegging the Chinese yuan—the base unit of the renminbi (RMB), the official currency of the People's Republic of China—to the U.S. dollar ensures the Chinese government that increased demand for Chinese goods will not drive the value of the Chinese yuan higher. If the Chinese yuan were to become more valuable, consumers in the United States would not be able to afford as many Chinese goods because they would all be more expensive. A decrease in demand from the United States would be catastrophic for the Chinese economy because the United States imports more goods and products from China than does any other nation. To combat this threat, the Chinese government made the commitment to peg its currency to the U.S. dollar.

We say "commitment" because the Chinese government, through the People's Bank of China, has already committed nearly three-quarters of its $711 billion in reserves, to the purchase of U.S. dollar–based assets. To put this in perspective, the United States—the world's largest economy—holds only $39 billion of foreign currency on reserve. You'll remember from our discussion earlier in the book that buying U.S. debt is one way the Chinese government suppresses the value of the Chinese yuan. As the value of the Chinese yuan rises against the U.S. dollar, the Chinese government goes into the open market and buys more U.S. debt. To do so, it has to sell Chinese yuan and buy U.S. dollars. This action serves two purposes: It increases the supply of the Chinese yuan in the Forex market, which drops its value. It also increases the demand for the U.S. dollar in the Forex market, which increases its value. During the first half of 2005 alone, the Chinese have injected $100 billion into the U.S. marketplace, mostly through buying Treasury bonds. For now, the Chinese government seems rather comfortable with the commitment it has made to manage the value of the yuan.

UNITED STATES' DEPENDENCE ON CHINA

The United States has developed a tight-knit symbiotic relationship with China. China needs the United States to buy the goods it produces, and the United States needs China to buy its debt and provide it with low-cost goods. This relationship has enabled the United States to spend and grow while keeping interest and inflation rates low. While this enabling cycle has endured for a few years without generating too many immediate problems, the long-term risks the United States faces if the nature of its relationship with China suddenly changes are paramount.

Inflation has remained surprisingly low during a period of relative economic success in the United States. Normally as the GDP grows and more money is injected into the economy, inflation will rise. During the past few years, however, China has changed the equation. Instead of consumer goods becoming more expensive because of inflation, they are becoming less expensive because China can produce them so inexpensively. In real terms, the price of clothing and shoes in the United States has declined nearly 40 percent during the past 10 years. So instead of U.S. consumers being forced to pay higher prices for fewer products, they are able to pay lower prices for more and more products.

The U.S. economy has also enjoyed unusually low interest rate levels for the past few years. This has allowed the economy to grow and pull itself out of the post-2000 recession rather quickly. That was a great boost for the economy, but we are starting to get accustomed to these low interest rates. Home buyers love them because it means they can afford to buy bigger homes. Businesses love them because they can finance purchasing, research and development, and expansion at an extremely affordable rate. As debt has become less expensive, more people have acquired increasing amounts of it. The United States economy as a whole is extremely leveraged, and at some point, we are going to have to pay off all that debt.

China, along with Japan, has made this low-interest environment possible. The Chinese government has not been a typical market investor during the past few years. Most investors are looking for a great return on their money, and they move prices around until they meet their objectives. In the case of U.S. debt, that means increasing the yield on the investment. *Yield* is the total amount you expect to receive from your entire investment. The higher the yield, the larger the percentage of return you make on your money. The lower the yield, the smaller the percentage of return you make on your money. There are only two ways to increase your yield. You can get a higher interest rate, or you can pay less for an investment than its face value says it is worth. For example, if you pay $1,000 for a $1,000 one-year note that pays you 10 percent interest, you will make a yield of 10 percent. You paid $1,000. You then earned $100 in interest. And you will ultimately get your initial $1,000 back when the note expires.

$$-\$1,000 + \$100 + \$1,000 = \$100$$
$$\$100 \div \$1,000 = 10\%$$

If you increase the interest rate, you can increase your yield. If you pay $1,000 for a $1,000 one-year note that pays you 15 percent interest, you will get a yield of 15 percent. You paid $1,000. You then earned $150 in interest. And you will ultimately get your initial $1,000 back when the note expires.

$$-\$1,000 + \$150 + \$1,000 = \$150$$
$$\$150 \div \$1,000 = 15\%$$

If you decrease the initial price you pay for the note, you can also increase your yield. If you had to pay only $950 for a $1,000 one-year note that pays you 10 percent interest, you will get a yield of 15.79 percent. You paid $950. You then earned $100 in interest. And you will ultimately receive $1,000 when the note expires.

$$-\$950 + \$100 + \$1,000 = \$150$$
$$\$150 \div \$950 = 15.79\%$$

If the U.S. government had been dealing solely with typical investors, it would have most likely had to raise interest rates faster than it did to attract more investors. But the Chinese government is not a typical investor. Remember, the Chinese government does not invest in U.S. debt and other U.S. dollar–based assets to make a good return on them. It is putting money into these investments to maintain the peg between the Chinese yuan and the U.S. dollar. The Chinese government makes much more money keeping the exchange rate pegged than it ever could by investing in the open market.

This relationship has been beneficial to both parties involved, but economies, governments, and global pressures have a way of changing over time, and we are beginning to see some of that now. Nobody knows how long the current peg to the U.S. dollar—and thus the subsequent dependence on U.S. debt—will last, but most people agree that its days are numbered. Every day the USD/CNY peg remains, U.S. producers suffer, the U.S. government sinks further in debt, and the governments of the other major global economies worry. Every country on Earth would suffer if the U.S. economy slid into recession or worse. Because the world is so interconnected, everyone is watching to see what will evolve between the United States and China.

THE FUNDAMENTAL TOOL: USD/CNY EXCHANGE RATE

The pegged exchange rate of the USD/CNY cannot last forever. Market forces are too powerful to be successfully manipulated indefinitely. We have already seen changes in the rate at which these two currencies are pegged. On July 20, 2005, the People's Bank of China announced that it would be moving the fixed peg on the exchange rate from 8.27 Chinese yuan per U.S. dollar to 8.11 Chinese yuan per U.S. dollar. This move increased the value of the Chinese yuan and decreased the value of the U.S. dollar—for a total movement of about 2 percent.

Let's take a look at our supply-and-demand graphs to see how this all works out. We begin with a basic supply-and-demand chart (see Figure 9.2).

When the People's Bank of China decided to reset the value of the USD/CNY peg to represent an increase in strength for the Chinese yuan, it meant that the Chinese government would not need to buy as much U.S. debt to maintain the new peg rate. A decline in the purchasing of U.S. debt will result in a subsequent decline in the demand for the U.S. dollar. As demand for the U.S. dollar decreases, the value of the U.S. dollar also decreases. You can see in Figure 9.3 how the price point for the U.S. dollar decreased as we decreased the demand for the U.S. dollar.

If the People's Bank of China decided to reset the value of the USD/CNY peg to represent a decrease in strength for the Chinese yuan, it would mean that the Chinese government would need to buy more U.S. debt to maintain the new peg rate. An increase in the

FIGURE 9.2

U.S. dollar—basic supply and demand

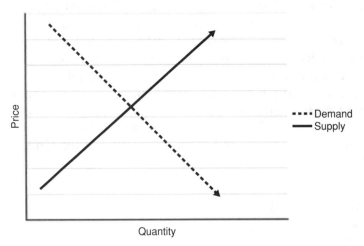

Source: Ouroboros Capital Management, LLC

FIGURE 9.3

U.S. dollar—demand falling, price falling

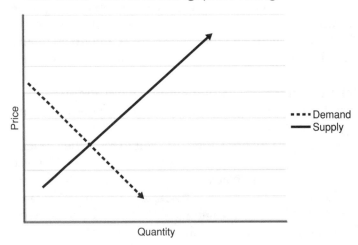

Source: Ouroboros Capital Management, LLC

purchasing of U.S. debt will result in a subsequent increase in the demand for the U.S. dollar. As demand for the U.S. dollar increases, the value of the U.S. dollar also increases. You can see in Figure 9.4 how the price point for the U.S. dollar increased as we increased the demand for the U.S. dollar.

FIGURE 9.4

U.S. dollar—demand rising, price rising

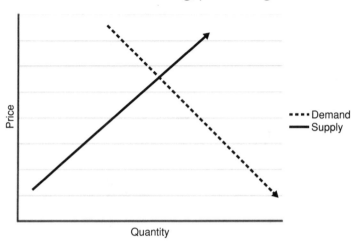

Source: Ouroboros Capital Management, LLC

You would be hard-pressed to find someone who believes that the peg rate on the USD/CNY will be changed to reflect a weaker Chinese yuan in the near future, but it is good to understand how both sides of the equation work. Most people, in fact, believe that the peg needs to be moved at least another 30 to 35 percent before the true exchange rate will be reached. Hopefully, however, that change will not happen overnight. Everybody will be much better off if the peg can be carefully managed until it reaches a stable market point within a year or two. If the peg were to move or be completely eliminated too quickly, the global economy would be devastated on a scale ten times as dramatic as the shock experienced after the Asian financial crisis.

THE ASIAN FINANCIAL CRISIS OF 1997

The Asian financial crisis began in Thailand in 1997 and soon spread through most of Southeast Asia. The affects of the crisis were felt the world over. During the Western economic boom of the late 1990s, investors began to invest heavily in the economies of developing countries—especially those in Asia. Asian economies were growing, and they seemed the perfect venue for expansion. Many of these countries, Thailand included, had also pegged the value of their currency to the value of the U.S. dollar. This made the exchange rate

FIGURE 9.5

EUR/USD, weekly intervals

Source: Prophet.net

simple, but it also made it quite easy for these developing countries to borrow money from abroad because lenders had discounted the exchange-rate risk. During this period, the value of the U.S. dollar was increasing, which meant that the value of these pegged currencies also was increasing. In the chart in Figure 9.5 you can see that the value of the EUR/USD (which serves as a proxy for the value of the dollar) declined during the period.

Everything seemed to be going well until investors started to lose confidence in the economies in which they had invested. Defaults in Latin America and the emergence of cheap labor and affordable products from China spurred on this drop in confidence. Once the first few investors began pulling their money out after government debt began being downgraded, the rest of the investors followed suit and demanded their money back. Suddenly Asian companies and governments lost their funding and were no longer able to meet their financial obligations. Forex speculators, sensing weakness, struck the exchange rate between the U.S. dollar and the Thai baht (USD/THB) and succeeded in breaking the peg. The Thai baht quickly lost value, and the Thai government and Thai businesses found themselves swimming in debt they could not repay. The Thai stock market

FIGURE 9.6

Dow Jones Industrial Average, October 27, 1997

Source: Prophet.net

plunged 75 percent, and the government had to seek aid from the International Monetary Fund (IMF). From Thailand, the wave of insolvency and chaos spread to the Philippines, Hong Kong, South Korea, Malaysia, Indonesia, and Singapore.

By the time the ripple effects of the wave that started in Thailand reached the United States on October 27, 1997, investors were poised and ready to take their profits from the stock market and run. By the end of the day, the Dow Jones Industrial Average had fallen 554.26 points, or 7.18 percent (see Figure 9.6). This loss ranked as the third largest in the history of the Dow. The New York Stock Exchange (NYSE) actually halted trading twice on this one day. The second time it halted trading, it actually closed the market early for the day.

This is only half the story. The very next day, the Dow turned around and posted a record gain of 337.17 points (see Figure 9.7). While this didn't restore all the profits that were lost, it did restore nearly $400 billion worth of equity back to the stock markets.

In the chart in Figure 9.8 we have identified the reaction from the currency market over the next 12 months as banks began collapsing under nonperforming loans and the Bank of Japan (BOJ) began intervening in the market. Government debt was being downgraded,

FIGURE 9.7

Dow Jones Industrial Average, October 28, 1997

Source: Prophet.net

FIGURE 9.8

USD/JPY, JPY collapses as banking crisis begins

Source: Prophet.net

and investors and speculators ran over each other trying to get out of those currencies that were most likely to suffer.

While the effects of the Asian financial crisis were relatively short-lived in the United States, countries like Thailand are only now starting to get back on their feet. If you drive around Bangkok and the surrounding areas, you will see skeletons of buildings and portions of elevated freeways that were never finished because funding dried up instantly. The question you have to ask yourself is what would happen in the United States if something like the Asian financial crisis occurred in a country that was a major trading partner of ours. The United States imports many things from Thailand and other countries in Southeast Asia, but the numbers are miniscule compared to the amount of goods the United States brings in from China every year. China was barely affected by the crisis in 1997, but what if investors begin pulling out of China in the future and the value of the Chinese yuan were to collapse? You will need to be ready to take action in the Forex market.

The most effective currency pair for taking advantage of movements in the USD/CNY we currently have available to us is the USD/JPY. Because the USD/CNY is not yet offered to retail Forex traders, you will need to place your trades using the USD/JPY. For example, if you had been watching the news on July 20, 2005, and seen that the Chinese government was going to revalue the Chinese yuan, you would have probably wanted to take advantage of that announcement. If you had access to the USD/CNY, you could have traded it and caught part of the 2 percent decline from 8.27 to 8.11 Chinese yuan per U.S. dollar. Unfortunately, this wasn't an option. If you look at the price action of the USD/JPY at this same time (see Figure 9.9), however, you will see that the Japanese yen also moved about 2 percent when compared to the U.S. dollar. The exchange rate for the Japanese yen moved from 112.88 to 110.24 Japanese yen per U.S. dollar.

You could have taken advantage of this movement as the USD/JPY is one of the most widely traded currency pairs in the Forex market. If the Chinese government continues to make movements toward a free-floating currency, we are confident that the USD/CNY will become more readily available for retail Forex investors. Until then, however, we will need to use the USD/CNY as a fundamental tool and take advantage of our findings using the USD/JPY pair.

FIGURE 9.9

USD/JPY, yuan revaluation, daily intervals

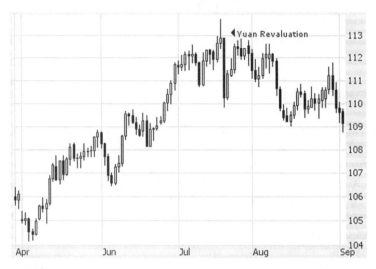

Source: Prophet.net

THE FUNDAMENTAL TOOL:
BALANCE OF TRADE

The balance of trade tells us how much the United States is importing compared to how much it is exporting. If the United States is exporting more than it is importing, it will have a positive balance of trade. If it is importing more than it is exporting, it will have a negative balance of trade. The last time the United States had a positive balance of trade was in the first quarter of 1992. And the last time before that was the first quarter of 1976.

Looking at the chart in Figure 9.10, you can see that the United States is certainly used to operating with a negative balance of trade. And as you can imagine, China makes up a large portion of the negative balance. The United States imports much more from China than it exports to China. In fact, the United States adds more to its negative trade balances through its dealings with China than with any other country. The United States also enjoys negative trade balances with Canada and other commodity and oil exporting countries.

The balance of trade affects the value of the U.S. dollar. Looking at our supply-and-demand charts, we will be able to see

FIGURE 9.10

U.S. Balance of Trade

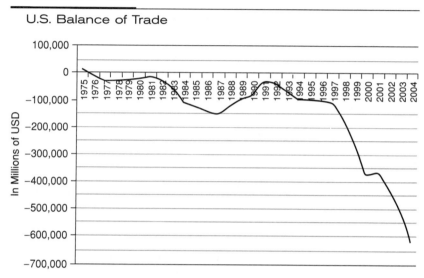

Source: U.S. Census Bureau

what affect the balance of trade has on the value of the U.S. dollar. We begin with a basic supply-and-demand chart (see Figure 9.11).

When the United States is importing more than it is exporting—creating a negative balance of trade—it has to convert U.S. dollars

FIGURE 9.11

U.S. dollar—basic supply and demand

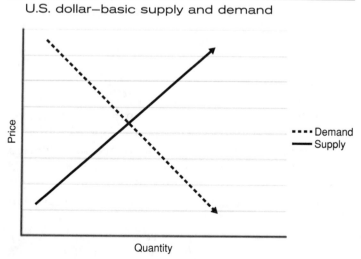

Source: Ouroboros Capital Management, LLC

FIGURE 9.12

U.S. dollar–supply rising, price falling

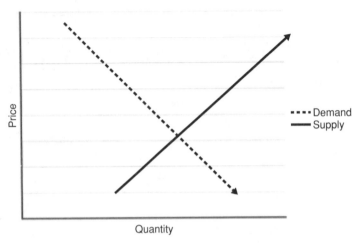

Quantity

Source: Ouroboros Capital Management, LLC

into foreign currencies by selling the U.S. dollars on the open market. This increases the supply of U.S. dollars. As the supply of U.S. dollars increases, the value of the U.S. dollar decreases. You can see in Figure 9.12 how the price point for the U.S. dollar decreased as we increased the supply of U.S. dollars.

When the United States is exporting more than it is importing—creating a positive balance of trade—foreign countries have to convert their currencies into U.S. dollars by selling their currencies on the open market. This increases the demand for U.S. dollars. As the demand for U.S. dollars increases, the value of the U.S. dollar also increases. You can see in Figure 9.13 how the price point for the U.S. dollar increased as we increased the demand for U.S. dollars.

During 2004, the United States increased its balance of trade deficit with China by $161,930,000,000.[1] As you can imagine, a number this large indicates that the United States had to sell a lot of U.S. dollars to buy Chinese yuan. However, it is no longer the sheer size of the trade imbalance that is important in the Forex market. The extreme changes in one direction or another are much more important when you are analyzing your trades. While the Chinese yuan

1 Bureau of Economic Analysis, News Release: Annual Revision International Trade in Goods and Services, U.S. Department of Commerce, www.bea.gov/bea/newsrel/ tradannnewsrelease.htm, March 17, 2006.

FIGURE 9.13

U.S. dollar—demand rising, price rising

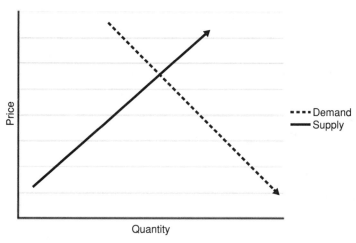

Quantity

Source: Ouroboros Capital Management, LLC

is pegged to the U.S. dollar, you won't be able to do much to profit from these trade imbalances. But you can use this information to help you trade other currency pairs. Any time you see a dramatic negative increase in the balance of trade, you know the U.S. dollar is probably getting weaker. Any time you see a dramatic positive increase in the balance of trade, you know the U.S. dollar is probably getting stronger.

USING THE TOOLS

Nobody knows when the Chinese government is going to revalue the Chinese yuan. Rumors will often circulate before something tangible and concrete actually happens, but nobody knows for sure. The only way you can track and use this fundamental tool is to pay attention to the daily news. You really should be reading a newspaper or news Web site or watching the evening news every day. You don't need to scour every article or digest every piece of information you possibly can. All you have to do is search the headlines for clues.

Balance of trade numbers come out on a much more predictable basis: once a month. Find out when these announcements will be made by the U.S. government each month, and find out what most analysts are expecting the report to say. Then all you have to do is see if the actual numbers match what analysts were expecting. If the numbers match, the Forex market is probably not going to move a lot as a result. If the actual number comes in well above or well below the estimated number, you have a great opportunity to make some money in the Forex market. Whenever a big economic announcement turns out to have different data from what was expected, the markets begin to move until they can find a place where everything seems right. Remember, the news itself isn't terribly important. What is important is how different the news is from expectations. The bigger the surprise, the bigger the subsequent move in the Forex market.

CHAPTER 10

Oil

Oil is a buzzword in the global economy. Whether bemoaning surging prices at the pumps or wondering if many of the problems in the Middle East would no longer be problems if the United States wasn't so entirely dependent on oil, somebody somewhere is always talking about oil. It's amazing that a greasy commodity can have such an amazing impact on our global economy.

THE FUNDAMENTAL FACTOR

Virtually every aspect of your life is touched by oil. Most of us only equate oil with the gasoline we pump into our cars. We pull up to the pump, see that gas prices have risen yet again, and curse under our breath wondering why the government, the oil companies, or the car companies can't do something to give our pocketbooks a break. This reaction is natural because it is what we hear all the time. The talking heads on the news programs tell us to equate rising gas prices with rising oil prices because that is all they equate it with. Sure, gas prices experience dramatic moves as oil prices move, but most of us have never sat back to look at what other prices are affected by changes in oil prices. If we had, we would realize that virtually every aspect of our lives is touched by oil.

Oil is the foundation for the gas in your car, the gas that fueled the trucks that delivered every piece of merchandise you have ever purchased at a store, the pesticides that protect the food you eat, the asphalt on which you drive, the propane you use in your barbeque grill, the Vaseline and other petroleum jellies you put on your chapped lips, the natural gas you use to heat your home, the dry-cleaning solutions your launderer uses to clean your suits and blouses, the lighter fluid you use to power your cigarette lighters, and the substance we seem to use as recklessly as we do gasoline—plastic. Yes, that's right. Plastics are made from oil.

See? We told you that every aspect of your life is touched by oil. And if oil is this pervasive in your life, it is bound to affect your portfolio as well. Fortunately for you, it doesn't matter if oil prices are going up or down; you can profit with the Forex.

WHAT IS OIL?

When most of us talk about oil, we are really referring to petroleum, or crude oil. Petroleum is a naturally occurring substance found in the upper layers of the Earth's crust—hence the name petroleum (from the Greek *petra* for "earth" and *oleum* for "oil").[1] Since none of us speaks Greek, however, we're going to stick with referring to petroleum as oil.

Basically, oil consists of various combinations of hydrogen and carbon that form hydrocarbons. The hydrogen and carbon that make up oil are generally believed to come from prehistoric plant and marine life. Over time, this organic material is compressed and heated by gravity and energy from the Earth's core until it turns into an oozing liquid that pools in cavities in the Earth's crust. And as you can imagine, these pools are the gold mines every oil company is searching for.

THE GENESIS OF BIG OIL

The first group of companies that was able to harvest the true wealth of oil was controlled by the Standard Oil Trust. John D. Rockefeller embraced the oil resources of the United States in a monopolistic stranglehold that allowed him to not only control the extraction of oil from its natural deposits in Pennsylvania, Texas, and elsewhere but also command the refinement and distribution of the oil-based products his Standard Oil Trust produced.

From 1870, when he formed the first Standard Oil Company (Ohio), through 1906, Rockefeller was untouchable. He controlled

---

1 Petroleum, Wikipedia, www.en.wikipedia.org/wiki/Petroleum, March 17, 2006.

big businesses by strong-arming them with oil supplies, and he controlled state governments simply by being bigger than they were
and doling out bribes and kickbacks. Even the federal government
seemed toothless against this raging oil behemoth when it passed the
Sherman Anti-Trust Act in 1890, yet it did nothing to address Standard
Oil's unfair business practices.

Finally, in 1906, Theodore Roosevelt's attorney general took a
stand and assigned special prosecutor Frank Kellogg to pursue the
case. The process continued for an arduous five years, but in May
1911, the Supreme Court ruled that Standard Oil was a monopoly
and that it had six months to divest itself of all of its subsidiaries.
This announcement seemed like a win for the government and small
business, but the executives of Standard Oil had already had plenty
of time to discover the benefits of tight controls and even tighter relationships throughout the production cycle.

Even as Standard Oil was carved up into myriad smaller companies, control of many of these companies was retained by the same
group of men who had controlled Standard Oil—including John D.
Rockefeller himself. To get an idea of the "effect" the breakup of the
monopoly had on the oil industry in the United States, Rockefeller
and his cronies still owned 38 of the smaller companies that had been
stripped off of the larger parent company. Rockefeller himself owned
a 25 percent controlling stake in each of those companies. Needless
to say, those companies worked closely with one another to ensure
that each of them would prosper in the future.

Three of the Standard Oil splinters went on to become three of the
Seven Sisters—the seven oil companies that would rise to dominate
and manipulate the global oil economy. The Standard Oil Company
of New Jersey went on to become Exxon, the largest and most powerful of the Seven Sisters. The Standard Oil Company of New York
became Mobil. And the Standard Oil Company of California, also
known as SOCAL, later became Chevron.

Two of the Seven Sisters found their beginnings in Texas. You
see, Texas had caught on to Standard Oil's under-the-table activities and had ousted the company from its borders. Unfortunately
for Standard Oil, Texas turned out to be the oil jackpot of the con-
tinental United States. Both Texaco and Gulf Oil rode this surge of
oil to corporate greatness.

The remaining two sisters sprung up across the pond in
Europe. The first was Royal Dutch Shell. This first European sister
actually came into being through a merger of a Dutch oil company

originally founded in the East Indies—Royal Dutch—and a British oil company—the Shell Transport and Trading Company, which was the first company to sail an oil-laden ship through the Suez Canal. As the story goes with all oil companies, Royal Dutch and Shell found that they could more effectively produce profits for their shareholders by working with each other rather than by being in competition with each other.

The second of the European sisters was the British Anglo-Persian Oil Company, which became British Petroleum (BP) sometime after Winston Churchill convinced the British government to buy a controlling interest in the company in 1914. The company started by cultivating oil fields in Burma and soon became the first oil company to take a controlling stance in the Middle East by negotiating a contract with the Grand Vizier in Iran. The company obtained a concession for the oil rights in an area of land that is almost twice the size of Texas. This step into the Middle East would be the first of many.

World War I was the catalyst that finally brought each of the Seven Sisters together into the incestuous relationship that dominated the global oil markets until the formation of the Organization of Petroleum Exporting Countries, or OPEC. You see, the Allies desperately needed oil to survive during and eventually emerge victorious from World War I. Royal Dutch Shell and British Petroleum were not able to meet the demands of the war on their own. This shifted focus to the American oil companies who ended up providing 80 percent of the Allies' oil. Exxon alone provided 25 percent of the oil that drove the Allies to victory. Lord Curzon is quoted as saying, "The Allies floated to victory on a wave of oil."

After World War I, the Ottoman Empire needed to be dismantled. The big oil men knew if they could get favorable treatment from the governments who were carving up the Middle East—namely those governments that had relied so heavily on the supply of oil during the war—the oil companies could enjoy a glut of oil and profits like they had never seen. They also knew that they would have to work together to achieve their objectives. There is an old Dutch saying, "Eendracht maakt macht," which means cooperation gives power. The big oil companies were ready. This understanding had been inbred into the oil industry for 50 years.

Their first collaboration was to look at the area along the Tigris River and decide that it, especially the areas around Baghdad and Mosul, was bound to contain huge oil reserves. They were right. And thus began the United States' obsession, via its oil companies, with Iraq.

British Petroleum, Royal Dutch Shell, Exxon, Mobil, and others became partners in the Turkish Petroleum Company. This company later became known as the Iraq Petroleum Company. And, sure enough, just as the geologists and engineers had predicted, Iraq proved to be a massive source of seemingly unending oil and profits. Unfortunately, in all the wrangling for position and ownership, the oil companies shut the Iraqi people out of the 20 percent share of the company and the profits that they had originally been promised.

This new black gold rush in Iraq, however, was soon to be outdone as oil companies moved into Saudi Arabia. Texaco and Chevron (still known as SOCAL in those days)—two companies that had been shut out of Iraq—stumbled upon what would turn out to be the largest oil finds in history because Exxon and the other players in the Iraq Petroleum Company were too busy with their newfound super wells along the Tigris. Plus, with so much oil on the market, the other companies weren't too interested in finding and producing more oil that would only add to the global glut.

King Ibn Saud had recently (1927) conquered the Arabian Peninsula and had promptly renamed it Saudi Arabia. With the other big oil companies preoccupied with Iraq, Texaco and Chevron wined and dined the king and received concessions to drill for oil. After all, the king was a former nomad who was in desperate need of money. That all changed shortly. By 1939, the Saudi oil fields were producing.

It wasn't long after Chevron and Texaco struck it big in Saudi Arabia that everyone else wanted a piece of the action. And, as it turned out, there was so much oil and such a huge demand for development funds in Saudi Arabia that Exxon and others were warmly welcomed into the fold. After all, the companies were used to working with one another.

The cartel of huge oil companies was crystallized in Iran in August 1954. Four years earlier in 1951, the prime minister of Iran, General Razmara, was assassinated by an Iranian nationalist group led by Dr. Mossadegh. The prime minister had supported sustaining the agreement the Iranian government had with British Petroleum. Mossadegh, however, convinced the Iranian people that they should be profiting from their oil fields and not the British.

After Razmara's assassination, Mossadegh—the nation's prime minister—took control of the government and nationalized Iran's oil fields. This move turned out to be the beginning of the end for Mossadegh. He had counted on being able to deal with the other big oil companies once he forced British Petroleum out of the country. He was gravely mistaken. The other big oil companies rallied behind British Petroleum, their partner in Iraq, and refused to deal in Iranian oil. Mossadegh was stuck with millions upon millions of barrels of oil and nobody to sell it to.

During this time, the Federal Trade Commission began looking into the monopolistic foreign agreements of the oil companies. Spearheaded by Attorney General James McGranery, the federal government deemed that the big oil companies had indeed formed an international oil cartel. On April 21, 1953, the U.S. government filed suit against Exxon, Mobil, SOCAL, Texaco, and Gulf.

By August 1953, however, President Eisenhower had crushed the antitrust case in the name of fighting against communism and the Soviet Union. Spurred on by fears of the Soviet Union moving into Iran and taking control of its oil fields, the U.S. government decided it would be better for the oil companies to act as a monopoly and secure Iranian oil rather than see it fall into the hands of the communists.

To ensure the success of the oil companies, the U.S. government—accompanied by the British government—orchestrated and financed the coup that would overthrow Mossadegh and reinstate the Shah of Iran, Mohammad Reza Pahlavi, who had been forced into exile by his former prime minister. The shah was sympathetic to Western governments and assured the United States that if he were returned to power, he would ensure a successful transition from a nationalized oil system to a privatized one. It worked, and each of the Seven Sisters took part in the development of Iranian oil.

And not to leave Kuwait out of the story, British Petroleum and Gulf made a behind-the-scenes deal to secure control of its oil fields.

So as you can see, the big oil companies, with the help of the U.S. and British governments, carved up and unilaterally controlled the Middle East's most profitable commodity: oil. And they did all of this while returning a disproportionately small percentage of the profits to the Middle Eastern countries themselves. While the new generation of oil tycoons fattened their bank accounts in the United States and Europe, the people of oil-producing countries watched their countries being stripped of their natural resources. All of that would soon change.

OPEC

The Organization of Petroleum Exporting Countries (OPEC) was the first organization, national governments included, to successfully wrest the control of oil from the Seven Sisters. On September 10, 1960, representatives from five oil-producing countries—Iran, Iraq, Kuwait, Saudi Arabia, and Venezuela—met in Baghdad to discuss what they could do to regain control of their countries' most profitable resource. Four days later, OPEC was born. OPEC now claims 11 countries in its membership. Qatar joined in 1961, Indonesia and Libya in 1962, Algeria in 1969, Nigeria in 1971, and the United Arab Emirates in 1974.

Of course, OPEC still needed to work with the oil companies if the member countries wanted to sell and distribute their oil to the rest of the world, but it was now in the driver's seat. Juan Pablo Pérez Alfonso, Venezuelan cofounder of OPEC, reveled, "Between us we control 90 percent of crude exports to world markets, and we are now united."

With a statement as bold as this, you would expect OPEC's leadership to take dramatic action. Unfortunately for OPEC, however, it did not fully realize the control it could now wield. For the next 13 years, OPEC did little more than negotiate fair treatment and compensation from the big oil companies. It wasn't until the beginning of the Yom Kippur War on October 6, 1973, that OPEC got its first taste of how much it could affect global oil prices.

Egypt and Syria attacked Israel to reclaim Sinai and the Golan Heights, respectively, which Israel had conquered six years earlier during the Six-Day War. The United States and many European countries threw their support behind Israel, while OPEC saw a chance to offset the profit losses it was experiencing caused by inflation in the United States and threw its support behind Syria and Egypt, fellow Arab countries. To show its support for Egypt and Syria and to bring profits back to preinflationary levels, OPEC imposed an embargo beginning on October 16 on those countries that supported Israel. This meant that the spigot that was delivering 5 million barrels of oil per day to the United States and others was instantly turned off. Suddenly, the supply of oil dropped off dramatically while demand remained steady. This shift in the balance between supply and demand caused oil prices to skyrocket. In less than a year, the price of oil had risen from about $3 per barrel to approximately $12 per barrel—an increase of 400 percent.

While this increase may appear exorbitant on the surface, it was actually quite reasonable. You first have to understand that leading up to the autumn of 1973, the U.S. dollar had lost approximately 75 percent of its value because of inflation compared to the price of gold. During this time, OPEC had continued to sell oil for around $3 per barrel. And as time went on, the $3 per barrel OPEC was receiving was becoming worth less and less—reaching somewhere around $0.75 per barrel. Boosting the price up to $12 per barrel only brought the value of oil back to its original level. If $3 in postinflationary dollars is worth only $0.75 in preinflationary dollars, then $12 in postinflationary dollars is worth only $3 in preinflationary dollars. So while OPEC did indeed discover how much power it could wield, it used that power responsibly.

OPEC took this newfound power and put it to good use, but not in the way you might expect. OPEC did not suddenly hike up the price of oil. In fact, the next four to five years saw relatively little increase in the price of oil. Rather, OPEC increased its political capital with the oil companies and foreign governments. OPEC had arrived as a force to be reckoned with.

One misconception most of us have about OPEC is that it is a cartel that is consistently raising oil prices. It isn't. OPEC never has and never will set oil prices. Prices are determined on oil futures exchanges. The only power OPEC has is to increase or decrease the amount of oil it puts out on the market. While supply restrictions and increases certainly will have an impact on the global price of oil, OPEC does not control 100 percent of the global oil supply. Currently, OPEC controls only about 50 percent of the world's oil exports. Plus, it is in OPEC's best interest to see acceptable oil prices. If oil prices get too high, people stop buying as much oil, and they start looking for alternatives. If people stop buying oil, OPEC's member countries don't make any money. And why would they want that to happen?

OPEC gets a bad rap for many things it doesn't deserve. Remember, profits drive the businesses of oil in oil-producing countries just like they do in oil-consuming countries. The problems the United States and other countries face because of rising oil prices are largely self-inflicted. We decide how dependent we want to be on oil—especially foreign oil. And since it appears we have made the decision to be heavily dependent on it, we need to be aware of how oil prices are going to affect our investments.

OIL AND YOUR PORTFOLIO

Wall Street watches oil prices like a hawk, and for good reason. As oil prices go up, consumers have to spend more money on oil-based products—like gasoline. The more consumers spend on oil-based products, the less they can spend on other products. The less they spend on other products, the less profit those other companies make. And, as you know, declining profits equal declining stock values.

The opposite is also true. During periods when oil prices decline, Wall Street becomes increasingly optimistic concerning the profit potential of U.S. companies. This increased optimism usually leads to increases in stock prices, and everybody is happy when that happens.

You should be watching oil prices just as closely as Wall Street does if you want to fill in the gaps in your investments. This doesn't mean that you have to have Bloomberg or CNBC running night and day so that you can see what oil prices are doing. You need to check prices only every now and then. And if you don't like looking at the paper or watching the news to see what oil prices are doing, just glance at the gas station marquees as you drive around your neighborhood. If the prices on the marquees are going up, chances are good that oil prices are also heading higher. If you notice that happening, you have to check some news sources and find out what is going on.

When you do check the oil markets, you've got to know what you're looking for. So here's a brief rundown.

The Oil Markets

Two large futures exchanges are used to determine the average price of oil: the New York Mercantile Exchange (NYMEX) and the International Petroleum Exchange (IPE). The NYMEX deals in West Texas Intermediate (WTI)—which comes from U.S. oil fields, and the IPE deals in Brent Crude—which comes from British oil fields.

You will notice that oil from the Middle East, Russia, and so forth is not mentioned here. That is because most oil in the world is not traded through an exchange. It is traded over the counter directly from the seller to the buyer. The oil exchanges are important though because they determine the price at which over-the-counter oil will be sold.

So when you watch the news and hear that oil has topped $70 per barrel, you know that the numbers being cited are those from the oil futures exchanges.

Rising Oil, Falling Markets

Rising oil prices have corresponded with falling markets on many occasions. Perhaps the most dramatic example of the relationship

FIGURE 10.1

S&P 500, monthly intervals, showing the dramatic
decline from November 1973 to October 1974

Source: Prophet.net

between oil and the markets occurred after the Arab oil embargo in October 1973. From November 1973 through October 1974, the S&P 500 dropped by more than 42 percent—from a value of 107.69 to 62.28. (See Figure 10.1.)

So as oil prices quadrupled, the stock market absorbed the brunt of the hit. The crisis also led to gasoline rationing, a national speed limit of 55 miles per hour, and the reinstitution of a federally mandated daylight savings time—all in an attempt to conserve oil.

The United States was trying to conserve oil because supply was drying up while demand was increasing. This imbalance between supply and demand is what caused the oil prices to rise so dramatically.

The question we need to be asking ourselves is whether this scenario could ever happen again. Could OPEC or another major oil exporter suddenly turn off the tap and decrease supply? Of course it could. But let's look at the other side of the equation. Oil producers may decide to never decrease their oil output, but oil consumers are guaranteed to increase their demand for more and more oil. Countries like China and India are experiencing dramatic economic growth and are demanding more and more oil and other natural resources.

Imagine what it would mean in terms of oil consumption if more than two billion people bought cars within the next 50 years.

If developing countries, like China, and economic powerhouses, like the United States, continue to increase their demand for oil, oil prices are bound to rise. And these rising oil prices will have an effect on the profitability of the corporations that are traded on Wall Street. Talk about a gap in the stock market that needs to be filled.

Imagine if you had been planning to retire in 1974, and you were forced to sit back and watch your nest egg dwindle before your eyes. The prospects would be grim. If you are unprepared, you may have to face the same situation in 2010, 2011, 2012, and so on. Fortunately for you, you don't have to sit back and do nothing.

THE FUNDAMENTAL TOOL: NYMEX CRUDE OIL FUTURES

The New York Mercantile Exchange (NYMEX) is the home of crude oil futures in the United States. You can bet that no matter what is happening in the world, somebody in New York is watching to see if it is going to affect the price of oil. And when this person and others see something significant happen, they invest in crude oil futures. As good things happen in the oil market, the price of oil futures goes down. As bad things happen in the oil market, the price of oil futures goes up. And whether the prices are going up or down, the movement is usually quite volatile. So much is wrapped up in the price of oil—both politically and economically—that it has to move big.

By monitoring the movement of crude oil futures on the NYMEX, you can get a feel for the future economic situation the United States is going to face. As oil prices go up, the U.S. economy generally suffers from the fall out. And as oil prices decline, the U.S. economy is usually able to take advantage of the lower energy prices. The affect all this has on the U.S. dollar, however, is a little more complicated. The biggest complication is the fact that oil is quoted and sold in U.S. dollars. Let's take a look at how this adds another layer to our fundamental analysis. We're going to use our supply-and-demand graphs again, and we begin with a basic supply-and-demand chart first in Figure 10.2.

When crude oil futures are increasing in value, the U.S. dollar should theoretically be getting more valuable. The more oil prices rise, the more U.S. dollars foreign countries are going to have to buy to purchase their oil. This increase in value of the U.S. dollar is the

FIGURE 10.2

U.S. dollar—basic supply and demand

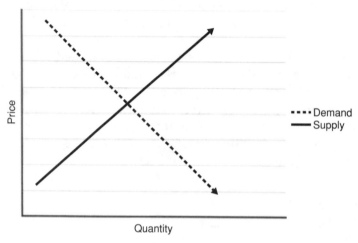

Source: Ouroboros Capital Management, LLC

result of increasing demand in the marketplace. As the demand for U.S. dollars increases, the value of the U.S. dollar increases. You can see in Figure 10.3 how the price point for the U.S. dollar increased as we increased the demand for the U.S. dollar.

When the price of oil does finally turn around and move lower, the demand for the U.S. dollar diminishes. As the demand for U.S. dollars decreases, the value of the U.S. dollar decreases. You can see in Figure 10.4 how the price point for the U.S. dollar decreased as we decreased the demand for the U.S. dollar.

This is not the whole story though. It is true that rising oil prices will increase the demand for the U.S. dollar, but rising oil prices also take their toll on the U.S. economy. The question is, which is more important in the Forex market. It depends on the currency pair you are watching. If you are watching a currency pair that involves the U.S. dollar and a currency representing a country whose economy does well during times of high oil prices, the affect high oil has on the U.S. economy is more important. If you are watching a currency pair that involves the U.S. dollar and a currency representing a country whose economy is hampered by rising oil prices, the affect rising oil costs have on the demand for the U.S. dollar is more important. Let's take a look at a few examples.

The most significant currency, when it comes to rising oil prices, is the Canadian dollar. This may surprise many of you, but

FIGURE 10.3

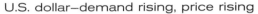

U.S. dollar–demand rising, price rising

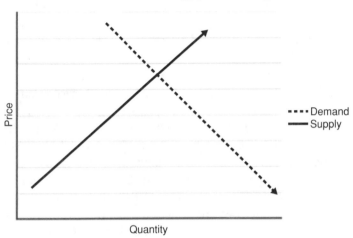

Source: Ouroboros Capital Management, LLC

FIGURE 10.4

U.S. dollar–demand falling, price falling

Source: Ouroboros Capital Management, LLC

the United States imports more oil from Canada than it does from any other country, including Saudi Arabia. What might also surprise you is that Canada has a larger oil reserve than any other country in the world, except Saudi Arabia. This wasn't always the case, but with oil prices rising so dramatically in the past few years, it has now become profitable to extract oil from oil sands—of which Canada has plenty.

China is also playing a role in Canada's success in oil. Big Chinese oil companies recognize, just as we do, that an increasingly affluent Chinese population is going to be demanding oil at ever-increasing levels. Taking this into account, these Chinese oil companies have been looking for oil resources they can tap into. And China has its sights set on Canada. So when you see oil prices rising, look for the Canadian dollar to be gaining in strength.

Take a look, for instance, at the USD/CAD pair. You will notice that when oil prices began to rise in 2003, the USD/CAD began to drop because the Canadian dollar was gaining strength. Since the Canadian dollar is listed second in this pairing, when it gets stronger, the chart of the currency pair goes down.

You would expect this movement because as the United States buys oil from Canada, it has to convert U.S. dollars into Canadian dollars. That means there is an extra supply of U.S. dollars, which makes their value go down, and an extra demand for Canadian dollars, which makes their value go up.

FIGURE 10.5

Comparison chart of USD/CAD (right axis) and Chicago Board Options Exchange (CBOE) oil index (left axis)

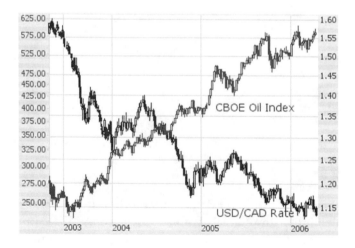

Source: Prophet.net

The currency pair that seems to have the strongest reaction to rising oil prices is the CAD/JPY pair. We've already talked about how the Canadian dollar gets stronger when oil prices go up. Now let's take a look at what happens to the Japanese yen when oil prices go up.

Japan imports nearly 100 percent of its oil. This affects the Japanese economy in two ways. First, when oil prices go up, Japan has to pay more for the oil it imports. Second, Japan's economy relies on its ability to export its goods. When oil prices go up, fuel to ship Japanese goods becomes more expensive, and it ends up costing more to ship those goods. And the more expensive Japanese goods are, the less goods foreign countries end up buying from Japan.

Knowing that oil can have such a positive impact on the Canadian dollar and such a negative impact on the Japanese yen, you are now ready to offset your rising gasoline bills and declining stock portfolio.

USING THE TOOLS

You will not have to try very hard to follow oil prices in your day-to-day life. If you don't hear about the price of oil on the news, you're bound to see gasoline prices changing at the pumps. Not to be pessimistic, but the prices are probably only going to continue to move in one direction: up.

When you see oil prices making major moves, watch for the currencies that have a strong relationship with oil to make major moves as well. Some currencies have a positive correlation with oil—meaning that when oil prices go up, the value of the currency also goes up. Other currencies have a negative correlation with oil—meaning that when oil prices go up, the value of the currency goes down. If you can, utilize those currency pairs that have one currency with a positive correlation and one currency with a negative correlation in the pairing, like the CAD/JPY. This will help you not only make profits in your Forex trading but also offset the additional expenses in your budget that will be brought on by rising oil prices.

CHAPTER 11

Breaking News

Breaking news is the wild card when it comes to trading in the Forex market. Record-breaking profits in the U.S. stock market may push the value of the U.S. dollar higher, and a terrorist attack may push the value of the U.S. dollar lower. Whether the news is positive or negative, it is important that you protect your account by always using a stop-loss order. Once you have that in place, you will quickly learn that breaking news is nothing you have to fear in your trading. You have a fifty-fifty chance that the breaking news will actually help you make money in the Forex market. But more importantly, breaking news eventually turns into yesterday's news, and it is easier to take advantage of the longer-term trends that are started by the breaking news.

THE FUNDAMENTAL FACTOR

Investors in any market, and especially those in the Forex market, are always watching the news to see if they can pick up any clues that will tell them in what direction the next big trend will be heading. Often when investors see something come out in the news, they will react immediately and hope they have made the correct decision. Sometimes they have, and sometimes they haven't. The important concept for you to remember is that eventually the Forex market comes to a consensus and determines what the correct response to the news should have been. Frequently the longer-term response is exactly the opposite of the immediate response. So if you're patient and give the market time to run its course, you can often pick up on the larger long-term movement.

To take an example from the world of liquid refreshment, let's take a look at the Coca-Cola Company's brief sojourn with "New Coke." The Coca-Cola Company was looking for a new product it could introduce to increase its competitive edge over various rivals, such as Pepsi. The company decided to experiment with new recipes for its cornerstone product Coca-Cola. Company managers had developers come up with various new recipes and then sent their marketing team out to see how people would react to the new flavors. Finally, after months of testing and retesting, the Coca-Cola Company unveiled New Coke to the general public. It bombed. Even though all the marketing tests had shown that people preferred the taste of New Coke to the original recipe, the general public rejected the new product. The one thing the company had failed to consider was the emotional attachment the Coca-Cola drinking public had to its product. It was more important to the public to be able to count on a familiar favorite than to have a drink that tasted a little better. In response to this debacle, the Coca-Cola Company removed New Coke from the shelves and rolled out Coca-Cola Classic to assure people that they could still have their old favorite. By reacting quickly to the rejection of New Coke, the Coca-Cola Company was able to maintain the value of its brand and has enjoyed its position of dominance in the soft drink world for a very long time. It was the company's reaction to the long-term trend that made the biggest difference.

Reactions from Forex investors to breaking news announcements are usually just as hard to predict as the general public's response to New Coke—even when you believe you have a lot of the facts. It doesn't matter how many facts you have if it turns out you don't have the right ones. Human beings are at the foundation of every financial market. Each person has his or her opinions and preconceived notions about what should and should not happen, and each person tends to act on those beliefs. The correct reactions in the Forex market turn out to be those that are in agreement with the majority of investors.

To illustrate how some initial reactions turn out to be the correct decisions over the long term and some don't, let's look at two examples: the reaction of investors to the USD/CHF and USD/CAD after the terror attacks of September 11, 2001, and the reaction of investors to the USD/JPY after China announced it was revaluing the Chinese yuan on July 20, 2005.

GUESSING RIGHT

After the attacks of September 11 and after the U.S. geared up to invade Afghanistan and Iraq, global investors began to run to two safe-haven currency pairs: USD/CHF and USD/CAD. Most investors believed that the U.S. dollar would continue to lose strength because the United States was still exposed to the threat of more terrorist attacks, and the U.S. government was certain to respond to the attacks with military force. Both these circumstances created an extremely volatile economic environment because investors don't like uncertainty. They like to know what to expect because they can then plan for it. When they don't know what to plan for, investors begin looking for safer havens in which to invest. This is exactly what happened after September 11, 2001. During the two-plus years following the attacks on the World Trade Center, the exchange rate between the U.S. dollar and the Swiss franc moved more than 4,000 pips in favor of the Swiss franc. During the same time, the exchange rate between the U.S. dollar and the Canadian dollar moved more than 3,000 pips in favor of the Canadian dollar.

The Swiss franc is considered a safe-haven currency because of the neutral stance Switzerland has taken and continues to take in global conflicts. Switzerland established itself as a neutral country during World War II when it decided not to side with or fight against Nazi Germany. *Sound of Music* enthusiasts will remember the von Trapp family was trying to flee to Switzerland to escape the Nazi regime. Switzerland's neutrality has proven to be one of its greatest assets. Since World War II, 35 percent of the world's investors have trusted Swiss banks to manage their funds.

While Canada does not share the same magnitude of investment management as Switzerland, it is still considered a safe-haven currency. Canada, while actively engaging in more military conflicts than Switzerland, still enjoys a level of neutrality. Canada never seems to be the one picking the fight and certainly does not hold itself out as the world's police force.

The advantage Canada has over Switzerland is that Canada is an enormous commodity-producing country. Plus, its economy is closely linked with the U.S. economy. The United States imports more goods from Canada than from any other nation. This means when the U.S. economy is doing well, the Canadian economy is most likely doing well also because the United States is probably importing billions of dollars worth of raw goods from Canada to support its burgeoning economy. This relationship provides a distinct advantage to Canada because it serves as a good proxy for the U.S. dollar. If the U.S. economy is performing well, but global investors suddenly lose confidence because of a terrorist attack, these investors can shift their money to Canada, vicariously enjoy the growth in the U.S. economy, and not have to worry about the value of the U.S. dollar going down. In fact, these investors want the value of the U.S. dollar to decrease.

The question now is how can you take advantage of the Forex market if global investors turn to Switzerland and Canada in times of terror-induced turmoil? The answer: sell either the USD/CHF or USD/CAD currency pairs. Let's take a look at why this works. Again, it is an economic question of supply and demand.

We look at the USD/CHF pair first. If global investors are moving their assets from the United States to Switzerland, they will have to convert their assets from U.S. dollars to Swiss francs. This action will increase the supply of U.S. dollars at the same time as it increases the demand for Swiss francs. The result will be a U.S. dollar that is losing value and a Swiss franc that is gaining value. When you apply these forces to the USD/CHF pair, they will cause the exchange rate to decline. As the U.S. dollar—being the base currency—weakens, it will cause the exchange rate to decline. As the Swiss franc—being the quote currency—strengthens, it will also cause the exchange rate to decline. So as you look at a chart of the USD/CHF in Figure 11.1, you will notice it is going down. When you believe the chart is going to be moving down, you sell the currency pair to make money.

The same concept applies to the USD/CAD pair. If global investors are moving their assets from the United States to Canada, they will have to convert their assets from U.S. dollars to Canadian dollars. This action will increase the supply of U.S. dollars at the same time as it increases the demand for Canadian dollars. The result will be a U.S. dollar that is losing value and a Canadian dollar that is gaining value. When you apply these forces to the USD/CAD pair, they will cause the exchange rate to decline. As the U.S. dollar—being the base currency—weakens, it will cause the exchange rate to decline. As the Canadian dollar—being the quote currency—strengthens, it will also cause the exchange rate to decline. So as you look at a chart of the USD/CAD in Figure 11.2, you will notice it is going down. When you believe the chart is going to be moving down, you sell the currency pair to make money.

FIGURE 11.1

USD/CHF, monthly intervals, showing the dramatic
decline after September 11, 2001

Source: Prophet.net

FIGURE 11.2

USD/CAD, monthly intervals, showing the dramatic
decline after September 11, 2001

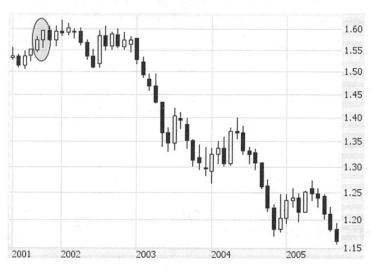

Source: Prophet.net

GUESSING WRONG

After the Chinese government announced that it would be revaluing the Chinese yuan on July 20, 2005, Forex investors started a fire sale on the USD/JPY. Because the Japanese yen is so closely correlated with the Chinese yuan, investors assumed that the Japanese yen would strengthen as much as the Chinese yuan did. So far, they were correct in their assumptions. As we discuss earlier in the book, both currencies strengthened by approximately 2 percent compared to the U.S. dollar. Unfortunately for Forex investors who had sold the USD/JPY and planned to hold that position for the long term, the move stopped there.

Many investors and economists around the world believed that the initial revaluation by the Chinese government was just the beginning and that the government was going to continue to revalue and revalue until the Chinese yuan strengthened by an additional 30 percent or so. But instead of making adjustments to bring the value of the Chinese yuan up to its true market value, the Chinese government sat still. Nothing else happened. In fact, directors of the People's Bank of China along with other government officials came out with strong statements emphasizing that the Chinese government was not even considering additional revaluations. This sent U.S.-dollar bears reeling, and the USD/JPY exchange rate sputtered around for a while until it finally made a 180-degree turn and started to head higher. Most of the investors who had sold the pair lost money, but many of them turned right around with the USD/JPY, bought the currency pair, and ended up making profits (see Figure 11.3).

The lesson Forex market investors should learn from these examples is that sometimes we will be right and sometimes we will be wrong. The important thing is to remain nimble enough to change your mind and go in the other direction when the situation dictates. And the easiest way to know when you have to change is by using the last fundamental tool.

THE FUNDAMENTAL TOOL: TECHNICAL ANALYSIS

We know that it may seem strange to refer to technical analysis as a fundamental tool, but this is where you can bridge the gap between

FIGURE 11.3

USD/JPY, daily intervals, showing the dramatic decline and subsequent rebound after the Chinese government revalued the Chinese yuan by 2 percent on July 20, 2005

Source: Prophet.net

fundamental and technical analysis. Technical analysis is the study of charts illustrating the movements of the Forex market. But technical analysis itself does not move the Forex market. Fundamentals move the market. So when you really get down to it, technical analysis is the study of how fundamentals move the Forex market.

While it does not affect the supply or demand for any particular currency, technical analysis tells us when the supply or demand is changing and how it will most likely affect the exchange rate between two currencies. Knowing this, you can take advantage of the subsequent movements. You will run across many pieces of breaking news where you have no idea how the news is going to affect the Forex market. We all do. When this happens, all we can do is wait to see how the majority of Forex investors is going to react to the news. Once investors have reacted, we can then make our decisions as to how we would like to profit from the market. Technical analysis enables us to see what others in the Forex marketplace are doing. It is also important for you to understand that most of the subsequent movements are going to happen during a longer time frame. Even though the Forex market reacts quickly to breaking news, most of the profits lie in the long-term movement brought on by the initial breaking news.

USING THE TOOLS

We introduce you to the various technical tools and techniques you can use to jumpstart your trading in Chapter 13, Technical Analysis Tools.

CHAPTER 12

Seesaw of Supply and Demand

You have probably noticed that we have used some of the same examples of a currency pair moving up or down to illustrate the effects of more than one fundamental factor on the Forex market. For example, we showed how the EUR/USD rose from 2002 through 2005, and we attributed it to both interest rates and the stock market. At first glance, this may seem like a misrepresentation because you wouldn't think you could attribute the same movement to two different things, but you can. We've spent a lot of time talking about individual fundamental factors that affect the Forex market, but the most important lesson to learn is that these fundamental factors don't operate in a vacuum. Each one affects the Forex market at the same time in its own way. The trick is weighing which ones are having the greatest effect on the market so that you can take advantage of them. To do this, we suggest using a tool we call the "Seesaw of Supply and Demand."

THE SEESAW AND INDIVIDUAL CURRENCIES

The Seesaw of Supply and Demand has two sides. The left side represents increasing demand and decreasing supply. The right side represents increasing supply and decreasing demand. (See Figure 12.1.)

As you are analyzing the U.S. dollar to determine how strong or how weak you believe it will be in the future, you need to stack up all the fundamental factors on the seesaw. If a fundamental factor

FIGURE 12.1

Balanced supply and demand

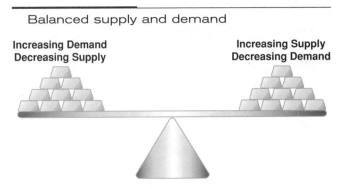

Increasing Demand   **Increasing Supply**
Decreasing Supply   **Decreasing Demand**

Source: Ouroboros Capital Management, LLC

is going to increase demand or decrease supply, you stack it on the left side of the seesaw. If a fundamental factor is going to increase supply or decrease demand, you stack it on the right side of the seesaw. As you stack more and more fundamental factors on the seesaw, you will notice that it begins to tip up or down depending on how many fundamental factors are on each side. If there are more factors on the left side of the seesaw, the left side will drop down while the right side rises. When this happens, you know that, fundamentally speaking, the U.S. dollar should be increasing in value. An easy way to remember this is by looking at the slope of the seesaw. You can see that it is rising from left to right. This is a positive slope and indicates strength in the U.S. dollar. (See Figure 12.2.)

If there are more factors on the right side of the seesaw, the right side will drop down while the left side rises. When this happens, you know that, fundamentally speaking, the U.S. dollar should be decreasing in value. Again, an easy way to remember this is by looking at the slope of the seesaw. You can see that it is tipping down from left to right. This is a negative slope and indicates weakness in the U.S. dollar. (See Figure 12.3.)

Using the Seesaw of Supply and Demand can help you distill complex economic information into a more manageable form. For example, when you are analyzing the relative strength or weakness of the U.S. dollar, it is easy to get sidetracked and lost when you are trying to keep track of the various factors that affect the value of the U.S. dollar—such as the unemployment rate, the trade balance, interest rates, and so on. However, if you look at each one of these factors individually to determine how it would affect the value of the U.S. dollar in a vacuum, it is much easier to decide if each indi-

FIGURE 12.2

Increasing demand

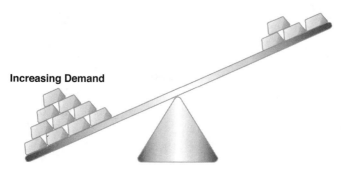

Source: Ouroboros Capital Management, LLC

FIGURE 12.3

Decreasing demand

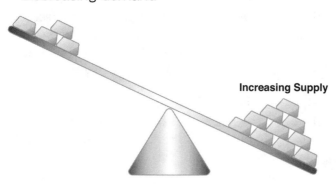

Source: Ouroboros Capital Management, LLC

vidual factor will have a positive or a negative impact. Once you have analyzed a factor, place it on the appropriate side of the seesaw and move on to the next factor. As you move through the various factors that are affecting the value of the U.S. dollar, you will begin to see which side of the seesaw is becoming overloaded, and you can form either a strong-dollar bias or a weak-dollar bias. This is a great way to get started in your fundamental analysis.

Determining on which side of the seesaw to place various economic factors and exactly how much weight to assign to any one economic factor will take some practice. As long as you avoid the pitfall of trying to make things more complicated than they need to be, however, you will do just fine. Remember that only when you combine all the fundamental factors can you conduct a thorough and meaningful analysis of what is affecting the value of the U.S. dollar or any other currency.

Analyzing a single currency using the Seesaw of Supply and Demand is extremely important, but it is still only half the equation. Once you have analyzed the first currency, you need to move on to your analysis of the second currency in the currency pair. Everything in the Forex market is relative, and the only way you can make money utilizing your fundamental analysis is by comparing the fundamental strength, or weight, of one currency with that of another and determining which one is stronger, or heavier.

THE SEESAW AND CURRENCY PAIRS

When you utilize the seesaw to analyze the strength of an individual currency, you place the fundamental factors that will strengthen a currency on the left side of the seesaw and those that will weaken the currency on the right side. When you are utilizing the seesaw to analyze the strength of one currency compared to that of another, however, you need to place each currency on its corresponding side— as indicated by the currency pair. For example, if you are analyzing the EUR/USD, you would place the euro on the left side of the seesaw and the U.S. dollar on the right side of the seesaw because the EUR is on the left side of the pairing, and the USD is on the right side. If you were analyzing the USD/JPY, you would place the U.S. dollar on the left side and the Japanese yen on the right side.

Analyzing the fundamental factors that affect each currency within a pair and then comparing the two currencies will help you make more informed investing decisions. Using the Seesaw of Supply and Demand in your analysis will help you keep your facts straight, and it will also help you visualize which way the value of a currency pair should be moving. If the currency on the left-hand side of the pair has a stronger fundamental outlook, the slope of the seesaw will be pointing up from left to right, and the value of the currency pair should follow that same direction. (See Figure 12.4.)

If the currency on the right-hand side of the pair has a stronger fundamental outlook, the slope of the seesaw will be pointing down from left to right, and the value of the currency pair should follow that same direction. (See Figure 12.5.)

One word of warning concerning fundamental analysis: the price movement of a currency pair will not always correspond with

FIGURE 12.4

Seesaw with positive slope

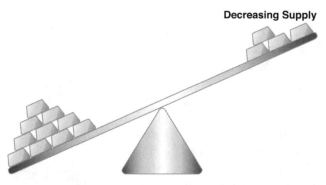

Source: Ouroboros Capital Management, LLC

FIGURE 12.5

Seesaw with negative slope

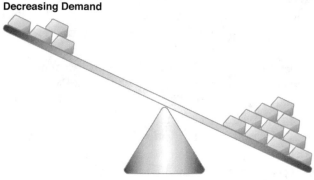

Source: Ouroboros Capital Management, LLC

the overarching fundamental influences in the Forex market. Sometimes currency pairs seem to have a mind of their own. Even when all the fundamental factors you have analyzed point to the currency pair moving in one direction or the other, something may happen to cause the currency pair to move in the opposite direction. Sometimes you will be able to easily identify the unexpected factor that caused the turnaround, but sometimes you won't. Regardless of whether you can identify the cause of every turnaround, you need to be prepared for them. Don't get so confident in your analysis that you believe it is foolproof.

INTEREST RATES AND THE GBP/JPY

The price movement of the GBP/JPY pair in 2003 and early 2004 provides an excellent example of a currency pair faithfully following the pressure applied by a major fundamental factor—interest rates—for more than a year and then experiencing a sharp 180-degree turnaround in a single month.

The GBP/JPY pair is quite sensitive to interest-rate changes and has been for the past few years. For the past decade, the United Kingdom has offered a substantially higher interest rate than Japan has offered, but each time the gap between the two rates has widened or narrowed, the movement has been reflected in the price of the currency pair. One such instance occurred in February 2003. The United Kingdom had held its interest rate at 4 percent for 15 months— beginning in November 2001—while Japan had held its rate at 0.1 percent. During that time, Forex investors had become accustomed to this wide spread and were moving the value of the GBP/JPY higher. In February 2003, however, the Bank of England decided to cut rates from 4 percent to 3.75 percent. Even though the rates offered in the United Kingdom were still much higher than those offered in Japan, this rate constriction caused Forex investors to devalue the GBP/JPY pair. (See Figure 12.6.)

At the beginning of February 2003, the GBP/JPY pair was trading at 197.39 Japanese yen per British pound. By the end of February— after the Bank of England had adjusted rates—the pair had fallen by nearly 1,200 pips to 185.82. Nobody, especially Forex investors, likes to see their investments decline in value. And when investors saw the Bank of England cut rates, they saw their future earning power from the interest-rate discrepancy diminishing. Even so, dropping the value of the pair nearly 1,200 pips was a bit extreme. And as the market started to adjust to the new interest-rate gap, the price of the GBP/JPY pair began to climb again. Unfortunately for GBP/JPY bulls, this rebound was short-lived. In July 2003, the Bank of England announced it was going to cut rates again, and it dropped the interest rate to 3.5 percent. Once again, the market pushed the value of the pair down. During the two months that followed the second interest-rate cut, the GBP/JPY pair dropped by 1,300 pips from an opening price of 198.15 to a closing price of 185.07. (See Figure 12.7.)

Again, the market stabilized as investors recognized that the spread between 3.5 percent and 0.1 percent was still a favorable spread, and the value of the GBP/JPY pair remained at around 185 for the next two months. In November 2003, the Bank of England finally released some good news as it announced it would be rais-

FIGURE 12.6

GBP/JPY, monthly chart through early February 2003

FIGURE 12.7

GBP/JPY, monthly chart through August 2003

ing interest rates to 3.75 percent. This announcement was immediately recognized in the market, and the value of the GBP/JPY pair increased by nearly 1,800 pips from the time of the announcement in November 2003 (186.15) through the end of January 2004 (203.68). (See Figure 12.8.)

FIGURE 12.8

GBP/JPY, monthly chart through January 2004

FIGURE 12.9

GBP/JPY, monthly chart through February 2004

The Bank of England decided to release more good news in February 2004 as it raised rates yet again to 4 percent. Based on the past price movement of the GBP/JPY pair, you would have assumed that the value of the pair would increase as the interest-rate spread continued to widen. However, even though the Seesaw of Supply and Demand indicated that rising interest rates should be beneficial, the value of the pair crashed down another 1,100 pips—from an opening value of 203.68 at the beginning of February 2004 to a value of 192.49 at the end of the month. (See Figure 12.9.)

Even though the interest-rate spread had been a major driving factor for years, this currency pair was still susceptible to other fundamental and nonfundamental factors.

CONCLUSION

You can be sure there were many investors who were caught off guard by this dramatic downward movement, and there will be times when you will be caught off guard in your investing. That is the nature of the market. You have to be ready for anything. The message of this chapter is to put the odds in your favor by conducting your fundamental analysis utilizing the Seesaw of Supply and Demand. But be ready for anything.

USD/GBP

USD becoming more valuable
than GDP.
      or
USD is bullish

USD↑/GDP↓

CHAPTER 13

Technical Analysis Tools

Technical analysis tools help you identify market sentiment—what the Forex market is doing and why. As Forex investors watch the markets, they begin to form opinions about what is happening, and these opinions ultimately drive their trading decisions. And as they do so, their trading decisions are reflected in the price movement of the currency pairs.

There are only two general market sentiments that you need to focus on in your trading: bearish and bullish. You are probably familiar with these two terms from the stock market, but in the Forex market, they carry slightly different connotations. In the stock market, "bullish" has a positive connotation because it means that the market is going up, and "bearish" has a negative connotation because it means that the market is going down. This is not the case in the Forex market. When a currency pair is going up on the chart in the Forex market, all it means is the first currency in the pair—the base currency—is becoming more valuable than the second currency in the pair—the quote currency. When a currency pair is going down on the chart in the Forex market, all it means is the quote currency is becoming more valuable than the base currency. So when you are talking about being bullish or bearish in the currency market, you have to take it one step further. You have to specify which currency in the currency pair you are referring to. For example, the trend on the chart of the EUR/USD (see Figure 13.1) could be going down, but you could still say you are bullish on the U.S. dollar because, as the U.S. dollar gains strength, it pushes the trend for that pair down.

FIGURE 13.1

EUR/USD, daily intervals

Source: Prophet.net

FIGURE 13.2

USD/JPY, daily intervals

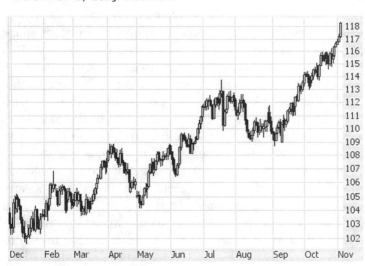

Source: Prophet.net

Now if you were looking at a currency pair in which the U.S. dollar was the base currency, such as the USD/JPY, the trend on the chart would have to be moving higher for you to say you are bullish on the U.S. dollar (see Figure 13.2).

Determining market sentiment is crucial when you are making your investment decisions, and technical analysis enables you to do so. There are times, however, when you are going to encounter periods of indecision in the Forex market, and you won't be able to determine if sentiment is bullish or bearish toward a given currency compared to another. Indecision is usually caused by too many impartial participants or a relatively even split between bearish traders and bullish ones. When this happens, the market will begin to trend sideways.

TECHNICAL INDICATORS

Technical indicators are the basic tools of technical analysis. They distill market movement so you don't have to deal with a lot of the static that comes with erratic price movements. There are literally thousands of technical indicators available to you as an investor. In fact, we even created one of our own called the Forex Forecast—a proprietary forecasting indicator that is available only through INVESTools at www.investoolsct.com. There is also an iteration of this forecasting indicator on www.investools.com that is used for investing in the stock market. But when it comes right down to it, most Forex investors stick to a repertoire of fewer than 20. Our goal is not to overwhelm you with thousands of technical indicators that you will have to weed through. We want to keep this as simple as possible because it is much easier to be profitable when you don't clutter things up too much.

Often you will see technical indicators classified into two categories: trending and nontrending (or oscillating). Practitioners divide technical indicators into these two categories because the trading signals produced by trending indicators are generally supposed to be more profitable during trending markets, and the trading signals generated by nontrending, or oscillating, indicators are supposed to be more profitable during nontrending, or flat, markets. While that is a nice way to conceptualize these indicators, most indicators usually perform best during trending markets. Fortunately for us, the Forex market usually has a lot of strong trends to take advantage

of. We are trend traders, and our strategies are trend-trading strategies so we tend to look at technical indicators a little differently.
Technical analysis for us is a two-step process. First, we identify
the current trend. Next, we sit back and wait until the market tells
us it is a good time to jump in and take advantage of the current
trend.

The trend is the single most important piece of technical information you can have. Once you are able to identify the trend of the
market, you are three-quarters of the way to a successful trade. When
you trade with the rest of the market, you exponentially increase
your chance of success. Let's look at the performance of the U.S. stock
market for the past decade to see how this works. If you bought
stocks or mutual funds from 1995 to 2000, you probably made a lot
of money. It doesn't really matter which stock or mutual fund you
bought because virtually all of them were going up. All you had to
do once you believed the stock market was going up was toss your
money into an account. After that, you were set. Month after month
the statements would roll in telling you how much money you had
made and how much earlier you could now retire. Everybody looked
really smart because everybody was choosing winning investments. But our success wasn't based on our genius; it was based on
the trend. The trend in the market was going up, and everyone just
rode the wave higher.

All that changed in 2000 when the market turned around and
lost huge amounts of money. Investors were certainly no less intelligent than they had been during the years of the mammoth
uptrend, yet they were still losing money. We all kept buying more
and more shares, but the value of our shares never seemed to go
any higher. Most investors were baffled and ended up losing quite
a bit of their money. So what happened? Well, the trend reversed
and started going down instead of up. Now, there were certainly a
great number of fundamental factors that affected the reversal of
the trend, but all we care about in technical analysis is that the trend
reversed. The point we want to make sure we drive home is that
you should always stick with the trend. Are there investors who
make money betting against the trend? Yes, there are. The more
appropriate question is, Are there *many* investors who make money
betting against the trend? No, there are not. Why would you struggle
and fight to swim upstream when you can enjoy life so much more
by swimming with the current?

TECHNICAL ANALYSIS TOOL:
THE MOVING AVERAGE

To identify the trend, we like to keep it simple. We use a moving average. If the moving average is pointing up, we know we are in an uptrend. If the moving average is pointing down, we are in a downtrend. It's as simple as that. Here is an example of the EUR/USD price chart with a moving average added to it (see Figure 13.3).

You can see how simple this analysis is. Whichever way the line is moving, that is the direction of the trend.

Once we have identified the direction of the trend, we then have to determine at what point we want to jump into the trend because some times are better than others. When you are getting on the highway, you know you are going to be moving with the trend, or flow, of traffic, but you have to determine when you are going to enter the flow of traffic. Most highway entrances take care of this decision for us. We have to wait for a green light before we can get on the highway. If we see a red light, we know it is not time to get on yet.

Oscillating indicators work like the traffic light at the highway entrance. They tell us when potentially profitable opportunities arise

FIGURE 13.3

↓ EUR/USD, ↑ daily intervals with 30-day moving average

Source: Prophet.net

so that we know it's time to enter the market. As you've probably noticed by looking at the price trends in the charts in this book, uptrends usually don't just go straight up, and downtrends usually don't just go straight down. They will move in one direction and then pull back in the opposite direction just a little bit before continuing on in the previous direction. These pullbacks are the ideal time to enter the trend, and oscillators help you identify when these pullbacks occur and when they are likely to turn back around.

TECHNICAL ANALYSIS TOOL: OSCILLATING INDICATORS

Oscillating indicators move back and forth, or oscillate, within a constrained range. They bounce up and down, up and down. When an oscillator bounces up too high, it is considered to be "overbought." When an oscillator bounces down too low, it is considered to be "oversold." And as the oscillator comes out of either one of these extreme areas, you get your green light to enter the trade.

Let's take a look at a few of the oscillating indicators you can use in your trading. We are going to illustrate four different oscillators here, but we want you to remember that there are many more you can explore. Also, we don't recommend trying to use too many oscillating indicators at one time. We want to avoid clutter in our technical analysis. Only use one, or maybe two, at a time in your trading. The oscillating indicators we look at are:

- The moving average convergence divergence (MACD)
- The stochastics indicator
- The commodity channel index (CCI)
- The relative strength index (RSI)

The *moving average convergence divergence (MACD)* is easiest to use when it is plotted as a histogram (see Figure 13.4). The MACD is overbought when the lines of the histogram are plotted above the flat, horizontal zero line in the middle of the indicator, and it is oversold when the lines of the histogram are plotted below the flat. During an uptrend, it is a great time to buy when the lines cross above the zero line. During a downtrend, it is a great time to sell when the lines cross below the zero line.

The *stochastics indicator* is plotted as two lines that move back and forth between 0 and 100 (see Figure 13.5). The stochastics indicator is

FIGURE 13.4

EUR/USD, daily intervals including MACD

Source: Prophet.net

FIGURE 13.5

EUR/USD, daily intervals including
stochastics indicator

Source: Prophet.net

overbought when the lines rise up above 75, and it is oversold when the lines drop down below 25. During an uptrend, it is a great time to buy when the lines cross back up above 25. During a downtrend, it is a great time to sell when the lines cross back down below 75.

The *commodity channel index (CCI)* is plotted as a single line that moves back and forth across a zero line (see Figure 13.6). The CCI is overbought when the line rises up above 100, and it is oversold when the line drops down below –100. During an uptrend, it is a great time to buy when the CCI line crosses back up above –100. During a downtrend, it is a great time to sell when the CCI line crosses back down below 100.

The *relative strength index (RSI)* is plotted as a single line that moves back and forth between 0 and 100 (see Figure 13.7). The RSI is overbought when the line rises above 80, and it is oversold when the line drops below 20. During an uptrend, it is a great time to buy when the RSI line crosses back above 20. During a downtrend, it is a great time to sell when the RSI line crosses back below 80.

Each one of these oscillating indicators is a great tool to use in your trading. As you noticed with each of these indicators, when you are in an uptrend, you want to watch for periods when the Forex market is oversold. This tells you that the dominant uptrend has

FIGURE 13.6

EUR/USD, daily intervals including CCI

FIGURE 13.7

EUR/USD, daily intervals including RSI

Source: Prophet.net

experienced a slight pullback. When you see the oscillating indicators moving back out of their oversold territories, you know that the dominant uptrend is resuming, and it is a great time to enter the trade. Conversely, when you are in a downtrend, you want to watch for periods when the Forex market is overbought. This tells you that the dominant downtrend has experienced a slight pullback. When you see the oscillating indicators moving back out of their overbought territories, you know the dominant downtrend is resuming, and it is a great time to enter the trade.

TERMS OF THE TRADE

You will need to know a few more terms for the specific trading examples in Chapter 15. Each one of these terms pertains to a specific part of the trading process. The more comfortable you are with these terms, the easier it will be for you to jump into the Forex market and be successful.

- *Stop loss.* This one is review, but it is so important that we threw it in again. A stop loss is an order that indicates a price at which you will automatically sell if the trade goes against you.

- *Limit, or price target.* A limit, or price target, is an order that indicates a price at which you will automatically sell if the trade goes your way. You set these orders for two reasons. The first reason is that it will automatically sell and collect your profits for you even if you aren't actively watching your account. The second reason is that it gives you an idea of what you are expecting to get out of the trade. This will help you determine your risk/reward ratio and whether you should even enter a trade.
- *Entry.* An entry is the price at which you entered your trade. It is the buy price if you are long the position, and it is the sell price if you are short the position.
- *Exit.* An exit is where you closed your trade. It is the sell price if you were long the position, and it is the buy price if you were short the position.
- *Risk/reward ratio.* The risk/reward ratio is a measure of how much risk you are willing to take for the chance to make a certain profit. If you were willing to risk 100 pips—which means setting your stop-loss order 100 pips away—in order to make 100 pips, you would have a risk/reward ratio of 1:1. This is not bad if you can be right more than 50 percent of the time. However, it is extremely rare for a trader to be right more than 50 percent of the time. We know that this doesn't sound like good odds, but we'll show you how you make up the difference. If you assume that you will be right less than half the time, you can offset your losers by making more money on your winners than you lose on your losers. In most cases, we are looking for a risk/reward ratio of at least 1:3—which means that we are risking 33 percent of what we stand to gain. For example, we would only be willing to risk 100 pips on a trade if we believed we could make 300 pips or more if we are right.

CHAPTER 14

Support, Resistance, and Fibonacci

In the previous chapter, we discuss several technical analysis tools that can help you identify both the trend and the sentiment of the market at any given time. Utilizing these technical indicators in your investing should increase your confidence in your analysis of what will be happening in the market in the future. However, technical indicators do have some limitations.

The largest drawback when dealing with technical indicators is that the equations used to calculate the indicators naturally cause the indicators to lag behind the market. This means that part of the price movement has already occurred before the movement is reflected in the indicator, which means that some of the profit potential in the current movement has already evaporated. Most technical analysts are willing to deal with this time lag because it is relatively easy to read the signals on technical indicators and to build trading rules around them. There is something quite appealing about eliminating ambiguity when you are trading in a dynamic market like the Forex.

Simplicity and usability aside, most technical analysts supplement the technical indicators they use with an analysis of various support and resistance levels—with Fibonacci levels being one of the most widely used forms of support and resistance analysis. Fibonacci levels and other levels of support and resistance are referred to as *leading indicators* because they lead the market in predictable paths. Now, certainly when we say predictable, we do not mean guaranteed. But it is pretty close.

Often as you read through any news regarding the Forex market or what institutional investors are looking at, you will see reference to Fibonacci levels and other levels of support and resistance. Seeing these references should encourage you to learn more about these technical tools so that you can utilize them in your own trading. If you aren't interested in utilizing these tools in your trading, you should nonetheless be aware of what other large investors are looking at. As you will see later in this chapter, support and resistance levels often become self-fulfilling prophesies. So knowing where the large investors are looking will help you in your trading.

Before we dive into Fibonacci analysis, let's take a look at the basic building blocks of a proper Fibonacci analysis: support and resistance.

SUPPORT AND RESISTANCE

Support is a price level that a currency pair has trouble breaking through to the downside. You will often hear support referred to as the floor of the currency pair price movement. *Resistance* is a price level that a currency pair has trouble breaking through to the upside. You will often hear resistance referred to as the ceiling of the currency pair price movement. Many new investors in the market are often surprised by the strangely predictable and reliable price action that occurs at levels of support and resistance. Although there is nothing on the chart itself or in the market to demand that all investors begin buying or selling at a given level of support or resistance, they do so just the same. While there are many explanations for this phenomenon, the most plausible is also the simplest: At support, the majority of investors believe that the currency pair is favorably priced and represents an excellent opportunity to buy once it reaches the support level. At resistance, the majority of investors believe the currency pair is not favorably priced and represents an excellent opportunity to sell once it reaches the resistance level. Whatever the reasons for the levels, you will have an excellent advantage in your trading if you are capable of accurately identifying support and resistance levels in the market.

We mentioned earlier that support and resistance levels are often self-fulfilling prophecies. Let us explain. As more and more investors begin to conduct technical analyses of the Forex market, they will inevitably begin to identify levels of support and resistance that are similar to one another. If only one investor believes that a particular level is a valid support or resistance level, that level probably won't hold up as support or resistance. However, if thousands of investors all identify the same level as a level of support or resistance, then it most likely will hold up as a level of support or resistance. So, as you can see, the level itself has no real force behind it. The only reason it serves as a support or resistance level is that thousands of investors say it should, and it acts accordingly. If enough investors prophesy that a certain price level will act as support or resistance, they can fulfill their own prophesy by buying or selling the currency pair when the price reaches the prophesied level.

Identifying Support and Resistance

Support and resistance levels exist on every chart you will look at in your investing career. As you can see on the EUR/USD chart (Figure 14.1), the price of the currency pair rose and dropped back down to the 1.2000 level multiple times without being able to break through that level of support. Nothing in the market insisted that the price had to remain above the 1.2000 level. But apparently, the majority of the investors in the market believed that the EUR/USD pair was a great deal at 1.2000. You will also notice we have drawn

FIGURE 14.1

EUR/USD, showing a horizontal level of support

Source: Prophet.net

in a heavy black line to identify where there is support. You will want to do the same thing when conducting your technical analysis to help you visualize these all-too-important price levels.

Understanding exactly what is happening in the market when you see the price drop down to support and bounce back up will help you in your future analysis. As investors begin to lose interest in the currency pair or as they begin to take profits, the price of the currency pair will begin to fall. As the price is falling, other investors who do not already own the pair will be watching to see how far it will fall. Most of these investors have run various calculations and simulations and have determined that if the pair drops to 1.2000, it is fairly valued and represents a good buy opportunity. Thus, when they see the price reach their predetermined level, they jump into the market and begin buying the currency pair. As buyers slowly enter the marketplace, they begin to outweigh the sellers, and the demand for the currency pair increases. This causes the previous downward price movement to reverse and begin moving higher.

Resistance levels are formed in much the same way as support levels. Looking at the GBP/USD chart (see Figure 14.2), you will see that the price of the currency pair hit a clearly defined ceiling at the 1.7800 price level. While this level is easily identifiable on the chart,

FIGURE 14.2

GBP/USD, showing a horizontal level of resistance

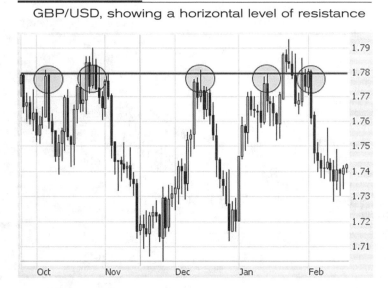

Source: Prophet.net

it is again important to ask yourself why this level of resistance exists. There is no market-governing body that decreed that the price of the GBP/USD should not rise above 1.7800, but nonetheless, the price obediently remained below this level. The simplest explanation is that a majority of market participants believed that the GBP/USD was too expensive when it reached 1.7800, and they began to sell the currency pair. Some of those market participants would have been long the pair as it was climbing higher, and their decision to sell the pair would have been spurred by a desire to take some profits. For those market participants who held no previous position in the currency pair, their decision to sell the GBP/USD pair would have been spurred by a desire to enter a potentially profitable position.

Regardless of each investor's individual motivations for selling, the selling started, and the currency price began to move back down. For most investors, properly identifying these levels of support and resistance is crucial because they are too small to move the market by themselves. And by knowing where support and resistance levels lie, they can make nimble adjustments to their trades that enable them to take advantage of the larger market movements.

One requirement of a support level, or a resistance level, is that the price level is reached multiple times but never breached. As you can imagine, if a large group of investors believed that a particular price level represented a fair price for the currency pair in the recent past, these investors will most likely believe it represents a fair price today. You can confirm that they believe it is still a fair price because, just as you can see in the EUR/USD chart (see Figure 14.1), the price continues to turn around and bounce back higher time and time again.

Support and resistance levels do not always have to be horizontal levels. They can also be diagonal levels—sloping up or down. As you can imagine, horizontal support and resistance levels are more than adequate when you are analyzing relatively flat market conditions. When the market is flat, prices tend to bounce back and forth between a horizontal support level and a horizontal resistance level. There may be intermediate levels of support and resistance in between the major levels that you identify, but all these levels remain horizontal. However, when the market begins to trend, as the Forex market often does, these horizontal support and resistance levels suddenly become less important.

If you try to continue using the same horizontal levels of support and resistance once the market begins to trend, you will find yourself frustrated and unable to properly manage your trades. As

FIGURE 14.3

EUR/USD, showing a diagonal level of support

Source: Prophet.net

you can see in the EUR/USD chart (see Figure 14.3), the currency pair
had dropped down to a horizontal support level of 1.1900 in early
July. After bouncing up off this level, the price continued to move
higher until it turned around and began moving lower in the middle
of the month. If the market were going to remain flat, you would
expect the price to drop down to the same support level at 1.1900. But
it didn't. The price dropped to a price level of only 1.2000 by the end
of July before it turned around once again and began moving higher.
This would be your first indication that the market has broken out
of its flat pattern and is now trending higher.

As the market establishes a new bullish trend, you must begin
to identify new support and resistance levels. Looking back at
Figure 14.3, you can see that instead of using a horizontal level of
support, we have identified a diagonal level of support. Remember,
you are looking for price levels that the currency pair is having trouble
breaking through. Once you see at least two points along a line that
have stood up to a threatening price movement, you can be confident
that you have a support or a resistance level. And the more times the
price bounces off that level, the stronger it becomes. In Figure 14.3,
the price dropped down to the new diagonal support level twice in
July and twice in August. And each time the currency pair dropped

down to that level of support and bounced back up, you would have become increasingly confident in the strength of that support level.

Resistance levels, just like support levels, will stray from their horizontal roots when a currency pair begins to trend. While you will still be able to identify various horizontal levels of resistance on the chart, the predominant levels of resistance you will see within a trending market are diagonal. The downward-sloping resistance level shown in the GBP/USD chart (Figure 14.4) is an excellent example of this. Looking at this chart, you could certainly draw a horizontal resistance level across the chart at the 1.8500 price level in early September, but this level would soon become momentarily obsolete as the price continued to fall without ever rallying back to that price level.

We recognize that the term "momentarily obsolete" may seem like a contradiction, but it actually does give quite an accurate description of what is happening on the chart. We want to emphasize that while the price of the currency pair may move away from a particular support or resistance level at any time, that particular support or resistance level doesn't necessarily go away. The market has an extremely long memory, and there may be a time in the future when the price of the GBP/USD will move back to that 1.8500 price level,

FIGURE 14.4

GBP/USD, showing a diagonal level of resistance

Source: Prophet.net

and that old resistance level may find new life. So as you are identifying various support and resistance levels, don't fall into the trap
of looking only at those levels that have appeared during the recent
past. Extend your analysis a little farther into the past to make sure
that you are aware of any support or resistance levels that may still
hold sway in today's market.

Perhaps the greatest benefit of utilizing support and resistance levels in your technical analysis is the universality of the concepts. It doesn't matter if you are looking at a one-hour chart or a
weekly chart; you can identify levels of support or resistance in any
time frame. The hourly chart of the EUR/USD (Figure 14.5) shows
a level of support that is just as dramatic and reliable as the support
levels shown on the daily charts in the previous examples. Of
course, you will notice that the subsequent rise in price from each
bounce was on a smaller scale than the price bounces you saw on
the daily charts, but an active trader could certainly take advantage
of the support level that was established and would profit from
each bounce.

This time-period universality applies to both horizontal and
diagonal levels of support and resistance. The 10-minute GBP/USD

FIGURE   14.5

EUR/USD, hourly intervals, showing a horizontal
level of support

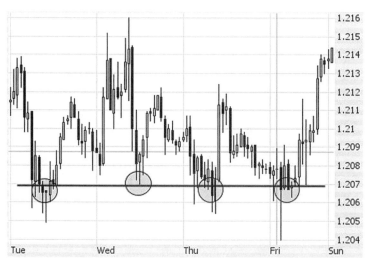

Source: Prophet.net

FIGURE 14.6

GBP/USD, 10-minute intervals, showing a diagonal
level of resistance

Source: Prophet.net

chart (Figure 14.6) illustrates the effectiveness of identifying a downward sloping level of resistance in an extremely short time frame.
The buyers in the market continued to try to push the price of the
currency pair back up, but each time they tried, they lost more and
more momentum as the sellers were able to push the price lower and
lower. It really doesn't matter which time frame you utilize in your
Forex investing. As you become more familiar with support and
resistance and how to identify various levels of support and resistance on your charts, you will improve your investing results.

Breaking Support and Resistance

Support and resistance levels enable investors to project how far they
believe a currency pair will move and at what points the price action
of a currency pair may turn around and start moving in the opposite
direction. But as with all good things in life, even the influence of particular support and resistance levels must come to an end. Sometimes
the market is strong enough to cause a currency pair to break through
a previously established level of support or resistance. Fortunately
for you as an investor, you know that for every level that is broken,

a new level will be established. Plus, the broken level may still have some influence on the market in the future—more details on that later.

Before we talk about breaking support and resistance levels, however, it is important to address a topic that frustrates many investors: attempted breakouts. As you learn how to identify levels of support and resistance relative to the currency pairs you are trading, it will become obvious that prices do not always stop at exactly the same point each time. In fact, it is virtually impossible to exactly identify a level of support or resistance. For example, it would be useless to try and say that support for the EUR/USD is exactly 1.2013 or is exactly 1.1958. If you tried to set such stringent requirements for your support and resistance levels, those levels would never hold up, and you would fake yourself out of a lot of valid price movements. If the price level, for instance, dropped two pips below the exact level you had identified, you would have to conclude that the price had broken through support and was on its way down. Unfortunately, that would be a foolish conclusion.

To avoid being too stringent in your analysis of support and resistance levels, try to identify a price range that is serving as either support or resistance. The time frame you are looking at on your chart will influence how wide you need to set this price range, but you should always try to give your levels a little room to breathe. One of our trading partners, Blake Young, puts it this way, "When you are drawing in levels of support and resistance, you should draw your lines with a thick crayon, not a fine-point pen." Giving yourself a little room will help you avoid making any rash decisions in your trading.

Even when you do take these precautions with your levels of support and resistance, you will still find that the market can have a sick sense of humor, and even all of the best-drawn lines won't be able to help you. To illustrate what we mean, imagine that the support and resistance lines you have drawn are like fences on a large cattle ranch and that the price of the currency pair is like the cattle on the ranch. Most of the time, the cattle will stay within the fences that outline their grazing lands. However, sometimes a cow will see a nice tasty patch of grass just outside the fence and will decide to take a bite or two. To do this, the cow has to stick its head through the fence and reach as far as it can before it is forced to come back. Technically, the cow is still inside the fence, but it has managed to breach the boundary just enough to appear as though it is on its way out.

You can see what a cow poking its head through the fence would figuratively look like on a currency chart in the daily EUR/USD chart (Figure 14.7). In the spirit of identifying approximate price levels for support and resistance, we will say that support on this chart was right around 1.2000. The price of the EUR/USD pair had dropped down to this level twice in June before dropping a third time and momentarily breaking through. For all intents and purposes, the 1.2000 support level was broken and no longer had any impact on the market price. However, within a few days, the price had rebounded, and the 1.2000 support level was back in vogue with the price bouncing off that level two more times during July before turning around and heading higher.

Stepping back for a moment, we promised to address the concept of momentary obsolescence, and here it is. Looking at this EUR/USD chart, you may have been tempted to write off the support level at 1.2000 once the price had broken through it at the end of June. However, instead of disregarding a support or resistance level once it has been broken, you need to look at it as a level that is not currently influencing the market but that may influence it at some time in the future. In other words, while the level may seem obsolete at the moment, it may not be so in the future.

FIGURE 14.7

EUR/USD, daily intervals, showing a momentary break in the level of support

Source: Prophet.net

Hopefully, looking at the EUR/USD chart has made you ask the question, "How can I tell when the price has truly broken through support or resistance?" The only answer to this question is to look for a secondary confirmation that the price action has changed enough to affect the historical levels of support and resistance. Two methods of establishing a secondary confirmation have proven to be quite accurate in the past: setting price-amplitude benchmarks and identifying role reversals.

Setting Price-Amplitude Benchmarks Setting price-amplitude benchmarks involves analyzing a chart to see if you can identify any moments when the price momentarily poked through the prevailing support or resistance level before pulling back and once again adhering to the previous level. In the EUR/USD chart (Figure 14.8), you can see that as the price was trending upward during July, August, and September, it would periodically dip below the main diagonal support level identified by the bold line. The dips below the predominant level were short-lived and didn't travel too far, but this doesn't mean that they aren't significant. If you draw in a secondary support level, like the dotted line you see in the figure

FIGURE 14.8

EUR/USD, showing a secondary support level—your price-amplitude benchmark

Source: Prophet.net

below the main diagonal line, you can then utilize this level as your price-amplitude benchmark.

A price-amplitude benchmark tells you that if the price breaks through the predominant support or resistance level but doesn't break through the benchmark, you probably don't need to worry about a change in the trend of the price movement. However, if the price breaks through primary support or resistance and has enough momentum behind it to breach the benchmark, it has a good chance of continuing in the new direction. You can see the break of the benchmark in September in Figure 14. 8. Holding true to form, once the price broke out of its previous trend, it continued to move in the new direction it had established with the breakout.

Identifying Role Reversals? Identifying role reversals involves watching for support levels to turn into resistance levels and resistance levels to turn into support levels. All too often, you will see the price of a currency pair bounce off of a level of resistance, turn around and start moving higher, break through resistance, turn around and start heading lower, and then bounce off the previous resistance level. More often than not, when a resistance level is broken, that same level will turn into support. Conversely, when a support level is broken, that same level will turn into resistance.

The USD/JPY chart (Figure 14.9) offers a perfect example of a role reversal. From the end of July through the middle of September, the price of the USD/JPY had been suppressed by a downward trending resistance level. Each time the price of the currency pair would rise up to that level of resistance—at points labeled A, B, and C, sellers would enter the market and drive prices back down. Finally in the middle of September, the buyers in the market were able to muster enough momentum to push the price of the pair up and through the prevailing level of resistance. Apparently, this upward push took a lot of strength out of the buyers in the market, and the price began to turn around and head lower. This price action is not an uncommon phenomenon. However, the psychological impact the previous break of resistance had had on the market cannot be ignored. Suddenly, all the market participants who believe the previous level of resistance was accurate begin to reevaluate their positions, and the level of resistance becomes a level of support—at point D.

One thing you may have noticed on the USD/JPY chart is the fact that you could have drawn in a benchmark level associated with these price movements as well. Had you drawn in a benchmark

FIGURE 14.9

USD/JPY, showing a role reversal from resistance to support

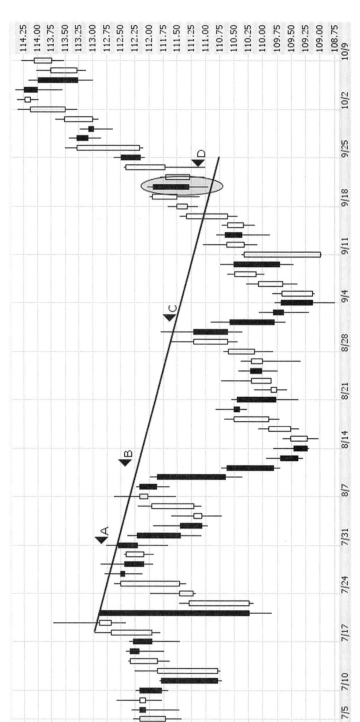

level above the primary level of resistance, the price would have reached that level when it broke through the primary resistance level in September. What this tells you is that you can use both the benchmark and role-reversal confirmations in your trading analysis. You do not have to limit yourself to either one. This concept of looking for as much information as you can find to support or discredit any given trade is one we hope you have recognized as a theme throughout this book. Whether you are looking at multiple fundamental factors and determining how they stack up on the Seesaw of Supply and Demand or you are looking at multiple technical indicators to confirm a price movement, don't ever sell your analysis short by consulting only one piece of information. Being aware of everything that is happening around them is what separates the successful investors from the unsuccessful ones.

Utilizing Support and Resistance in Your Trading

You have learned how to identify both horizontal and diagonal levels of support and resistance. You have also learned how to identify when those levels are merely being tested and when they have been broken. Now, we need to connect the dots and apply the theory to trading to see how these levels of support and resistance may affect your investment decisions.

Let's review a few basic tenets of utilizing support and resistance levels in your trading:

- Focus on support levels when identifying entry points during uptrends
- Focus on resistance levels when identifying exit points during uptrends
- Focus on resistance levels when identifying entry points during downtrends
- Focus on support levels when identifying exit points during downtrends
- Always wait for confirmation of both support or resistance bounces and breakouts

Whenever the price of a currency pair reaches a support or resistance level, market participants begin to get a little anxious because they know the current trend has a heightened potential of turning around and moving in the opposite direction. For investors who are trading with the current trend, this is a tenuous situation because they have to decide whether they should stay in their current positions and hope that the support or resistance levels don't hold up. For investors who are looking for a possible entry point into their next trade, this is also a nerve-racking situation because they have to decide whether they should bet on a bounce or a breakthrough. Needless to say, the tension is tangible in the market whenever a currency pair nears support or resistance.

The best thing you, as an individual investor, can do at this point is wait for the market to come to you. Do not try to outguess, outthink, or outfox the market. Wait for the market to decide what it is going to do with a particular support or resistance level, and then jump on the bandwagon. When you are investing in the Forex market, you have everything to gain from going along with the herd just as long as you are actively managing your positions.

Waiting for the market simply means that you watch the price action of the currency pair to see how it reacts. For example, if the price moves up to a resistance level, bounces off it, and begins heading lower, you know that the market believes this resistance level is legitimate, and you can place or manage your trades accordingly. Additionally, if the price moves down to a support level and breaks down through that support level, you know that the market no longer believes this support level is legitimate, and you can place or manage your trades accordingly.

The most effective way to illustrate these concepts and how you can apply them in your own investing is through a case study. This case study involves the USD/CHF pair and its price action during the latter half of 2005 (see Figure 14.10). From the beginning of September, the price of the currency pair had been trending upward. At the beginning of October, the price of the pair began to pull back until it paused at the 1.2700 level.

As you look at this price movement, you need to step back and try to get into the mindset of the market participants at this time. When you see a prolonged trend, such as the uptrend you see in the USD/CHF chart during September, you know that a majority of the market participants believed that the price of the pair should be moving higher, and they all jumped onboard to take advantage of the movement. Any good investor always establishes a targeted exit point before entering a trade. In the case of the USD/CHF pair in this example, that target was the 1.3000 price level. (As a side note, it is not uncommon for large institutions to focus on nice round numbers when determining their profit and loss projections. And clearly, 1.3000 is a nice round number.) Once the price reached this predetermined

FIGURE 14.10

USD/CHF, September–October 2005

Source: Prophet.net

level, those investors who had been riding the previous uptrend decided it was time to realize some profits, and they began exiting their positions. As this happened, more sellers began to enter the market, which pushed the price even lower. As the price began to drop, investors began looking for established levels of support that might prevent the currency pair from falling any farther. As you look at the chart toward the end of September, you can see a black candlestick that shows the price falling to the 1.2700 level. The next trading day, the price rebounded and continued its upward trend for the next two weeks. However, this drop to the 1.2700 level is significant because it established a possible level of support. And sure enough, that level of support held firm at the beginning of October because the majority of the market participants at the time believed it would.

Of course, it would be quite aggressive to buy the currency pair just as the price reached the 1.2700 level because the market hadn't yet confirmed that it was going to respect that level of support. Again, you are looking for confirmation. The following trading day, the price of the USD/CHF pair did rebound and you receive your initial confirmation that the market looks to be holding strong at support. At this point, you could choose to enter a trade by buying the currency pair, but let's assume that you are an extremely conservative investor and you would like to wait for another entry point.

FIGURE 14.11

USD/CHF, September–December 2005

Source: Prophet.net

By looking at an extended chart of the USD/CHF (Figure 14.11), you can see that after the price of the currency pair bounced up off the 1.2700 level at the beginning of October, it rose back up to the 1.3000 level. After a brief stay at this newly confirmed level of resistance, the price turned back around and dropped back down to the 1.2700 level at the end of October. Knowing that a support or resistance level becomes stronger each time the price bounces off it, you decide that the 1.2700 support level is legitimate when you see the price begin to bounce up off it, and you decide to enter a trade by buying the USD/CHF pair.

As you enter the trade, you know two things: one, the price has just bounced off the 1.2700 support level; and two, the price is moving up toward the established 1.3000 resistance level. Because you know that resistance levels are price levels at which the currency pair is likely to be a little more volatile, you determine to set your price target at that level. If the price moves up to the 1.3000 level of resistance and the market decides to honor that level of resistance by sending the price of the currency pair back down, you can exit your trade and enjoy your profits. If the price moves up to the 1.3000 level of resistance and the market decides not to honor that level of resistance and the price continues higher, as it did in this example, you can stay in your trade and accumulate additional profits. The important thing was not to know exactly what you were going to do when the price reached the 1.3000 level of resistance. The important thing was to know that this level of resistance existed and that you would probably have to take some action as the price neared that level.

In the previous case study, we showed a nice trade setup using horizontal support and resistance levels. Had you placed a trade during this time, you would have most likely been successful. Our examples wouldn't be complete, however, if we didn't show you a case study utilizing diagonal support and resistance levels. The next example will do just that. The primary benefit you have when you are analyzing diagonal support and resistance levels is that the market is already trending. As you learned previously, the trend is your friend, and when you trade with the trend, you increase your odds of success.

This case study involves the CHF/JPY pair (see Figure 14.12). Beginning in late June, this pair began to trend higher. And as you've seen before, the trend rarely moves straight up. Often, you will see it move up for a while before it pulls back down to prepare for another strong move upward. As it pulls back down at the end of July, hits support, and turns around to move higher again, you can see that

FIGURE 14.12

CHF/JPY, creating a diagonal level of support

Source: Prophet.net

the new level of support is higher than the previous level of support the price established in late June. This indicates that you should utilize a diagonal support level in your analysis.

Once again, let's assume that you are an extremely conservative investor and that instead of buying right now during this uptrend, you would like to wait until you see one more support bounce to confirm the validity of this diagonal level of support. Fortunately, you don't have to wait very long because in late August, the price of the CHF/JPY pair drops back down to the established diagonal level of support, turns around, and begins to move higher. Seeing this, you decide to jump in and take advantage of a confirmed support bounce during an uptrend. By looking at the updated CHF/JPY chart (Figure 14.13), you can see that entering your trade on this support bounce would give you plenty of room to grow on the upside—based on the previous high established earlier in August. It also provides you with a conservative price point at which to set your stop loss—based on the previous low established during the most recent support bounce.

While the two trades we have analyzed in these case studies would have been wonderful profit-generating opportunities, we want to make sure we stay in touch with reality. Anyone can find

FIGURE 14.13

CHF/JPY, showing a confirmed diagonal level of support

Source: Prophet.net

examples of trades that worked out well. But as we do so, we want to acknowledge that not all trades will work out as you expect them to. Even when you utilize the trend to put the odds in your favor, you can still have trades that don't perform as expected. One example of a trade gone awry is called a "whipsaw." A whipsaw gets its name from the feeling of being whipped around in the market you will be left with after losing your money. You get whipped around when you enter a trade, the price of the currency pair immediately turns around, and you end up losing the money you invested in the trade. In most cases, a whipsaw happens quite quickly and illustrates how temperamental the Forex market can be—even when you have conducted a thorough fundamental and technical analysis. While losing trades can be frustrating, we discuss a few techniques you can implement in your trading to help you keep your long-term perspective in Chapter 16 on money management.

Before moving onto our discussion of Fibonacci analysis, we would like to look at one more case study in which we can roll in a little fundamental analysis with our technical analysis. This case study involves the USD/CAD pair. During the time period illustrated on the chart (Figure 14.14), commodity prices—especially oil prices—were rising. These rising prices caused an increase in demand for the

FIGURE 14.14

USD/CAD, establishing a downward-sloping level of resistance

Source: Prophet.net

Canadian dollar. In response to this increased demand, the value of the Canadian dollar increased when compared to the value of the U.S. dollar, and the USD/CAD pair began to move lower. In May and June, you can see that the price began to establish a downward-sloping level of resistance as it continued to move lower and lower.

By the time the price had moved up and hit the diagonal resistance line for a third time, you probably would have been ready to enter a trade by selling the USD/CAD pair. Once again, you would have placed the odds in your favor by trading with the trend and waiting for a fresh bounce off of resistance. Plus, you know that you have the economic factors identified in your fundamental analysis working in your favor. Knowing all this, you recognize you have no guarantee of success, but you are confident you have an excellent chance of getting out of this trade with a tidy profit. By looking at the highlighted chart of the USD/CAD pair (Figure 14.15), you can see that your entry point would give you plenty of room to move as the price continues to fall toward your target rate. Your entry point is also close enough to your stop-loss level to keep you from losing too much money if the trade does indeed go against you.

Support and resistance are incredible weapons in any investor's technical analysis arsenal. Having the ability to project levels where

FIGURE 14.15

USD/CAD, showing entry point and target rate

Source: Prophet.net

the price of a currency pair may turn around without having to wait for the lag associated with technical indicators is priceless. But if you thought that simply drawing support and resistance levels on a chart based on previous levels where the price of a currency pair turned around was revolutionary, wait until you see what you can do with a little math inspired by an Italian rabbit-breeding monk— Leonardo Pisano, or Fibonacci.

FIBONACCI

Fibonacci analysis is an exercise in identifying levels of support and resistance during both trend retracements and trend continuations based on a series of numbers and ratios derived from the Fibonacci sequence. This sequence was discovered by the Italian mathematician Leonardo Pisano, or Fibonacci. The Fibonacci sequence starts with 0, 1, and 1 and is calculated by adding the two most recent numbers in sequence to arrive at the next number in the sequence. For example, if you take the first two numbers in the sequence, you get $0 + 1 = 1$. If you then take the two most recent numbers in the sequence, you get $1 + 1 = 2$. Repeating the process, you get $1 + 2 = 3$, and so on. As you continue on with this process, the sequence begins to take shape and ends up looking like this: 0, 1, 1, 2, 3, 5, 8, 13, 21, 34, 55 . . .

While this sequence alone is a fascinating discovery, the relationships between the numbers in the sequence are what we, as investors, are really interested in. Pisano showed that the ratio between the numbers in the sequence at specific intervals would consistently be the same regardless of how high you counted. The two most important ratios found within the sequence from an investor's point of view are 38.2 percent and 61.8 percent. These two ratios appear over and over again in nature—such as in the concentric rings of sunflowers, conch shells, and pine cones—and in such architectural masterworks as the Parthenon. These ratios also make very interesting appearances in the Forex market.

The first ratios we look at are those ratios investors utilize when forecasting retracement levels. The first ratio, 38.2 percent, is approximately the ratio of any number in the sequence divided by the number two places higher in the sequence. For example, the sequence goes . . . 13, 21, 34, 55 . . . If you were to take 21 and divide it by the number two places higher than it in the sequence, 55, you would get the ratio 38.2 percent ($21 \div 55 = 0.382$, or 38.2%). The second ratio, 61.8 percent, is approximately the ratio of any number in the sequence divided by the number directly following it in the sequence. For example, looking once again at the sequence . . . 13, 21, 34, 55 . . . , if you were to take 34 and divide it by 55, you would get the ratio 61.8 percent (34 ÷ 55 = 0.618, or 61.8%).

In addition to the two ratios discussed above, which are the ratios investors use when they're identifying support and resistance levels during retracements, most investors use three additional ratios—0 percent, 50 percent, and 100 percent. These ratios have no real correlation with the Fibonacci sequence, but when used in conjunction with the two primary Fibonacci ratios, these ratios round out your retracement analysis tools.

Two secondary Fibonacci ratios we discuss below also draw their values from the Fibonacci sequence. These ratios are most effective in projecting trend continuations. The first ratio, 161.8 percent, is approximately the ratio of any number in the sequence divided by the number directly preceding it in the sequence. For example, looking at the sequence . . . 13, 21, 34, 55 . . . , if you were to take 55 and divide it by 34, you would get the ratio 161.8 percent (55 ÷ 34 = 1.618, or 161.8%). The second ratio, 261.8 percent, is approximately the ratio of any number in the sequence divided by the number two places lower in the sequence. For example, looking again at the sequence . . . 13, 21, 34, 55, 89 . . . , if you were to take 89 and divide it by the number two places lower in the sequence, 34, you would get the ratio 261.8 percent (89 ÷ 34 = 2.618, or 261.8%).

Investors use Fibonacci ratios to project future levels of support and resistance based on previous moves in the market. In other words, previous moves in the market dictate where the Fibonacci levels will be placed. Since all the Fibonacci levels are discussed in terms of percentages, you first need to determine what you will be referencing with those percentages. Simply saying a "retracement level at 38.2 percent" doesn't mean much on its own. The question you need to ask is 38.2 percent of what? Once again, the best way to illustrate how Fibonacci retracement and projection levels work is through case studies.

Fibonacci Retracement Levels

Trends in the Forex market never travel in a straight line. Uptrends never go straight up, and downtrends never go straight down. The price will always retrace along the way as buyers and sellers enter

FIGURE 14.16

GBP/USD, showing a downward price movement

Source: Prophet.net

and exit the market. The question on every investor's mind, however, when these retracements occur is how far the retracement will penetrate into the previous movement. This is where Fibonacci retracement analysis becomes so useful.

The first case study we look at involves the GBP/USD (see Figure 14.16). The first step in any Fibonacci analysis is identifying the price movement you would like to analyze. In the GBP/USD chart, you can see we have drawn in a line covering the downward price movement that began in early September and concluded in early October. This is the movement we are going to utilize in our Fibonacci retracement analysis.

The line we have drawn may seem a little arbitrary, and to a certain extent identifying peaks and valleys does take a little experience and finesse, but with enough practice you will gain the confidence you need to accurately identify appropriate price movements. Also, as you move forward in your own trading, don't be afraid to adjust your analysis as a trade progresses and you obtain new information.

Once you have identified the price movement you would like to analyze, you should place your predetermined Fibonacci retracement levels on your GBP/USD chart. You will see we have drawn in levels for each of the retracement levels we discussed previously—

FIGURE 14.17

GBP/USD, showing Fibonacci retracement levels

Source: Prophet.net

0, 38.2, 50, 61.8, and 100 percent (see Figure 14.17). Your Fibonacci retracement levels will be populated according to the rules determined by your charting system, but they should look similar to the lines drawn on the GBP/USD chart.

Once again, you are trying to identify how far the price of the currency pair may pull back after having dropped approximately 1,000 pips during the previous month. Having the Fibonacci retracement levels drawn in on your chart gives you a few projections you can base your expectations on. One important reminder is that the support and resistance levels projected by a Fibonacci retracement analysis act just like support and resistance levels you draw in on your own. The levels are not significant until the market reacts to them. Keeping this in mind, you should always wait for confirmation of a support or resistance bounce off of a Fibonacci retracement level. In the GBP/USD chart (Figure 14.17), you can see that the market was watching the 38.2 percent retracement level and that when the price of the currency pair reached that point, sellers entered the market and began pushing the price back down.

Many market participants debate whether the price action around Fibonacci levels is based on normal market behavior that

Fibonacci levels are extremely adept at identifying or on self-fulfilling prophesies. While this may be an interesting theoretical debate, when it comes down to market application, it doesn't really matter. All you, as an investor, need to worry about is what the market chooses to do with the information available to it. If the market decides to turn around when it reaches a particular retracement level, go with the market.

Once you see the market reacting to a particular retracement level, you can jump into action by selling the GBP/USD pair. You would want to sell because the overall trend is down, even though the price did experience a slight retracement. Of course, more aggressive traders may try to profit from the price movement in the retracement itself, but this is certainly more difficult and risky. An additional advantage you have when trading with the overall trend is that the other Fibonacci retracement levels give you excellent stop-loss and profit targets. Looking on the GBP/USD chart (Figure 14.18), you can see where we have identified potential entry and stop levels. We determined the entry level by placing it just below the 38.2 percent retracement level. We determined the stop level by simply placing it at the next highest retracement level—the 50 percent level. The profit

FIGURE 14.18

GBP/USD, indicating potential entry and stop levels

Source: Prophet.net

target for this trade will be the 0 percent level. With this trade setup, you will be profitable if the market resumes its previous trend and drops back down to the 1.7400 level.

In the next case study, we are going to enhance the analysis with a simple trick of the trade involving market psychology. Often in the market, you will see the price of a currency pair make a dramatic movement within a short period of time. These movements are usually the result of some fundamental factor changing, which results from an economic announcement or the like. When the market sees this change, everyone tries to be the first one to react, and the price changes dramatically. As the price changes, the numbers of buyers or sellers in the market are quickly exhausted, and the market has to regroup. Usually during a regrouping period like this, the price will slip back in the direction it just came from as investors decide whether to continue on with the new trend. These momentary retracements often coincide with the Fibonacci retracement levels. Plus, if there was a news event so dramatic that it could spark such a pronounced move in the price of the currency pair, chances are that same news event will have a longer-term effect on the value of the currency pair. If all this is true and the first volatile movement is just a precursor to the larger sustained move that awaits, you should be able to take advantage of the new trend. So here's the trick of the trade: look for large volatile movements, draw your Fibonacci retracement levels, wait for the price to pull back and bounce off of one of the levels, and then enter the trade in the direction of the newly established trend.

The chart of the USD/JPY pair (Figure 14.19) provides an excellent example of this type of market reaction. The USD/JPY pair was trading at a multiyear high of 121.00 at the beginning of December when Japanese consumer confidence reports came out at surprisingly high levels. This caused the value of the Japanese yen to increase overnight, and the price of the pair dropped dramatically. After just a few days and an incredible drop to 115.50, the sellers in the market had exhausted themselves and needed to pull back and regroup. Using the strategy outlined above, you would take this opportunity to draw your Fibonacci retracement levels.

Once you have your retracement levels drawn, all you can do is sit back and see which level the market decides to react to. After a steep drop like the one you see in the USD/JPY chart, the most common retracement level the market will react to is the 38.2 percent level. This is because it is the nearest level. A steep price move is

FIGURE 14.19

USD/JPY, with Fibonacci retracement levels placed after a surprising economic announcement

Source: Prophet.net

usually an indicator of more moves to come, and investors want to jump on this price movement as quickly as they can.

Once you see the price of the currency pair start to bounce off the 38.2 percent retracement level, you can set up to enter your trade. This trade will be just like the one you saw in the previous GBP/USD case study. First, you have to determine when to enter the trade. When you are placing trades based on support or resistance bounces, you want to make sure you give the price of the currency pair enough room to confirm that it truly is bouncing off of the predetermined level. However, you do not want to give the price of the currency pair too much room because this will cause you to miss out on too much of the profits from the trade. To find a happy medium, consider setting your entry point at 10 percent above a support level or 10 percent below a resistance level. In the case of the USD/JPY chart you are looking at (Figure 14.20), you would place your entry point at 10 percent below the 38.2 percent retracement level—somewhere around 117.50. This will give the price room to move but will still get you into the trade early enough to take advantage of any continuations of the previous trend.

Fibonacci retracement levels also provide excellent guidance for your setting your stop losses. If you did sell the USD/JPY pair when

FIGURE 14.20

USD/JPY, showing the established entry and stop points

Source: Prophet.net

the price bounced back down from the 38.2 percent resistance level, you would want to protect your trade just in case the previous downtrend didn't resume and your trade went against you. Using the Fibonacci levels you established, you could set your stop loss at the 50 percent retracement level. By utilizing the 50 percent retracement level, you give yourself a firm exit point that is not very far away from your entry point. Knowing that you have set a predetermined exit point if the trade goes against you will help you stick to your investing plan.

The last decision you have to make is determining when you will exit the trade if it moves in the direction you have predicted. Once again, the Fibonacci levels you have drawn in can be quite helpful in your decision making. In this case, even though you believe the currency pair is going to resume its previous downtrend, you will probably set a more conservative profit target. There is always a chance that you may be at the bottom of a trend, and you want to take that into consideration by setting your expectations at realistic levels. You can always readjust your profit targets as the trade progresses, but it is better to be more conservative from the outset.

The 0 percent retracement level is set at an excellent price point for a conservative profit target. The reason this level is considered conservative is that the price of the currency pair already reached this level in the recent past. Because the currency pair was recently at this price level, it wouldn't have to break through any new levels of support or resistance to get back to this same level. That is great news for you as an investor. The easier it is for you to reach your profit targets, the better off you will be.

By setting your entry and exit points using the Fibonacci retracement levels you have identified, you put the odds in your favor that you will be successful over the long run. Though you may lose some money on this particular trade, if you continue to set up your trades in a similar fashion, you should be profitable over the long run. We talk about why that is more fully in Chapter 16 on money management. For now, just know that if you stand to gain more than you have at risk, the odds are in your favor over the long run.

One of the most convenient features of technical analysis, including Fibonacci analysis, is the ability to use the same strategies in both upward trending and downward trending markets. Looking again at a chart of the USD/JPY pair (Figure 14.21), you can see that the same relationship between the price movement and the Fibonacci retracement levels that existed during a downward trending market

F I G U R E   14.21

USD/JPY, indicating Fibonacci retracement levels and entry, stop, and target points

Source: Prophet.net

also exists during an upward trending market. First, the price of the currency pair rose dramatically from the beginning of May through the beginning of June. After reaching a high for the movement at approximately 109.00, the price for the USD/JPY pair turned back around and retraced a portion of its previous movement. In this case, the price fell all the way back down to the 50 percent retracement level before the buyers reentered the market and began pushing the price higher.

Once again, you would have been focusing on the 38.2 percent retracement level for your trade entry point. However, in this case because the previous trend you were analyzing was an uptrend, you would have been looking to set your entry point at 10 percent above that retracement level instead of 10 percent below the retracement level. Setting your exit points also follows the same pattern we have been discussing in the last two case studies. You would set your stop-loss exit point at the 50 percent retracement level, and you would set your profit target exit point at the 0 percent retracement level. Of course, your stop-loss exit point would be below your entry point, while your profit target exit point would be above your entry point in this case because you are anticipating that the currency pair will resume its previous upward trend, but the idea is the same.

Now, in looking at the previous three case studies, you have probably noticed that the price of the currency pair has moved well beyond the initial profit target set at the 0 percent retracement level in each example. This should not be a surprise because, as we mention earlier, if a currency pair has established a new trend, it will most likely continue in that direction until something in the market changes. Knowing that this is generally the case, we want to show you how you can project future continuations of a previous trend utilizing Fibonacci projection levels.

Fibonacci Projection Levels

Fibonacci levels apply not only to trend retracements but also to trend continuations. But to make the switch, you need to start using different Fibonacci ratios. While you have been using the Fibonacci ratios of 38.2 percent and 61.8 percent to analyze trend retracements, you must shift your attention to the Fibonacci ratios of 161.8 percent and 261.8 percent to analyze trend continuations. Along with shifting from one set of Fibonacci ratios to another, you will also have to shift your attention from analyzing a previous trend to analyzing the retracement of that trend. When you are setting your Fibonacci retracement levels, you base your levels on the previous trend. When you are setting your Fibonacci projection levels, you base your levels on the previous retracement.

There is no better way to illustrate this concept than with case studies, so let's get started with our final two case studies in this chapter. You will recognize these case studies because they are the same case studies we just looked at with the USD/JPY. We are using the same examples because, when we first went through these examples, we stated that you should set your initial profit target at the 0 percent retracement level, but that you should be willing to reevaluate your profit target as the trade progresses. Well, both of these trades progressed quite well, and the price moved well past the 0 percent retracement level. In an effort to leave as little money on the table as possible in each trade you place, we want to show you how you could have squeezed even more profit out of each of these trades.

By looking back at the first USD/JPY setup we analyzed, you can see that once the price of the currency pair had retraced, it turned back around and started moving lower again. This was not a surprise because, while investors expect momentary retracements, they also expect the overall trend to continue over the long run. The trick now is projecting how far you believe the price will move. As you can see on the USD/JPY chart (Figure 14.22), to project levels associated with the future movement, we analyzed the retracement of the previous down trend. By doing so, the levels are flipped upside down from our previous example, and you can see an additional support level at 161.8 percent.

Assume you had entered this trade by selling the USD/JPY pair after the retracement occurred at the end of December. Your original profit target would have been 115.50 or so. But once the price reached that level, instead of immediately exiting your position, you could have run this Fibonacci projection analysis and seen that the 161.8 percent level was at around the 114.00 price level. At this point, you could have moved your stop loss down to protect some of your profits, and you could have remained in the trade to see if it would continue down to the 161.8 percent projection level. We know we have talked about this before, but it is incredibly important to have concrete profit and loss projections in your trading. If you know ahead of time where you are going to be getting out of your trade, regardless of which direction it moves, you will be less likely to make foolish, emotionally based decisions in your investing.

FIGURE 14.22

USD/JPY, indicating Fibonacci retracement levels and projection levels

Source: Prophet.net

As you can see from the USD/JPY chart, the price did move right down to the 161.8 percent projection level before catching some support. And while it may seem that we got lucky on this one and that it sure is a coincidence that support showed up right at the level we identified, we can assure you this is another classic example of a self-fulfilling prophesy. Remember, large institutional traders are closely watching these Fibonacci levels, and they know that everyone else in the market is watching them as well. And in an effort not to be left out of any trade, everyone is poised to move together once someone flinches. This herd mentality can be a gold mine for individual investors.

The second projection level we mentioned is the 261.8 percent level. If you ever find yourself using this level in your trading, you know you are in the middle of an extensive trend and the odds are definitely in your favor. Any time a currency pair has enough momentum to make an extended price move in any direction, you are bound to make some great profits as long as you are trading with the trend. The important thing to remember here is you may have been in this trade from the beginning of the retracement, or you could have just entered it as the price of the currency pair passed the 161.8 percent projection level. It doesn't matter when you entered the trade. All you need to be concerned with is analyzing the information you have in front of you today.

Seeing how the price reacts with each of these projection and retracement levels should also give you a lot of confidence as an investor because you can see that you have multiple price points at which you can enter a trade. You don't always have to get in right at the beginning of a movement. There will be many opportunities to get in during any one trend. So if you miss the first chance, don't give up. Keep watching the currency pair and wait to get in at the next level.

By looking at the chart of the upward trending USD/JPY pair (Figure 14.23), you can see that the price of the pair barely even blinked as it encountered the 161.8 percent projection level. Instead, it kept climbing higher and higher until it reached the 261.8 percent level. Now, let's look at this from two perspectives. First, if you had entered this trade earlier, all you would have had to do was sit back and move up your stop loss as the price of the currency pair climbed higher and higher. It is as simple as that. There is no use complicating issues. Second, if you weren't in this trade previously and you saw the price break up and through the 161.8 percent projection

FIGURE 14.23

USD/JPY, moving upward toward established projection levels

261.8% ($112.53)

161.8% ($110.21)

100.0% ($108.78)
61.8% ($107.90)
38.2% ($107.32)
23.6% ($106.96)

0.0% ($106.47)

Source: Prophet.net

211

level, you could have entered a new trade the next day. To do so, you would follow the same procedures we outlined when you're looking at entering a trade after a retracement. When you enter the trade at the 161.8 percent projection level, you set your profit target at the 261.8 percent projection level, and you set your stop loss at the 100 percent level. This gives you plenty of room to grow on the upside while you still protect your trade from any unexpected turnarounds.

Although the market was very choppy for most of July, you will notice that it was unable to substantially break the 261.8 percent level. Apparently, the major market participants were watching this level, and they determined that the price should not head any higher. With that, the 261.8 percent projection level served as an excellent level of resistance for the next month. At this point, you would probably have to switch your tactics and analysis on this pair. Although you could continue to extend the Fibonacci projection levels out farther and farther, it doesn't make a lot of sense to do so. Once the price of a currency pair reaches the 261.8 projection level, the odds of the price moving past that level decrease. But if you have enjoyed the profits up to that point, it doesn't really matter.

USING THE TOOLS

Regardless of whether you decide to actively employ Fibonacci retracement and projection levels in your trading or not, being aware of these levels in the market will help you both understand the news commentary referencing Fibonacci levels and avoid entering trades when the price of a currency pair is coming up to a Fibonacci level. However, we hope you have recognized the incredible advantages you gain as an investor when you are actively analyzing Fibonacci levels in the market. When you have a tool that is this clear and concise in forecasting support and resistance levels, it seems silly not to implement it in your own investing. And to get you started, we want to provide a little help. We will be highlighting additional methods utilizing Fibonacci levels and illustrating them for you in real time at www.profitingwithforex.com. Stop by and check it out.

Putting It All Together—
Trading Techniques

Okay, you've got your fundamental tools, and you've got your technical tools. Now what? Now, you have to put them together. This chapter focuses on specific techniques you can implement using the tools you've been given. We have actually used the strategies in this chapter. They work and can help you grow your portfolio faster than you may have thought possible. We also want to be up front in ensuring that you understand that sometimes these techniques will work better than others. Part of becoming a good investor in the Forex is learning to understand that the market evolves and changes. As it does, your trading strategies must also evolve and adjust. You may need to make a little tweak here or a little tweak there sometimes. There will always be periods of lower returns or losses during the transitions, but once you have made the change and you have adjusted your strategies, you will continue to make great profits.

In each of the following examples, we include both a good trade and a bad one. We are not always right, and neither is anyone else. We want to illustrate that so you don't develop any unreal expectations of yourself. It's a lot easier to work through the bad trades if you know that some are going to come your way. In the examples we show you, the analysis of the trade was valid and correct, but some trades work out and some just don't. Consider our earlier discussion about your risk/reward ratio carefully before you enter any trade. It will make all the difference.

These strategies are not comprehensive. They are wonderful strategies for the market today, but the Forex market is never the same two days in a row. As economic conditions change and the Forex market evolves, we will continue to discuss new and revised strategies on our Web site at www.profitingwithforex.com. It is also important to understand that the specific strategies we outline here are representative of larger categories of trading strategies. For example, when we discuss a strategy that focuses on trading a specific currency pair based on a specific news event, we are trying to draw your attention to the fact that certain currency pairs are more responsive to particular news events than others. Don't get stuck following only that one news event and that one currency pair. Start looking at other news events and analyzing how various currency pairs react to them.

The same principle applies when we illustrate trades you can make based on a particular technical indicator—like the MACD (moving average convergence divergence). The MACD is certainly not the only technical indicator you can use in your trading. Our examples are a great way to get started and should be great profit generators, but we hope they will be only a springboard into other trading techniques. Consider expanding your Forex education with additional training courses and books, and think about consulting with professional investors in your trading. We have personally taught thousands of investors to trade the stock, options, and currency markets. We have seen many of our students become so successful that they quit their jobs and do it full time. Others achieve their objectives and continue to invest profitably part time. Whatever your situation, you can profit with the Forex market.

Okay, here we go. This is where it gets to be fun.

TRADING TECHNIQUE 1: THE CARRY TRADE

The carry trade is an opportunity to make some extra income from the daily interest payments you can receive when you trade a currency pair. Earlier in the book, we talk about how some economies offer higher interest rates than others. Naturally, if you were putting your money into an account somewhere, you would want to put it in the account that offers the highest rate of return. The same concept applies in the Forex market.

When you buy a currency pair, the EUR/USD for instance, you are buying euros and selling U.S. dollars. If you were to sell this pair, you would be selling euros and buying U.S. dollars. Whenever you sell a currency, you have to pay the daily interest rate charged by that economy. And whenever you buy a currency, you are paid the daily interest rate set by that economy. Imagine that the interest rates in both the United States and the European Union are set at 2 percent. If you bought the EUR/USD pair, you would receive 2 percent for buying the euro, and you would have to pay 2 percent for selling the U.S. dollars. In this case, the interest rates would offset each other, and you would neither pay nor receive interest.

In most cases, however, one economy has a higher interest rate than the other. This is where the carry trade comes in. When you are placing a carry trade, you are looking to buy the currency with the higher interest rate and sell the currency with the lower interest rate. As you do so, you can expect to receive an interest payment every day. It doesn't matter if the exchange rate is going up or down, you still receive your interest payment. One exciting side note is that the exchange rate usually moves in the direction of the currency with the higher interest rate. So if you stay in the trade for the long term, you can make profits from both the interest payments and the pips you gain in the trade.

As you evaluate potential carry trades, you will need to identify whether you need to sell or buy the currency pair to receive the interest payment. In most cases, your dealer will have a list that is continually updated that tells you if you have to buy or sell to receive the payment and how large the payment will be. Once you find an interest rate that looks good, make sure the trend is going in the right direction. If you receive the interest payment only when you sell the currency pair, you want to make sure that the currency pair is currently in a downtrend. If you receive the interest payment only when you buy the currency pair, you want to make sure that the currency pair is currently in an uptrend. Let's look at an example.

Let's say that you saw the interest rate differential on the GBP/JPY, which currently enjoys quite a large one. You now have an opportunity to make some money from interest payments by trading this pair. Because you are currently paid when you buy this currency pair, you will be looking for opportunities to buy it. Remember, you don't want to just arbitrarily enter the position because you can receive an interest payment. The interest payment is not going to offset a major loss. You want to put the odds in your favor. You want to wait until you see an uptrend and a good entry signal based on your technical analysis.

Because the carry trade relies on interest rate differentials, the larger the differential the better. During 2004, a huge differential existed between high interest-bearing currencies like the British pound, the Australian dollar, and the New Zealand dollar and very low interest-bearing currencies like the U.S. dollar, the Japanese yen, and the euro. The Japanese yen was the currency with the lowest rate, and the New Zealand dollar was the currency with the highest available rate. Therefore, this was a very popular pair to use in a carry trade. As of this writing, this differential still exists. Different pairs will move in or out of favor with carry traders as interest rates change, but fortunately they don't change very often, and you can usually use the carry trade strategy on a single pair for a few years at a time.

Entering a carry trade is a four-step process. In this strategy, we are using a moving average to identify our trend and an MACD to identify our trade entry signals.

- *Step 1.* Identify a pair with a large interest rate differential. In this case, we are using the GBP/JPY.
- *Step 2.* Determine if you have to buy or sell the currency pair to receive the interest payments. In this case, you have to buy the GBP/JPY to receive the interest payment because the British pound is the currency offering the higher exchange rate.
- *Step 3.* Identify the current trend of the currency pair. Make sure it is moving in the same direction as the trade you will have to place to enter the carry trade. In this case, you want to see an uptrend because you have to buy the GBP/JPY.
- *Step 4.* Enter when the MACD indicates it is a good time to buy. In this case, we are investing in an uptrend so we would be looking for the MACD to cross up from below the zero line. This tells us that the currency pair is no longer oversold and is resuming its previous uptrend.

To exit this trade, you will be looking for the MACD to cross back down below the zero line. This indicates that the positive momentum that existed in the market has dissipated, and it is probably safer to take your profits and sit on the sidelines for awhile.

Successful Trade

Using these rules, you would have had a signal to enter a trade on the GBP/JPY on January 24, 2005, as the MACD crossed up from below the zero line. You would have been watching for crosses back above the zero line because you want to buy the GBP/JPY to take advantage of the carry trade. Seeing the crossover occur at the end of the day on January 24, you would have entered the trade at the beginning of the day on January 25. (See Figure 15.1.)

You would have then held the trade until the MACD crossed back below the signal line. This occurred on March 8, 2005. When you saw this happen on March 8, you would have exited your trade at the beginning of the day on March 9, 2005.

Had you placed this trade, you would have made about 620 pips in profit. Plus, you would have earned interest for each of the 43 days you were in the trade. Assuming that the average profit per pip was $9 and the average interest payment per day was $15, you would have made approximately $6,225 on the trade.

$5,580 (profit from pips) + $645 (profit from interest) = $6,225

Unsuccessful Trade

Using these rules again, you would have had a signal to enter a trade on the GBP/JPY on May 29, 2005, as the MACD crossed up from below the zero line. You would have been watching for crosses back above the zero line because you want to buy the GBP/JPY to take advantage of the carry trade. Seeing the crossover occur at the end of the day on May 29, you would have entered the trade at the beginning of the day on May 30. (See Figure 15.2.)

You would have then held the trade until the MACD crossed back below the signal line. This occurred on June 5, 2005. Seeing this happen on June 5, you would have exited your trade at the beginning of the day on June 6, 2005.

Had you placed this trade, you would have lost about 185 pips. You would have offset some of your losses with the interest payment for each of the five days you were in the trade, however. Assuming that the average profit per pip was $9 and the average interest payment per day was $15, you would have lost approximately $1,590 on the trade.

−$1,665 (loss from pips) + $75 (profit from interest) = −$1,590

You will win some and lose some in your trading, but if you follow a good system, you will ultimately come out on top. We specifically highlighted the GBP/JPY pair in these examples because this pair is currently enjoying a large differential between the interest rates in the two economies. However, different currency pairs will

FIGURE 15.1

GBP/JPY, entry and exit signals for successful trade example, including MACD

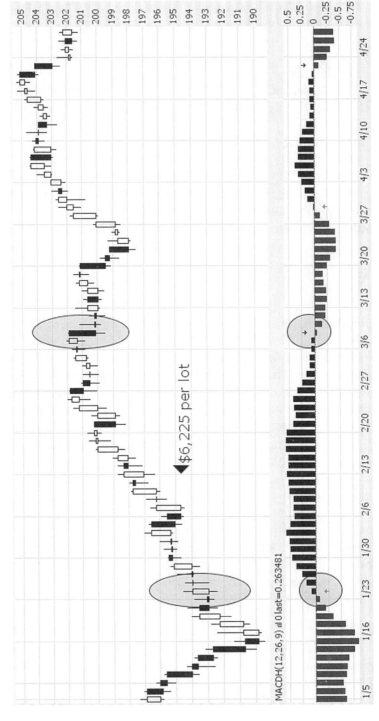

$6,225 per lot

MACDH(12,26,9) .ıl 0 last=0.263481

Source: Prophet.net

FIGURE 15.2

GBP/JPY, entry and exit signals for unsuccessful trade example, including MACD

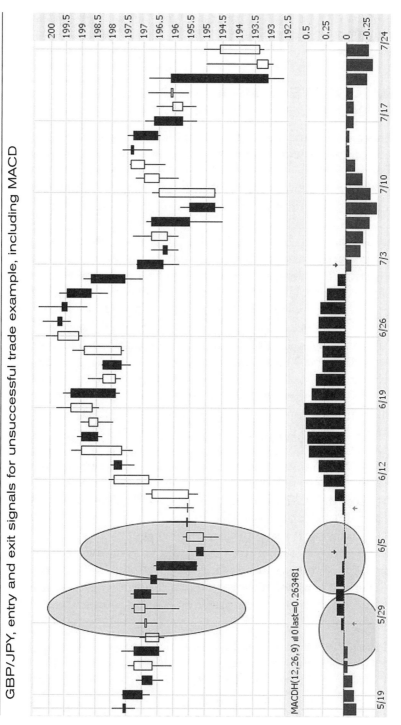

Source: Prophet.net

emerge in the future that have similar interest-rate relationships. Watch for these relationships to develop so that you can take advantage of them in your future trading.

TRADING TECHNIQUE 2: TRADING ECONOMIC ANNOUNCEMENTS

Economic announcements tend to move in trends. If one announcement brings particularly good or bad news, the next announcement will most likely bring more of the same. Macroeconomic forces usually change direction very quickly. It is difficult to put the brakes on an economy, turn things around, and start moving in another direction. For example, if the balance of trade numbers come out and show that the trade gap between the United States and other countries is getting worse, the next balance of trade announcement will most likely show a widening trade deficit. Let's take a look at an excellent example of the balance of trade announcements involving the largest importer in the world—the United States—and the largest exporting region of the world—Asia. We use the Japanese yen as a proxy for all the currencies in Asia. As the U.S. economic recovery kicked in during 2003 and 2004, U.S. consumers began buying more inexpensive Asian goods. This caused the balance of trade between the two economies to widen. As we learned earlier, as the balance of trade widens and the supply of U.S. dollars increases, the U.S. dollar loses value. Knowing this, you would assume that the currency pair would start to move lower, and so you would want to take only those trades that were headed in the same direction. Conversely if the trade balance narrowed, you would want to look for a strengthening U.S. dollar. This means that if the pair is trending down and the announcement is strong for the U.S. dollar, you will pass on the trade. Likewise, if the announcement is negative for the U.S. dollar and the pair is trending up, you would pass on the trade. We want to make sure that we are trading only with the highest probability.

Let's take a look at how you could set up your parameters for this trade. Entering a trade based on economic announcements is a four-step process.

- *Step 1.* Determine which currency pair you are going to use in your trade. In the case of the balance of trade information, we chose to use the USD/JPY because both currencies play such a large roll in the announcement figures.

- *Step 2.* Identify the current trend. Again, we use the moving average to do this—only take trades that are moving in the direction of the trend.
- *Step 3.* Watch the announcement. If it comes out as you thought it would, place your trade. Because balance of trade numbers are released only on the second Thursday of each month, we only have to pay attention once a month to play this strategy.
- *Step 4.* Set a close stop and a reasonable limit or target. In the case of the balance of trade announcements, we set a 50-pip stop loss and a 200-pip limit order to take our profits. This gave us a 1:4 risk/reward ratio—which means we would have to be right only one time out of four to make money.

Unsuccessful Trade

Using these rules, you would have had a signal to enter a trade on the USD/JPY on January 11, 2005, as the balance of trade announcement was released as expected. The balance of trade between the United States and other countries grew, which should weaken the value of the U.S. dollar. The moving average was also pointing down at the same time. This confirmed the trade. (See Figure 15.3.)

You would have been in this trade for only two days, however, as the USD/JPY experienced a volatile upward swing during the day on January 13, 2005. During this upswing, the price of the pair would have hit your stop loss of 50 pips, and you would have been taken out of the trade.

Had you placed this trade, you would have lost about 50 pips, which would have amounted to a loss of about $500 per contract.

$$-50 \text{ pips} \times \$10 \text{ per pip} = -\$500$$

Successful Trade

Using these rules, you would have had another signal to enter a trade on the USD/JPY on March 8, 2005, as the balance of trade announcement was released as expected. This time, the balance of trade between the United States and other countries shrunk—which should strengthen the value of the U.S. dollar. The moving average was also pointing up at the same time. This confirmed the trade. (See Figure 15.4.)

FIGURE 15.3

USD/JPY, entry and exit signals for unsuccessful trade example, including moving average

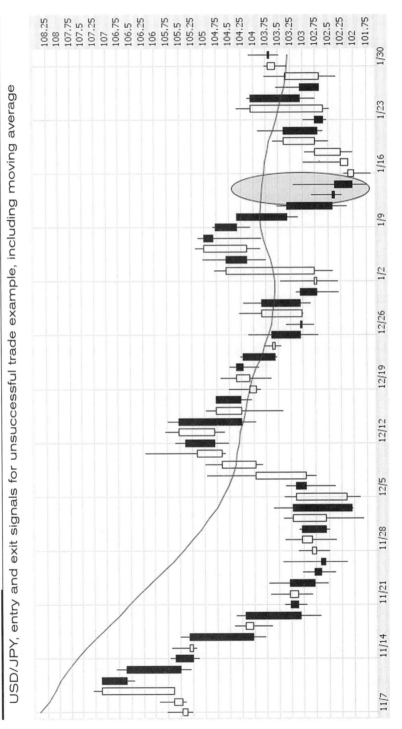

Source: Prophet.net

FIGURE 15.4

USD/JPY, entry and exit signals for successful trade example, including moving average

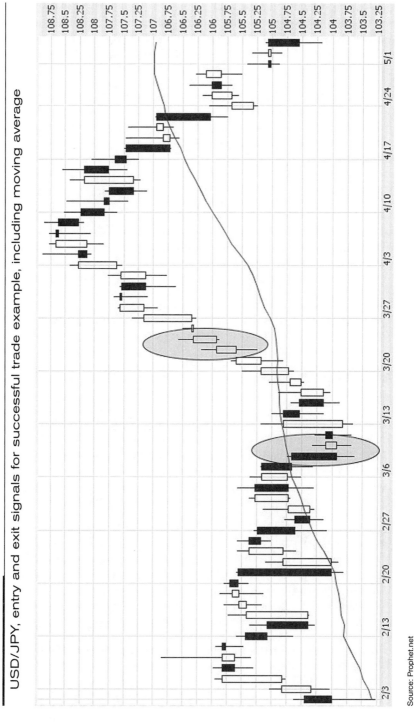

Source: Prophet.net

Once again, you would have been in this trade for only a few days. It didn't take too long for the market to react. During the upswing that occurred the next few days, the price of the pair would have hit your limit order of 200 pips, and you would have been taken out of the trade.

Had you placed this trade, you would have made about 200 pips, which would have amounted to a profit of about $2,000 per contract.

$$200 \text{ pips} \times \$10 \text{ per pip} = \$2,000$$

You can use similar rules to take advantage of various economic announcements. Look at placing trades like these around TIC (Treasury International Capital) data announcements or FOMC (Federal Open Market Committee) interest-rate decisions. One thing you need to note is that these trades are longer-term trades. Often, Forex traders will try to guess which way the news is going to come out and jump on very short-term trades in the hopes of making a quick 100 pips. This is extremely risky and difficult. Successful Forex investors don't gamble. They wait until all the factors line up before they will enter a trade so that the odds are definitely in their favor. They are not interested in chasing a quick buck.

TRADING TECHNIQUE 3: FOLLOWING OIL

There are many sources of oil, but some currencies react more strongly than others when oil prices change. Fortunately for you, oil prices usually trend for extended periods. When oil prices are rising, they are likely to continue rising for several months. Likewise, if oil prices are declining, they tend to continue declining for several months. Some of the currencies that are most sensitive to the changes in oil prices are the GBP and the CAD. We focus on the USD/CAD in this example. As the United States imports more oil from Canada, the value of the Canadian dollar should increase in relationship to the U.S. dollar. This means that the pair should begin trending down. This strategy is another trend trade, and we are using the CCI (Commodity Channel Index) to trigger our entries.

Let's take a look at how you could set up your trading parameters for this trade. Entering a trade to follow oil is a three-step process.

- *Step 1.* Watch for times when oil prices are increasing and the exchange rate of the USD/CAD is decreasing. You can also watch for times when oil prices are decreasing and the exchange rate is increasing, but we are focusing on trades that occur as oil prices are going up in these examples.

- *Step 2.* Watch for the 14-period CCI to cross above 100 and then cross back below 100. Enter the trade by selling the USD/CAD pair. This tells you that buyers have made a temporary upward push on the currency pair but were not able to turn the trend around.
- *Step 3.* Set a limit order of 300 pips and a stop-loss order of 75 pips. This gives you a risk/reward ratio of 1:4, which allows you to be wrong a few times without ruining your chances of being profitable.

Successful Trade

Using these rules, you would have had a signal to enter a trade on the USD/CAD on the candlestick beginning on July 28, 2005, as the CCI crossed back below the 100 line (see Figure 15.5). When you are looking at the dates on the charts, it is important to remember that daily candlesticks begin at 5 p.m. Eastern and end the following day at 5 p.m. Eastern. So the candlestick labeled July 28 began on July 28 at 5 p.m. Eastern and ended on July 29. The USD/CAD was in a downtrend, and the price of oil was climbing steadily (see Figure 15.6)—just what you are looking for. Seeing this, you would have entered your trade at the beginning of the trading day on July 31, 2005. You would have waited until July 31 because the market is closed each week from Friday at 4 p.m. Eastern through Sunday at 2:15 p.m. Eastern.

This trade moved back and forth for a while, and you would have stayed in it for nearly one month. You would have finally been limited out for a profit of approximately 300 pips on August 23, 2005.

Had you placed this trade, you would have made about 300 pips, which would have amounted to a profit of about $3,000 per contract.

$$300 \text{ pips} \times \$10 \text{ per pip} = \$3,000$$

Unsuccessful Trade

Using these rules again, you would have had another signal to enter a trade on the USD/CAD on the candlestick beginning on October 6, 2005, as the CCI crossed back below the 100 line. The USD/CAD was in a downtrend, and the price of oil was climbing once again. Seeing this, you would have entered your trade at the beginning of

FIGURE 15.5

USD/CAD, entry and exit signals for successful trade example, including CCI

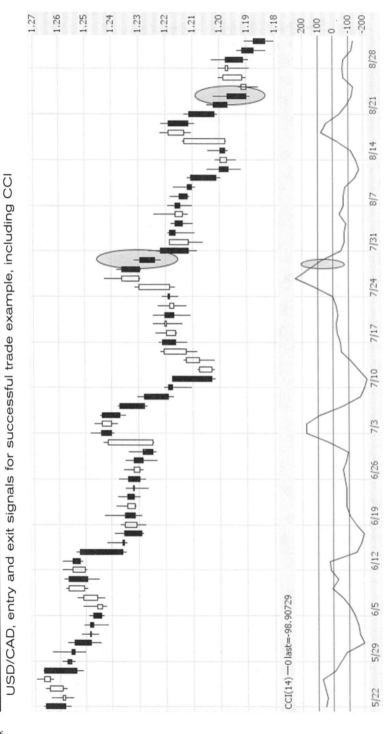

CCI(14) —0 last=-98.90729

Source: Prophet.net

FIGURE 15.6

CBOE oil index, daily intervals

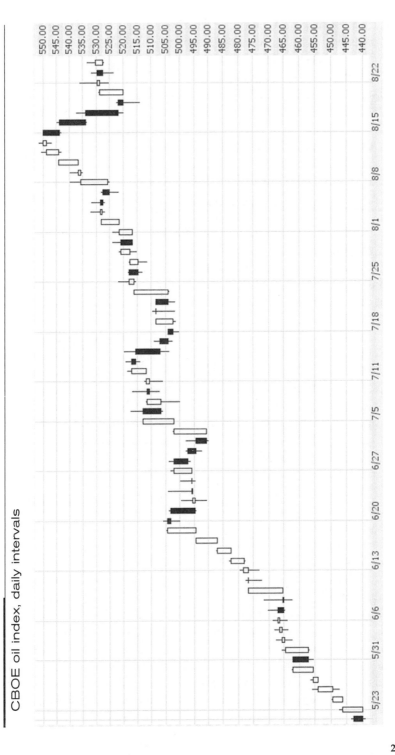

Source: Prophet.net

the trading day on October 9, 2005 (see Figure 15.7). Once again, the weekend would have played a role in determining when you would enter the trade.

Shortly after you would have entered this trade, the price of oil began to decline, and the price of the USD/CAD began to move higher in response. Suddenly, the conditions that made the trade look like such a good one changed. You would have been stopped out for a loss of approximately 75 pips on October 12, 2005.

Had you placed this trade, you would have lost about 75 pips, which would have amounted to a loss of about $750 per contract.

$$-75 \text{ pips} \times \$10 \text{ per pip} = -\$750$$

Trades that move against you like this are not uncommon. What you will notice, however, is that you would have to be wrong quite a few times at 75 pips per losing trade to make a dent in the profits you make when you are correct at 300 pips per winning trade. It takes a lot of the pressure off knowing that you have such a large cushion to work with.

You should also look to trade the USD/CAD in the opposite direction if oil prices ever start to decline. Though it is unlikely that we will ever see a prolonged downtrend in the price of oil, we can take advantage of momentary pullbacks. As the price of oil decreases, we may see the value of the USD/CAD move higher. Remember, we are not hoping the price of oil moves in one direction or another in our trading. We just want to make sure we know which way it is moving right now so that we can take advantage of it.

TRADING TECHNIQUE 4: FOLLOWING GOLD

The Australian dollar is known for its strong correlation to gold prices. Most of this is caused by the amount of gold that Australia produces and exports. In any case, this relationship provides us with another way we can take advantage of the fundamental factors in the Forex market. It is also important to note that the U.S. dollar has an inverse relationship with gold. This generally means that when the U.S. dollar falls in value, gold will rise in value—which will also cause the price of the AUD/USD pair to rise. The opposite is also true. As the U.S. dollar gains value, gold usually loses value. So when gold prices are rising, we can execute long trades on the AUD/USD, and if gold prices are falling, we can sell short the AUD/USD.

The trading example we use here utilizes the RSI (Relative Strength Index). You may ask why we chose to use the RSI in these

FIGURE 15.7

USD/CAD, entry and exit for unsuccessful trade example, including CCI

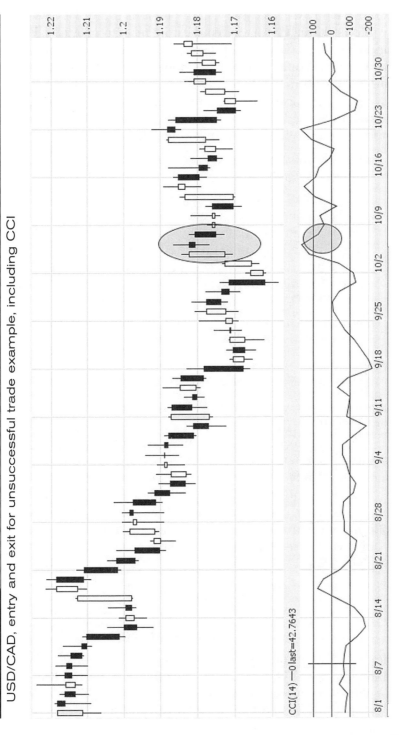

Source: Prophet.net

examples while we used the CCI in previous examples. It all comes down to how quickly the two indicators react to volatility. We have found that the CCI gives quicker signals, which is good for less volatile pairs, while the RSI gives slower signals, which is ideal for more volatile pairs like the AUD/USD.

Let's take a look at how you could set up your trading parameters for this trade. Entering a trade to follow gold is a three-step process similar to that of our examples for following oil.

- *Step 1.* Use a moving average to determine if gold is in an uptrend or a downtrend.
- *Step 2.* Watch for the seven-period RSI on the AUD/USD chart to enter one of its reversal zones and then move back out of the reversal zone in the same direction as gold is trending. Enter a long trade on the AUD/USD if gold prices are rising and the RSI is crossing back above the 30 line. Enter a short trade on the AUD/USD if gold prices are declining and the RSI is crossing below the 70 line.
- *Step 3.* Set a limit order of 200 pips and a stop-loss order of 50 pips. This gives you a risk/reward ratio of 1:4.

Successful Trade

Using these rules, you would have had a signal to enter a trade on the AUD/USD on July 10, 2005, as the RSI crossed back up above the 30 line (see Figure 15.8). At the same time, gold was in an uptrend and gaining strength (see Figure 15.9). Seeing this, you would have entered your trade at the beginning of the day on July 11, 2005.

This trade moved back and forth for about one week before it broke out higher. You would have finally been limited out for a profit of approximately 200 pips on July 20, 2005.

Had you placed this trade, you would have made about 200 pips, which would have amounted to a profit of about $2,000 per contract.

$$200 \text{ pips} \times \$10 \text{ per pip} = \$2,000$$

Unsuccessful Trade

Using these same rules, you would have had another signal to enter a trade on the AUD/USD on August 21, 2005, as the RSI crossed back above the 30 line. At the same time, gold was still in an uptrend. Seeing this, you would have entered your trade at the beginning of the day on August 22, 2005 (see Figure 15.10).

FIGURE 15.8

AUD/USD, entry and exit for successful trade example, including RSI

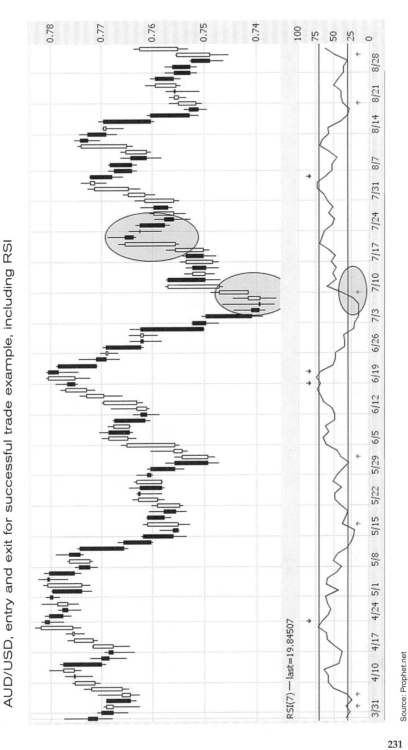

Source: Prophet.net

231

FIGURE 15.9

CBOE gold index, including moving average

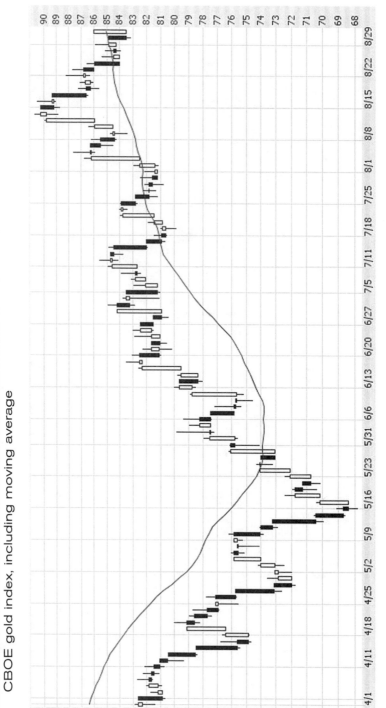

FIGURE 15.10

AUD/USD, entry and exit for unsuccessful trade example, including RSI

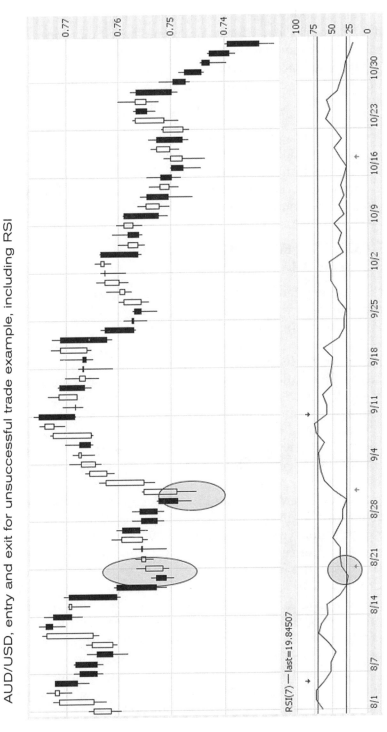

RSI(7) — last=19.84507

Source: Prophet.net

This trade bounced back and forth for about one week again and then dropped back down. You would have finally been stopped out for a loss of approximately 50 pips on August 29, 2005.

Had you placed this trade, you would have lost about 50 pips, which would have amounted to a loss of about $500 per contract.

$$-50 \text{ pips} \times \$10 \text{ per pip} = -\$500$$

The very next signal using these rules would have come a day later on August 30, 2005. Had you taken this next trade, you would have once again made approximately 200 pips, or $2,000. It is not uncommon to have a trade go against you only to find yourself right back in a trade that goes your way.

TRADING TECHNIQUE 5: TECHNICAL DIVERGENCES

Technical divergences occur when a technical analysis tool begins to move in the opposite direction from the price of the currency pair. For example, if the price of the currency pair is moving higher and the CCI is moving lower, the two are diverging from each other as one goes up while the other one goes down. Technical divergences are a great indication that the currency pair may be changing direction shortly. This is one area where technical analysis has a distinct advantage over fundamental analysis. Fundamental factors usually don't give a lot of warning that the market is going to switch directions. You usually have to wait until the fundamental announcement is made to get an idea of what is going on. Technical analysis does give advanced warning in some situations.

We don't want to discount fundamental analysis though. While a technical divergence suggests that the currency pair may be reversing its direction, you still want to see if you can find confirmation of the reversal from another source. If your fundamental analysis tells you that the price reversal would bring the price of the currency pair back in line with the current fundamental factors, you should have even more confidence in the coming reversal. You can see an example of this type of confirmation in the USD/CAD as it was trending up while oil prices were also moving higher. Normally, you would expect to see the USD/CAD moving lower as oil prices are moving higher because rising oil prices tend to strengthen the Canadian dollar. So if you were to see a technical divergence telling you that the USD/CAD was going to turn around and head lower at the same

FIGURE 15.11

USD/CAD, bullish technical divergence

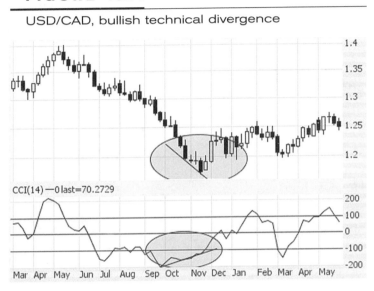

CCI(14) — 0 last=70.2729

Source: Prophet.net

time oil prices were rising, wouldn't you feel more confident it was going to happen?

Technical divergences can be either bullish or bearish. When you see a bullish divergence, you can anticipate that the currency pair is going to turn around and move higher. When you see a bearish divergence, you can anticipate that the currency pair is going to turn around and move lower. To qualify as a bullish divergence, you have to see the currency pair creating lower lows on the chart while you see the technical indicator creating higher lows. (See Figure 15.11.)

To qualify as a bearish divergence, you have to see the currency pair creating higher highs on the chart while you see the technical indicator creating lower highs. (See Figure 15.12.)

Let's take a look at how you could set up your trading parameters for a trade like this. We use the MACD as our technical indicator in these examples. Entering a trade to take advantage of a technical divergence is a three-step process.

- *Step 1.* Identify whether the currency pair and the MACD are forming either a bullish or bearish divergence.
- *Step 2.* If the currency pair and MACD are forming a divergence, enter the trade as the MACD crosses over the zero line. Buy the currency pair as the MACD crosses back above

FIGURE 15.12

USD/CAD, bearish technical divergence

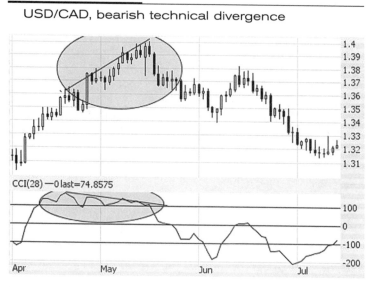

Source: Prophet.net

the zero line if you see a bullish divergence. Sell the currency pair as the MACD crosses below the zero line if you see a bearish divergence.

- *Step 3.* Exit the trade as the MACD crosses back over the zero line in the opposite direction from the divergence.

Successful Trade

Using these rules, you would have had a signal to enter a bullish trade on the EUR/USD on February 13, 2005, as the MACD diverged from the price of the currency pair and crossed back above the zero line. Seeing this, you would have entered your trade at the beginning of the day on February 14, 2005. (See Figure 15.13.)

After the technical divergence, the EUR/USD moved steadily upward for the next month or so. You would have finally exited your trade as the MACD crossed back below the zero line for a profit of approximately 181 pips on March 21, 2005.

Had you placed this trade, you would have made about 181 pips, which would have amounted to a profit of about $1,810 per contract.

$$181 \text{ pips} \times \$10 \text{ per pip} = \$1{,}810$$

FIGURE 15.13

EUR/USD, entry and exit, bullish technical divergence

Source: Prophet.net

Successful Trade

We are showing you two successful trades in this example because the bullish divergence signal was immediately followed by a bearish divergence signal in this case. Using these rules, you would have had a signal to enter a bearish trade on the EUR/USD on March 20, 2005, as the MACD diverged from the price of the currency pair and crossed back below the zero line. Seeing this, you would have entered your trade at the beginning of the day on March 21, 2005—the same day you got out of the bullish trade we discussed above. (See Figure 15.14.)

The EUR/USD continued moving lower for approximately three weeks. You would have finally exited your trade as the MACD crossed back above the zero line for a profit of approximately 243 pips on April 13, 2005.

Had you placed this trade, you would have made about 243 pips, which would have amounted to a profit of about $2,430 per contract.

$$243 \text{ pips} \times \$10 \text{ per pip} = \$2,430$$

F I G U R E   15.14

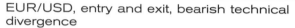

EUR/USD, entry and exit, bearish technical divergence

Source: Prophet.net

MORE TRADING TECHNIQUES

Combining the fundamental and technical tools you have at your fingertips provides you with numerous opportunities to profit in the Forex market. You can see that from the five trading techniques we just discussed. These are five of our most effective techniques, but they are only five techniques. You can combine other fundamental and technical tools to create hundreds of trading techniques. We're sure some of these tools look more appealing to you than others. Try taking those tools that look the best to you and combining them to develop you own techniques.

If you would like more examples of effective trading techniques, visit the companion Web site to this book, www.profitingwithforex. com. You will find a free supplement to this chapter outlining more of our favorite trading techniques. With all these trading techniques— plus a few you have created on your own—you will be ready to profit with the Forex.

CHAPTER 16

Money Management

Before you go out, open an account, and dive into the Forex market, there is one more thing you need to know: the most important aspect of your investing is your money management. Money management involves determining how much of your overall portfolio you are willing to put at risk in any one trade, how many contracts your risk tolerance warrants, and how you can improve your investing results by making small changes to your investing strategies. We know that this doesn't sound as exciting or as sexy as some of the other concepts we've covered in this book, but often in life, the bland and routine activities and concepts make the biggest difference.

Proper money management can be the difference between a successful account that you are able to manage far into the future and an unsuccessful account that you decimate in six months. If you've ever watched a poker tournament on television, you have seen money management in action. Rarely will you see players push all of their chips into the middle of the table on a single bet. In most cases, it would be foolish to do so. If poker players risk only a portion of their money in any one bet, they know that win or lose, they will have the means to play the next hand. On the other hand, if poker players bet everything in one hand, the only way they will be able to play the next hand is if they are right. That is a lot of pressure, and you have to be looking at some pretty good cards to justify making a bold move like that.

The most important difference between our poker analogy and your management of your investment account is that a poker game has a limited number of inputs. Each deck only has 52 cards, and you can weigh your odds in a finite universe of risk. Financial markets, in contrast, have thousands of variables that you need to account for, and determining your odds is much more difficult. Hurricanes, government scandals, terrorist attacks, and the like can all have an incredible impact on the Forex market, and you have to try to take them all into consideration when placing your trades. While taking every variable into account is virtually impossible, the lesson remains the same—you want to survive to trade another day, regardless of what happens today.

MONEY MANAGEMENT PITFALLS

To properly implement a successful money management system, you need to be aware of some of the most common pitfalls investors encounter. The following are three of the most common pitfalls you may run across in your trading:

1. Swinging the risk pendulum
2. Making decisions on the go
3. Misunderstanding what is truly at risk

Swinging the Risk Pendulum

Swinging the risk pendulum means that you vacillate between risking too much in your trades and not risking enough. This back-and-forth movement stems from the two great emotions that drive the financial markets: greed and fear. When greed takes over and begins to cloud your judgment, you start to risk too much money in each trade because you believe, for whatever reason, that this next trade is the one you are going to strike it rich on. When fear takes over and impairs your decision making, you fail to risk enough money in each trade because you have no confidence in your decision making. Let's take a look at the impact this can have on your trading results.

Most investors will experience a run of successful trades at the beginning of their investing careers that gives them a boost of confidence. This alone is a great thing for investors—as long as they know how to control their emotions. The pitfall lies in investors becoming overconfident in their trading ability and risking too much in each trade. Inevitably when this happens, a trade will turn south, and investors will take a large loss in their accounts or find that their accounts are completely wiped out. For example, most investors won't risk more than 2 percent of their accounts in any one trade. They do this because they know they are not going to be correct on every trade, and if they are wrong, they want to have plenty of money left in their accounts to make up for the loss over the long run. However, when investors become overconfident in their trading ability, they begin to feel invincible and start risking more and more in each trade. Why wouldn't they? If they are such great investors, there is no point in waiting around for slow steady growth and a conservative risk plan. If they are such great investors, they can afford to risk more and increase their profits exponentially. However, most successful runs come to an end, and you end up with a loss or two. If you have been conservative in your risk management, those losses shouldn't faze you too much. But if you've put too much on the line, even one loss can be devastating.

Let's assume that these overconfident investors started by risking only 2 percent of their accounts in any one trade. As time went on, however, they began to see more success and wanted to accelerate their earnings. To meet their new objectives of supersonic growth, they start to risk more and more in each trade because the more they have in the trade, the more they will make when they are right. So they started by risking 2 percent of their accounts, then 5 percent, then 10 percent, and finally 25 percent. Unfortunately for them, on the trade they finally decided to risk 25 percent of their accounts on, they lost. That means they lost one-quarter of their total accounts in a single trade. And this is a deeper pit to dig out of than most investors believe.

When you lose 25 percent of your account, you have to make more than 25 percent on your remaining account balance to get back to where you were before your initial loss. That may seem counterintuitive, but let us explain. Assume that you have a $100,000 account and you foolishly risk 25 percent of your account, or $25,000, in a single trade, and you lose the entire amount. You now have an account with a balance of $75,000 ($100,000 − $25,000 = $75,000). Although you lost 25 percent to reach your current account balance of $75,000, if you want to get back to the original account balance of $100,000, you will have to earn 33 percent on your current account balance. Running through the numbers, if you have an account balance of $75,000 and you want to increase that account balance to $100,000, you must earn an additional $25,000, or 33 percent ($25,000 ÷ $75,000 = 33.333, or 33 percent). So you had to lose only 25 percent to drop down to $75,000, but you must earn 33 percent to climb back up to $100,000.

Unfortunately, many investors realize this a little too late, and they are left either scrambling to rebuild their portfolios or eliminating as much risk exposure as they can. For those investors who believe they must scramble and recover all their losses immediately, they begin risking even more than the foolish 25 percent they risked in the first place just to try and make up for the 25 percent blunder. This downward spiral causes investors to lose more and more money, which causes them to take bigger and bigger risks, which again, causes them to lose more and more money, and on and on it goes. Eventually, these investors destroy their accounts, and they are out of the investing world forever. You probably know some of these investors, and you have probably never heard a positive thing about the financial markets come out of their mouths.

Those investors who fall on the other side of the equation are better off in that they don't lose their entire accounts, but they divorce themselves from any opportunity for meaningful growth in their accounts. As investors panic after a large loss, many will attempt to eliminate as much risk exposure as they can. Instead of risking 25 percent, 10 percent, or even 2 percent, these investors scale back their trading so that they are risking virtually nothing in each trade. As you can imagine, even if these investors are right and make sound decisions, the profits will be so small that they will never be able to make up the gap and rebuild their accounts. Of course, these investors may be able to rebuild some of their confidence in some of these smaller trades. But if they are not careful, they will find themselves becoming overconfident once again, risking too much, and ending up right back in the same place. Only those investors who learn how to avoid swinging the risk pendulum are able to sustain long, profitable investing careers.

Making Decisions on the Go

Making decisions on the go implies that you have no set game plan for your investing activities. You may feel a little more confident in one trade than you do in another so you decide to risk more in the one trade than you do in the other. Or you may not keep track of how much you risk in any one trade so you just come up with a different risk amount each time you pull the trigger to enter a trade. Whatever it is you are doing, if you don't have a game plan beforehand, you are setting yourself up for failure.

Failure in investing comes in two forms: failure to maintain your principal and failure to effectively grow your principal. The first form of failure is one we have already discussed. Investors who swing the risk pendulum often fail to maintain their principal. They risk too much, lose a large portion of their principal, and either lose the rest in subsequent trades or fail to make up the initial loss. The second form of failure can be deceptive because it can look like success. For example, suppose you see investors who have been able to grow their accounts by 20 percent each year for the past few years. On the surface, they may look like successful investors with great accounts—and they are. However, what if you knew that these investors didn't have a money management game plan and that if they did have a money management game plan, they would have been growing their accounts by 40 percent each year for the past few years? Would you still think that their 20 percent was a success? Hopefully, you are looking to maximize your investing results to their fullest. And if 40 percent is your maximum potential, you probably aren't going to be too happy with 20 percent.

Investors who make decisions on the go cripple themselves by not taking the time or showing the discipline to understand, develop, and trade according to a detailed money management system. As we go through the rest of this chapter, these money management failures will seem even more tragic as you learn how simple and easy it is to apply a money management system to your own investing.

Misunderstanding What Is Truly at Risk

Misunderstanding what is truly at risk is usually the result of an investor not understanding the concept of margin in the Forex market. Margin is the amount of money you have to set aside to assure the dealer you have enough money in your account to cover any losses you may incur in your trade. Most dealers require you to set aside somewhere around $100 per contract in a mini account or $1,000 per contract in a full-size account. Where many investors get confused is that they believe the $100 or the $1,000 they have set aside is the maximum amount they can lose in the trade. This couldn't be farther from the truth.

Imagine that you have a $10,000 account, and you buy one full-size EUR/USD contract. Your dealer will require you to set aside approximately $1,000 in margin. This means that $1,000 of your money is tied up as a guarantee for your dealer and that $9,000 is available for use in your trading. The question now is how much of your money is at risk. Again, common sense for some investors would say that you only have $1,000 at risk. However, just the opposite is true. You would actually have $9,000 at risk. If the trade were to go against you, you could lose up to $9,000 in your portfolio before you receive a margin call. A margin call is an order in which your dealer automatically takes you out of the trade because you have no more money. When a dealer exercises a margin call, you not only get out of the trade but you also receive your initial margin deposit back—$1,000 in this case.

So how could you lose $9,000? First, you have to establish the value of a single pip. Every pip on the EUR/USD pair is worth $10 when you are trading full-size contracts. If you enter a trade to buy one contract of the EUR/USD pair and the price of the currency pair begins to fall, you will lose $10 for every pip the pair drops in value. Next, you have to determine how far the EUR/USD pair could fall before you lose the entire $9,000. All you have to do is divide the amount you have at risk—$9,000—by the value per pip—$10. That gives you 900 pips ($9,000 ÷ $10 = 900 pips).

Hopefully, you are looking at this and thinking that something is missing because there is—a stop loss. You don't have to risk 900 pips in any trade if you don't want to. One of the benefits of the Forex market is you have guaranteed stop losses that you can set to protect yourself from adverse price movements. Knowing this, you can dramatically reduce the amount you are risking in any one trade. You could set a stop loss 50 pips away so that you are risking only $500 (50 pips × $10 per pip = $500) on the trade, or you could set a stop loss 100 pips away so that you are only risking $1,000 (100 pips × $10 per pip = $1,000) on the trade. But no matter where you decide to set your stop loss, the amount of money you set aside to meet your margin requirements with your dealer does not tell you how much you have at risk unless you are planning on getting a margin call.

Understanding and recognizing these common money management pitfalls is the first step to avoiding them in your own investing. But unless you take the time to develop a few trading and money management rules that you can personally apply, you will most likely slip into one or more of these pitfalls. Fortunately, coming up with a few money management rules is an incredibly simple process. So let's get started.

MONEY MANAGEMENT RULES

The investors who enjoy the greatest amount of success in their trading are those investors who have established clearly defined rules that govern their trading. These rules help them avoid the money management pitfalls you just learned about and keep their emotions under control. Following are three money management rules you will want to incorporate in your own trading:

1. Live to trade another day
2. Know what you are willing to risk
3. Know how to determine trade size

Live to Trade Another Day

Live to trade another day is perhaps the greatest piece of advice you could receive in your investing. Regardless of whether you are right or wrong in your trade analysis, if you live to trade another day, you know that you will always have another chance to make more money. The subsequent two rules we discuss will show you exactly what you must do to survive every day in the Forex market, but as long as you understand and believe this first rule, you will already have an advantage over most investors.

The single factor that causes most investors to overextend themselves and blow up their accounts is greed. When investors get greedy, they take unnecessary risks. They also spend countless hours trying to find the one technical indicator or the one economic announcement that is the "Holy Grail" of investing. They believe that if they only follow what that one indicator says or what that one economic announcement points to, they will never have to worry about being unprofitable in their trading again—they will always be right. You will also hear this referred to as the "secret" of investing.

Unfortunately, all this searching and hoping is unproductive simply because there is no secret. Sure, they may be able to identify a technical indicator that provides outstanding returns during a given period in market history, but the market changes, and soon another technical indicator will come into vogue. Or they might find an economic announcement that the market has been paying particularly close attention to for the past few months and believe they have found the key to their investing success. But once again, the market will change, and they will be left looking for a new key to success. To help you avoid the frustration that always comes from chasing your tail, we are going to show you how to live to trade another day so that no matter what changes take place in the market, you can be successful.

Know What You Are Willing to Risk

Know what you are willing to risk before you ever enter a trade. This rule is the basic tenet of living to trade another day. If you don't risk too much of your account in any trade today, you know you will have enough in your account tomorrow—even if you lose money on your trades today—to place another trade. In other words, it is not sound investing practice to put all your money into any one or two trades. Because you never know what is going to happen in the market, you never want to risk everything you have on one position.

The first thing you have to do is determine what percentage of your account you are willing to lose in any one trade. Once you have decided that, the rest is a simple math formula. Most investors feel comfortable risking approximately 2 percent of their total account balance in any one trade. While this is a general rule of thumb, you will need to determine how aggressive or conservative you want to be in your individual account. If you want to be more aggressive, you would risk a larger percentage of your account in any one trade. If you want to be more conservative, you would risk a smaller percentage of your account in any one trade. It is up to you to determine how much you are willing to risk, but we will say one thing—avoid going to either extreme. If you want to be more aggressive, consider risking 2 to 5 percent in any one trade. If you want to be more conservative, consider risking 1 to 2 percent in any one trade. If you risk too much, you probably won't be around to trade another day much longer. If you risk too little, you probably won't make very much money in your investing.

Once you have determined the percentage of your account you feel comfortable risking, all you have to do is plug that number into the following equation:

Account balance × risk percentage = amount at risk

Here is an example of how this would work. Imagine that you have an account balance of $50,000 and that you would like to risk 2 percent of your account in any one trade. If you plug these numbers into the equation, you will see you should not risk more than $1,000 in any one trade.

$$\$50,000 \times 0.02 = \$1,000$$

One point to remember is that this is the maximum amount you want to risk in any one trade. You may have more than this at risk in your overall account if you are in more than one trade. If you were in three trades at once, for example, you would want to risk only $1,000 per trade, but this may add up to a total amount at risk of $3,000. Once you have determined how much you are willing to risk, you are ready to determine your trade size.

Know How to Determine Trade Size

Know how to determine trade size to prevent unnecessary exposure to risk. Trade size is the number of contracts you purchase in any one trade. Once you know how much you are willing to risk, you need to know how to set up your trades so that you don't end up risking more than you are comfortable with. It doesn't do you any good to know what your risk tolerance is and then enter a trade that exposes too much of your account to risk.

To determine your trade size, you must first decide where you are going to set your stop loss. Once you have determined where to place your stop loss, you have to figure out how many pips lie between the point where you are going to enter the trade and the point you have determined to use as your stop loss. Now all you have to do is plug that amount into another simple equation that builds on the equation you just used to determine the amount you want to have at risk in any one trade.

$$\text{Amount at risk} \div (\text{pips at risk} \times \text{value per pip})$$
$$= \text{number of contracts}$$

Note that while you would use this same approach in any market you were investing in, you have an added advantage in the Forex market because you know that your stop-loss levels are guaranteed. That is an incredible benefit when you are defining your money management rules.

Here is an example of how this would work. Imagine you were willing to risk $1,000 in any one trade and you saw a trade setup on the EUR/USD pair (see Figure 16.1). You would be entering this trade by buying the currency pair at 1.1900. Looking at the trade, you decide to set your stop loss at 1.1850, or 50 pips away (1.1900 – 1.1850 = 0.0050, or 50 pips). If each pip on the EUR/USD pair is worth $10 in a full-size contract, your equation would look like this:

$$\$1,000 \div (50 \text{ pips} \times \$10 \text{ per pip}) = 2 \text{ contracts}$$

or

$$\$1,000 \div \$500 = 2 \text{ contracts}$$

FIGURE 16.1

EUR/USD, determining your trade size

Source: Prophet.net

Once you have calculated these two equations to determine how much you are willing to risk and what your trade size should be, you have taken all the guesswork out of your investing. You can sleep comfortably at night knowing exactly how much of your account is at risk and that you are going to be able to trade tomorrow no matter what happens today.

CONCLUSION

Understanding and actively applying consistent money management rules will help you avoid the common pitfalls that plague most individual investors. All too often, we find ourselves talking with investors who have lost a majority of the money in their accounts because they became greedy or overconfident. And if they would have simply set and adhered to a few simple money management rules, they would have not only avoided substantial losses but they also could have made a profit in many cases. Sometimes it sounds overly simplistic, but understanding your risk so that you can live to trade another day can help your trading take a quantum leap to the next level of profitability.

CHAPTER 17

Getting Started

There you have it. You now probably know more about the Forex market than 99 percent of the people in the United States. The question now is, what are you going to do with that knowledge? You basically have three choices:

1. You can say that the things you have learned in this book were nice, but you really don't believe the Forex market is a great place to put your money, and you are going to ignore it.
2. You can say that you are extremely interested in the concepts outlined in this book and would love to jump in and take advantage of the Forex market, but you don't have the time to dedicate to trading in the Forex market on your own.
3. You can say that you are interested, you have the time, and you have the inclination to learn more about the Forex market and trade your money on your own.

THANKS, BUT NO THANKS

The Forex market is not for everyone. Some people aren't comfortable with the sheer size and global scope of the market. Some people aren't comfortable with the new terminology and increased leverage. Some people just don't want to branch out into anything different—they are quite content with the status quo. We understand. If you don't think the Forex market is for you, we hope you've at least learned something by reading this book. And remember, if you ever change your mind, the Forex market will always be there generating profits for those who are patient enough to invest correctly.

PROFIT WITH A PROFESSIONAL

There is no more exciting or profitable market in the world than the Forex market. Of course, it takes some time to master the fundamental factors that drive the Forex and apply what you have learned in your trading. If you're excited about the tremendous profit-generating power of the Forex market but just don't feel like you have the time to devote to learning everything you need to know to be successful, you can still participate in the market and take home your share of the profits.

Professional Forex traders are involved in the market every day and offer their services to those who want to stick with the experts. The Forex professionals who can help you are called *commodity trading advisors (CTAs)*. CTAs are similar to mutual fund managers in that they do all the work for you. You just have to sit back and watch your account balance. The added advantage you get from working with a CTA, however, is that you get all the benefits associated with the Forex market. You get the special tax treatment and the increased leverage. You also have access to your account any time, day or night.

For those of you who are interested in living your life while your money grows in the Forex market, visit www.OuroborosCapital.com and see how our CTA can help you profit from the greatest market in the world. But remember, the Forex market is most effective when you are using it as a part of a diversified portfolio. Keep investing in the stock market. Keep buying bonds. Keep doing the successful things you're doing. Then you can truly enjoy the unparalleled advantages of the Forex market.

I'M READY TO DIVE IN

For those of you who can't believe you haven't gotten involved in the Forex market until now and want to dive in on your own, the best thing you can do is practice. The biggest mistake you could make is to start trading real money too quickly. If you are patient and make sure you've learned the things you need to know, you can enjoy the successes you're looking for.

When we say practice, we are referring to opening a practice, or demo, account with a Forex dealer. Every reputable Forex dealer will give you access to a demo account with paper, or fake, money in it so you can practice and perfect your trading. So the first step is identifying a Forex dealer through whom you would like to trade. We've put together an alphabetical list of the Forex dealers we believe deserve a further look.

CMC Markets	www.cmcmarkets.com
CMS Forex	www.cmsfx.com
Direct Forex	www.directforex.com
Forex Capital Markets	www.fxcm.com
Gain Capital Group	www.forex.com
Global Forex Trading	www.gftforex.com
HotSpot FX	www.hotspotfx.com
Interbank FX	www.interbankfx.com
MG Financial Group	www.mgforex.com
Oanda	www.fxtrade.oanda.com
RJO Futures	www.rjofutures.com

Take a look at these dealers, and register for a demo account. Follow the instructions you will receive from the dealer once you have registered telling you how to download and start trading in your demo account. Utilize the tools and techniques we have discussed in this book, and see what kind of profits you can generate. Remember to visit www.profitingwithforex.com to make sure you have all the free additional tools, techniques, and reports.

While you are practicing, you will probably also want to be enhancing your Forex education. If you are serious about turning your Forex trading into a full- or part-time endeavor, you will need to get all the information and training you possibly can. We recommend you check out the program at www.INVESToolsCT.com. We feel comfortable recommending this program because we created it. You'll receive comprehensive training materials, new insights into the Forex market, and most importantly, a coach who will be there every step of the way to make sure you avoid major pitfalls and take advantage of all of the opportunities that lie before you.

Conclusion

The Forex market is the greatest financial market on Earth. Globalization continues to make the world smaller and smaller, and the more that various nations and economies exchange goods and services among one another, the more active and vibrant the Forex market is going to become. How many times in your life have you seen a once-in-a-lifetime opportunity pass you by and wish you had only had the courage or the foresight to have taken advantage of it when you had the chance? This is one of those times. Every day that you sit back and watch the Forex move on by without you, you are missing out on profits that could be increasing the value of your portfolio.

Free yourself from worrying about the performance of the stock market and the U.S. economy. If the stock market goes up, you can make money in all your accounts. If the stock market goes down, you can balance things out by making money in the Forex market. Whether you're a seasoned investor with a large portfolio or a new investor who is just starting out, you can take advantage of the profit-generating power of the Forex market. The Forex market is for everybody. Come see what it can do for you.

APPENDIX

Fat Tails

One of the most basic concepts of statistics is the bell curve. The bell curve received its name because of its bell shape—the highest point is in the middle, and then it drops off fairly quickly until it flattens out at the tails until it eventually disappears (see Figure. A.1). It is the tails of the curve that we are concerned with in this book.

The middle part of the bell curve represents the area where most of the action takes place. For example, when you roll a pair of dice, you have the highest odds of rolling a 7 because there are more different combinations of numbers you can have that add up to 7 than any other number: you could roll a 6 and a 1, a 5 and a 2, a 4 and a 3, etc. Six different combinations lead to your rolling a 7. The next two numbers you are most likely to roll are 6 and 8. Both these numbers, just like the number 7, can be reached with a variety of combinations but not as many. There are only five possible combinations that would lead to your rolling a 6 or an 8. The next two numbers you are most likely to roll are 5 and 9. These two are followed by 4 and 10, and so on. The two numbers you are least likely to roll are 2 and 12. That is because each of these numbers can be reached by rolling only one combination of numbers—1 and 1 for a total of 2 and 6 and 6 for a total of 12. So if we were to graph the statistical likelihood of rolling any of these numbers, it would look like the bell curve in Figure A.2.

In the standard and ideal version of a bell curve, the tails are flat and narrow. But what would happen to our bell curve if we

FIGURE A.1

Standard bell curve

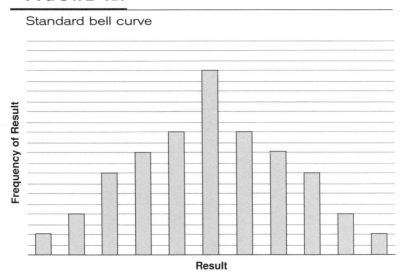

Source: Ouroboros Capital Management, LLC

FIGURE A.2

In 500 rolls of the dice, the odds of rolling one of eleven numbers are demonstrated in a bell curve

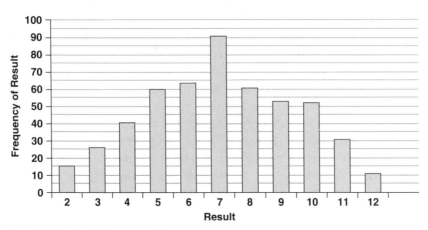

Source: Ouroboros Capital Management, LLC

FIGURE A.3

In 500 rolls of the dice, the actual occurrences of rolling
one of eleven numbers are demonstrated in a nonstandard
bell curve

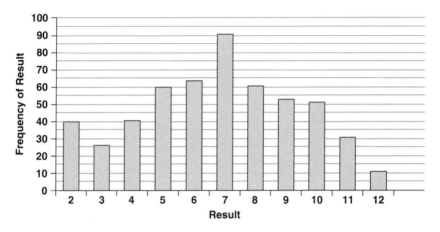

Source: Ouroboros Capital Management, LLC

were lucky, or unlucky, enough to roll snake eyes twice instead of
just once? It would make the tail on the left-hand side of the chart
get fatter, as you can see in Figure A.3.

The bell curve in Figure A.3 has a fat tail. And fat tails are a
result of all of the unexpected things that happen in life. The one
thing you can count on in life is the fact that you will never be able
to predict or account for everything that is going to happen to you.
So you might as well prepare for the unexpected.

Index

ABOUT THE AUTHORS

John Jagerson has worked in the capital markets and private equity for most of his career—including investing, writing, money management, and as vice president of content for INVESTools, Inc. (IED), the leading investor-education company in the United States.

John earned his B.S. in business administration in 1997 and funded his first private placement in 1998. His experience in the Forex began as the owner of an import/export firm, and it quickly became a major focus for risk control and profit opportunities.

He has been a featured profile in *BusinessWeek*'s Stock Trader newsletter and has been published several times in numerous online and offline periodicals. He is actively involved in managing his own stock, options, futures, and Forex portfolio and is a managing principal of Ouroboros Capital Management, LLC, a National Futures Association member firm.

John lives in Orem, Utah, with his wife and two children.

S. Wade Hansen is a managing principal of Ouroboros Capital Management, LLC, where he created the firm's proprietary trading system. He is registered with the National Futures Association as a commodity trading advisor. His articles have appeared in *Technical Analysis of STOCKS & COMMODITIES* magazine, *BusinessWeek*'s Investor Education program, and CNBC's Investor Education program.

Wade has been investing in the Forex market for years and has been a featured speaker at multiple Forex-trading workshops and seminars. He has also helped train tens of thousands of investors as the cocreator of the INVESTools Currency Trader, Advanced Options, and Advanced Technical Analysis education programs.